"A fascinating collection of brilliant essays—m(
by this most remarkable and original of twenti
ting to the heart of the relationship between th
between death and life. It is an indispensable resource, complementing the
reading of Bulgakov's major works."

—JOHN BEHR
Regius Chair of Humanity, University of Aberdeen, and Metropolitan Kallistos
Chair of Orthodox Theology, Vrije Universiteit, Amsterdam

"In this judicious selection of Bulgakov's eschatological essays, which tra-
verse the speculative, political, pastoral, dogmatic, and personal, Roberto
De La Noval offers Anglophone readers a true gift. His graceful translation
retains throughout the urgency, force, and bright delicacy of Bulgakov's singular voice as the volume extends an invitation—even an imperative summons—to contemplate together the griefs and consolations of endings in
history, time, and death."

—JENNIFER NEWSOME MARTIN
Associate Professor, Department of Theology, University of Notre Dame

"A master of multiple sources—philosophical, theological, liturgical, scriptural, and patristic—which he synthesizes in order to leave no theological
stone unturned without a response, Sergius Bulgakov is the Aquinas of our
time. Roberto J. De La Noval's masterful translation of these essays further
reinforces Bulgakov's genius and ongoing relevance for our contemporary
questions."

—ARISTOTLE PAPANIKOLAOU
Professor of Theology, Archbishop Demetrios Chair in Orthodox Theology and Culture, cofounding director, Orthodox Christian Studies Center, Fordham University

The Sophiology of Death

The Psychology of Death

The Sophiology of Death

Essays on Eschatology: Personal, Political, Universal

SERGIUS BULGAKOV

Edited and translated by
ROBERTO J. DE LA NOVAL

Foreword by
DAVID BENTLEY HART

CASCADE *Books* • Eugene, Oregon

THE SOPHIOLOGY OF DEATH
Essays on Eschatology: Personal, Political, Universal

Cascade Books
An Imprint of Wipf and Stock Publishers
199 W. 8th Ave., Suite 3
Eugene, OR 97401

www.wipfandstock.com

PAPERBACK ISBN: 978-1-5326-9965-8
HARDCOVER ISBN: 978-1-5326-9966-5
EBOOK ISBN: 978-1-5326-9967-2

Cataloguing-in-Publication data:

Names: Bulgakov, Sergiï, 1871–1944, author. | De La Noval, Roberto J., translator | Hart, David Bentley, foreword writer.

Title: The sophiology of death : essays on eschatology : personal, political, universal / Sergius Bulgakov, translated by Roberto J. De La Noval, with a foreword by David Bentley Hart.

Description: Eugene, OR: Cascade Books, 2021 | Includes bibliographical references and index.

Identifiers: ISBN 978-1-5326-9965-8 (paperback) | ISBN 978-1-5326-9966-5 (hardcover) | ISBN 978-1-5326-9967-2 (ebook)

Subjects: LCSH: Bulgakov, Sergiï, 1871–1944 | Eschatology | Orthodox Eastern Church—Doctrines | Restorationism—History of doctrines | Apokatastasis (The Greek word) | Universalism—History of doctrines | Death—Religious aspects—Christianity

Classification: BT821.3 B8513 2021 (paperback) | BT821.3 (ebook)

05/10/21

To John and Ashley and Sonya and Brian,
for making your homes outposts of heaven

Contents

Foreword

JUST TWO DECADES AGO, the thought of Sergius Bulgakov was still a fairly recherché interest among Anglophone theologians. And even among the small number who had heard anything about it, none but a tiny minority were aware that its reputation as something exotic and wantonly hermetic was a silly caricature. For one thing, few of Bulgakov's books had appeared in English, and those that had were hardly exemplary of the extraordinary range, richness, originality, or sheer genius of his accomplishments (at best, they provided tantalizing hints of something splendid and mysterious, but inaccessible behind an opaque Cyrillic veil). Since then, however, and rather unexpectedly, a largely unorganized collective labor of translation has arisen, and grown from a steady trickle into a positive inundation. As a result, a great number of Christian scholars are only now coming to discover and appreciate one of the true titans of twentieth-century theology—arguably, in fact, the one whose thought achieved the most impressive balance between speculative audacity and logical precision. In the process, they are also discovering a thinker who speaks to—but from outside of—most of the standard Western models of doctrinal, hermeneutical, and metaphysical theology, but who is also anything but a conventional representative of the Eastern models with which they are already familiar. In truth, this is perhaps the most delightfully unanticipated aspect of the late springtime that Bulgakov's thought is just now enjoying: his theology simply cannot be fitted easily into any of the more common genres of modern systematics.

On the one hand, Bulgakov's work was something of an anomaly in Orthodox thought. It was to a great degree shaped by the very special conditions of late nineteenth- and early twentieth-century Russian "religious philosophy," a loosely affiliated "movement" that constituted the most brilliant and original development in Orthodox thought since the days of the Church fathers; and it was this tradition of which Bulgakov's mature theological writings were the last great flowering and synthesis. But, of course, even in the Orthodox world, this places him in a fairly rarefied class, inasmuch as that entire remarkable tradition was nearly extinguished by the rise and triumph of the neo-Palamite movement in Orthodox thought, which at its worst can become a kind of historically unrefined neo-patristic scholasticism that all too often strives to stifle any genuinely creative Orthodox theology, or any attempt at a dynamic engagement with modern thought.

On the other hand, Bulgakov's theology could *only* have been a product of the Orthodox world. Although he possessed an extraordinarily comprehensive mastery of the entirety of Western philosophy, including the whole of the modern continental tradition, and although he was profoundly learned in and appreciative of Western theological traditions, he was very much a child of the Christian East. All of his most fundamental theological premises and habits of mind—his understanding of grace, nature, and supernature, of redemption, sin, and guilt, his emphasis upon the inseparable rationality of divine incarnation and human deification, his vision of creation as a true theophany, his pervasive sacramentalism, and so on—are derived from the Greek and Semitic sources of the tradition, with little admixture of distinctively Western Christian themes. Moreover, while very much a thinker of his time, entirely comfortable with the critical schools of modern theology, he was also frankly insistent upon the reality of the miraculous and the mystical. He was keenly conscious of the difference between pre-critical and post-critical naivetés, and of the tension between biblical myth and history, but he did not take this as a warrant for abandoning spiritual interpretations of scripture, or for any project of thoroughgoing demythologization. He understands modernity neither as an imperative nor as an enemy to be overthrown, but rather as an occasion to think the tradition anew.

In any event, Roberto de la Noval has given us an invaluable contribution to this still emerging Bulgakovian moment. A number of the pieces included here, I suspect, as substantial as they are, might not otherwise have seen publication in English. And, in bringing them together, as exemplary of one great guiding theme in Bulgakov's thought, he has provided a very particular but indispensable perspective upon the whole "system." In concentrating upon writings dealing specifically with death, the last things, and the eschatological horizon of history, he has opened a perspective upon the entire trajectory of Bulgakov's thought. It really is amazing how many of the most crucial of Christian theological themes pour through these essays, like sunlight pouring through a prism and refracted by it into new and dazzling patterns. And, cast against a backdrop of such profound and ultimate urgency, those patterns take on an altogether absorbing richness. The insights and aperçus and inspirations defy enumeration, and the final result is a kind of tutelage in how to see every discrete aspect of theological concern in the light of history's last end and of creation's eternal meaning within the totality of God's revelation of himself. Even Bulgakov's own encounter with death—or with its menacing proximity—becomes the occasion of remarkably profound but also extraordinarily rigorous meditations on creation as an eternal and "Sophianic" act, on Christology, on divine kenosis, on Christ's abandonment on the cross, and on countless related matters of dogma and theology.

It seems especially clear that Bulgakov sees these issues of death and of history's encounter with its own ending as opening a privileged view of the threshold at once separating and joining time and eternity. And by this I mean more than the border between the here-and-now and the hereafter. I mean also the difference between the kind of time we know within the fallen world and that creaturely aeon that in a sense comes both before and after this life—or, rather, that is neither before nor after in a merely temporal sense, but that is instead the "moment" where the creation and the deification of the creature prove to be one and the same event. It is that eternal reality where creation's end and beginning coincide, and where humanity's eschatological praise of the God who is All in All is also each person's original free assent to his or her own creation in Christ. But, further yet, these same themes also grant us a glimpse of the still more mysterious threshold between the creaturely aeon and the divine eternity beyond the ages, and thus between God as disclosed in creation and God as he is in himself. And here, for Bulgakov, fittingly and inevitably, we discover that humanity has been created *as* divine, but also as called to *become* divine, precisely because there is a Divine Humanity that is always already both an eternal truth of God's own life and also the source and end of all creation.

It is worth noting, incidentally, all this having been said, that the essays collected here also very much concern life in this world, and the concrete realities of cosmic and human history. For Bulgakov, the eschatological pervades every aspect of our lived existence, and inflects every moment with a kind of additional stress, away from the flow of time and toward the eternal. And death is the unique experience of eternity as at once interrupting and encompassing time as we know it. Seen in its light, and with a properly theological orientation, all of history acquires its meaning and its inner narrative from its relation to the incarnation, death, and resurrection of the Son of God, and specifically from the way in which the death of "Adam" is taken up in the death of Christ and, through it, the life of the age to come. And, in learning to see death and history entirely in the light of Christ's cross, Christians find themselves addressed by a practical call to dwell within the logic of history with a creative will toward a future, and to seek models of social life that might make the age to come proleptically manifest. This means both taking real responsibility for the social order as judged in the light of the kingdom of God, but also accepting the verdict of history upon the failed accommodation of Christendom. It means never succumbing to nostalgia for a vanished imperial arrangement that was always a corruption of the gospel. It also means, however, that Christians should not seek a fantastical reprise of the ahistorical apocalypticism of the nascent Church, which was necessary in the early days of the Church as a means of survival, but which would now be a mere dereliction of what the gospel demands of believers in *this* moment.

But I should stop here. I am making a scrupulous attempt to indicate some of the content of these essays without actually divulging any of the arguments, principally out of fear of either misrepresenting or banalizing them. Bulgakov is quite able to speak for himself, even if he makes more than ordinary demands on the reader, and his translator here has captured both his voice and his brilliance with exemplary fidelity. This book is invaluable, and in some places it sounds the depths of Bulgakov's theology in a way that no other text available in English does.

David Bentley Hart

Translator's Preface
and Bibliographic Information

TRANSLATING BULGAKOV PROVES AS exciting as it does challenging. Anyone who has had the pleasure of reading his Russian knows that even in the driest and most straightforward of passages one hears echoes of a deeper music beneath the surface. I have tried to preserve some of the rhythm of Bulgakov's Russian by replicating his asyndeton and run-on sentences as much as (my sense of) English style would permit. I hope this reflects for the English reader something of the pressure of the thought incessantly cascading forth from Bulgakov's prodigious mind. Additionally, the reader will encounter in this translation the use of the male singular pronoun as well as instances of "man" to render Bulgakov's frequently appearing *chelovek* (human being). In order to escape infelicity in the trnaslation's style, I have reverted to this older English convention in places where "the human person" (my typical rendering for the word) was less than ideal; this is unfortunate, and so I ask the reader's indulgence and pray that it will not prove too distracting.

For various key words in Bulgakov's lexicon I have followed the precedents set by translators of such stature as Thomas Allan Smith and Boris Jakim. On that note, when preparing my own translation of the text I have consulted to great benefit Jakim's 1995 translation of "On the Question of the Apocatastasis of the Fallen Spirits (in Connection with the Teaching of Gregory of Nyssa)," first appearing in *Apocatastasis and Transfiguration* (Variable Press, 1995). Readers should be aware that between "Hades" and "hell" and "divinization" and "deification" in this text, there is no difference in the underlying Russian. Bulgakov's many, many italicizations have been preserved in almost all instances, and I confess that I have added a few of my own (in keeping with the master's style) where I thought it might help to clarify a difficult syntactical structure or to render the appropriate emphasis. Also, I have added numerous paragraph breaks to aid the reader in digesting Bulgakov's lengthy paragraphs.

When Bulgakov's footnotes in these texts illuminate his argument, I have kept them; few other footnotes from the original remain. In square brackets I translate Bulgakov's occasional comments written in other languages, both ancient and modern. Also in square brackets the reader will find references to the plethora of biblical texts that Bulgakov tirelessly interweaves into his prose. I have added these especially so that readers new to Bulgakov may recognize how deeply shaped by the sacred page was the language of this minister of the Word. Additionally, I have registered Bulgakov's biblical citations with respect to the Masoretic instead of the Septuagintal numbering; where the verse numbering differs between Bulgakov's versions and those common to English-language Bibles, I have followed the latter system for the reader's ease. Bulgakov's not infrequent miscitations of biblical verses—both in Russian and in Greek—have been corrected, though in the translations I note this only sparingly. With respect to translating scriptural quotations in these essays, I have tended to translate them myself, in order to represent the original as faithfully as possible, though where Bulgakov quotes the Slavonic readings, I have preferred the King James Version. Regarding the liturgical texts and patristic writings Bulgakov cites, I have employed English translations wherever possible and have indicated their provenance as well as whatever changes I have made to them. Finally, whenever Bulgakov quotes the text of other authors, I offer my own translations of these passages; in exceptional instances when I do not, I indicate that I am quoting a published translation.

Full bibliographic information is provided at the end of this book for texts that I have cited in my own editorial introduction and footnotes, yet only if they exist in English translation. The sources for the texts translated herein are as follows. "The Foundational Antinomy of the Christian Philosophy of History" constitutes the final chapter of Bulgakov's book *Apocalyptic and Socialism*, which appeared in his 1911 collected volume *Two Cities* (Dva Grada). I have used the 1997 reprint of *Two Cities* (Sankt–Peterburg: Izdatel'stvo russkogo khristianskogo gumanitarnogo instituta), 243–47. "On the Kingdom of God" was included in the July 1928 issue of the Russian émigré journal *The Way* (Put') 11 (1928) 3–30. "The Soul of Socialism (Part II)" appeared in the journal of political theology, *New City* (Novy Grad) 3 (1932) 33–45. Rowan Williams translated this article into English nearly twenty years ago for his volume on Bulgakov, *Towards a Russian Political Theology* (Edinburgh: T. & T. Clark, 1999). Given its thematic unity with the present volume, I considered it worthwhile to offer a fresh translation of this seminal essay. "The Problem of 'Conditional Immortality'" was published in two parts in *The Way* (Put') 52 (1936) 3–23 and 53 (1937) 3–19. The following four studies served as appendices to Bulgakov's posthumously released conclusion to his major dogmatic trilogy *The Bride of the Lamb* (1945): "On the Question of the Apocatastasis of the Fallen Spirits (in Connection with the Teaching of Gregory of Nyssa)," "Apocatastasis and Theodicy," "The Redemption and Apocatastasis," and "Augustinianism and Predestination." The latter text has been significantly edited and redacted for inclusion in this collection, with the sections not directly relevant to eschatology having been removed. The interested reader can find my translation of the entire excursus, with all of Bulgakov's footnotes intact, in the *Journal of Orthodox Christian Studies* 2.1 (2019) 65–99. For my translation of these last four writings from *The Bride of the Lamb* I employed the 1971 reprint of the Russian version (*Nevesta Agntsa*) from Gregg International Publishers. "The Sophiology of Death" (1939) was also published posthumously, in two parts, by *Le Messager* of the Russian Christian Student Movement: IV.127 (1978) 18–41 and I–II.128 (1979) 13–32.

Bulgakov's posthumously released commentary on John's Apocalypse (Paris: YMCA Press, 1948)—from which I translated the appendix, "Even So, Come"—was reprinted by Pravoslavnoe Bratstvo Trezvosti "Otrada i Uteshenie" (Moskva: 1991). To the great benefit of the Anglophone theological world, an English translation of Bulgakov's entire commentary on the Apocalypse has just recently appeared (edited by Barbara Hallensleben, Regula M. Zwahlen, and Dario Colombo, and translated by Mike Whitton and Michael Miller. *Sergii Bulgakov: The Apocalypse of John: An Essay in Dogmatic Interpretation* [Münster: Aschendorff Verlag, 2019]). It is highly recommended. Bulgakov's homily on the Dormition of Mary included here was delivered in 1943, a year before his death, and it too was printed by *Le Messager* III (1952) 5–7. The final piece of this collection, not strictly speaking a work of theology, is the short note "Concerning My Funeral," written by Bulgakov in 1941 and giving instructions for his burial arrangements. The note became available to the public a decade later in St. Serge Theological Institute's publishing organ, *La Pensée Orthodoxe: travaux de l'institute théologie orthodox* à Paris/ Zhurnal "Pravoslavnaya Mysl'" ("Orthodox Thought") 8 (1951) 8–9. I thought it a fitting conclusion to this collection of texts centered on death.

All these works are in the public domain.

Acknowledgements

THIS PROJECT BEGAN OVER three years ago, and in that time I have accrued many debts. As I will inevitably fail to remember all those to whom many thanks are owed, I apologize in advance.

It is right first to acknowledge Thomas Allan Smith and Boris Jakim. Without their commitment to bringing Bulgakov to an English-speaking audience, my professional (and personal) life would have taken a quite different direction. In matters of translation I have often followed their own insightful English renderings, and the Anglophone public is fortunate to enjoy the fruit of their efforts.

Many thanks to Matthew Wimer and Robin Parry, my editors at Wipf and Stock, who showed enthusiasm for this project from our first conversation and who worked with me to see it through to the end. I am most grateful.

To Yulya Milogradova and Valentina Kurenshchikova, for helping me over the years to make progress in their beautiful mother tongue. To the extent I enjoy its pleasures, it is in large part due to them. Annie Rhodes and Florian Tatschner also deserve grateful mention for their help in checking my translations from French and German.

My thanks also to Deacon Mark Roosien for help in identifying Bulgakov's liturgical quotations. He has a share of the spirit of the Bulgakov, and his scholarship and ministry will undoubtedly enrich many. Regula Zwahlen—a veritable master on all things Bulgakov—has over the years afforded me her time and knowledge; her influence is felt in these pages too.

My gratitude goes out to David Bentley Hart for his support of this project and for writing the foreword. I can think of no living theologian who has carried forward Bulgakov's theological vision quite like David, and so it is a genuine delight and privilege to have him contribute to this volume.

Yury P. Avvakumov deserves many thanks for his unfailing help in reviewing this translation, catching errors, pinpointing quotations, and making helpful suggestions. His learning is matched only by his generosity—both are staggeringly wide and deep.

Finally, my heartfelt thanks to John and Ashley Wallace and Sonya and Brian Cronin. Your nurturing care in my life began over a decade ago, and your friendship has continued since. I hope to continue in the eschatological joy I have experienced in your presence—and we know that hope does not disappoint.

Introduction

THE THEOLOGY OF FR. Sergius Bulgakov (1871–1944) is decisively and thoroughly eschatological, even apocalyptic.[1] From a purely biographical perspective[2] this is unsurprising: in the Bolshevist Revolution he lived through the collapse of one of the last outposts of Christendom only to see a new world rise from its ashes, one soaked in the blood of Christian martyrs and worthy of the most dramatic montages of John's Apocalypse.[3] The revolution ended more than just the political, cultural, and ecclesial world Bulgakov had known for fifty years; it also closed the chapter of his life spent in his beloved Russia and sent him abroad into exile. He settled ultimately in Paris, where he died two decades later, never to see his homeland again. If the beginning of his life as a priest (ordained 1918) coincided with an event of such apocalyptic proportions, then his death came near the end of the cataclysms shaking Europe during World War II. A life lived in the midst of such violent disruptions provided regular opportunity for reflection on the inbreaking of other, more otherworldly kingdoms, be they bestial or divine.

But Bulgakov's interest in the end-times was hardly jump-started by the Bolshevist revolution: already in 1911, seven years before his ordination to the priesthood, Bulgakov was contemplating in his book *Apocalyptic and Socialism* the relationship between Jewish Messianism, Christian chiliasm

1 . English-language studies of Bulgakov's eschatology are few. For a fine introduction to Bulgakov's general eschatological thought, with criticisms, see Paul Gavrilyuk's "The Judgment of Love: The Ontological Universalism of Sergius Bulgakov (1871–1944)." Cyril O'Regan situates Bulgakov's eschatology in nineteenth- and twentieth-century theology in his Père Marquette lecture, *Theology and the Spaces of Apocalyptic*. A more specific contextualization of Bulgakov in the trends of nineteenth- and twentieth-century Russian eschatology can be found in the introduction to Bulgakov, *The Apocalypse of John: An Essay in Dogmatic Interpretation*.

2. For a brief biography of Bulgakov's life, see Slesinski, *The Theology of Sergius Bulgakov*, 11–34.

3. For more on the martyrdom of Christians under the Soviet regime, see Pospielovsky, *The Russian Church under the Soviet Regime 1917–1982*.

and eschatology, and the immanentized eschatology of Marxist revolutionary thought. Vladimir Soloyov (whom Bulgakov called his "philosophical guide to Christ") had already spurred this turn to eschatology in Russian religious thought with his important final treatise, *A Short Story of the Anti–Christ*,[4] and Bulgakov followed him down this path. Nonetheless, the push that the new Soviet reality gave Bulgakov towards more explicitly eschatological dogmatic theologizing is recognizable in a short work he wrote from Crimea in his first, "internal" exile under the Bolshevists: *On Relics (In Connection with Their Desecration)*.[5] In this treatise, Bulgakov responds to the Soviet practice of exposing before the eyes of the faithful the decomposed bodies of saints, with the aim of scandalizing believers who thought these holy remains could suffer no corruption. Such a practice was, in Bulgakov's words, "fanaticism" and "the breath of the anti-Christ," and it required in response a serious theological reflection on the Orthodox doctrine of relics. What Bulgakov proposed was a systematically explicated realized eschatology in which the saints, because of their profound sanctity, become capable of maintaining their connection with their bodily matter even beyond the grave. As such their bodies are already, in a significant sense, *resurrection bodies*, transparent to the will of these saints in heaven who procure on behalf of God answers to the prayers of the faithful. If the resurrected Christ displayed absolute control over matter in his resurrected and divinized state, so too the spirits of the saints demonstrate a power over their remains on earth to make of them sites of blessing and knowledge of God.

Realized eschatology intersects here with anthropology, the metaphysics of spirit and matter, and most importantly, Christology. This interpretive nexus for eschatology remains operative for Bulgakov throughout his theological career, although with differing emphases depending on the period and the issue in question. This bears emphasizing in light of how easy it is to focus solely on the more provocative aspects of Bulgakov's eschatology, such as his unequivocal and extensive argumentation for universal salvation, and to lose sight of the more subtle and pervasive influence of eschatological thinking in all of his theological production. It is realized eschatology, and the real difference that Christ's historical advent has made, that drives his entire project.

When turning to consider Bulgakov's explicit reflections on eschatology, however, it is helpful to divide his thought into three categories: the personal, social, and the apocalyptic. These three intermingle at all stages of his writing, yet key themes can be distinguished in relation to each.

4. Solovyov, *War, Progress, and the End of History*, 159–94.
5. Bulgakov, *Relics and Miracles: Two Theological Essays*.

Beginning with the personal, we note how particular encounters with death in Bulgakov's life functioned as a revelation of the eschatological tension constantly though hiddenly present in human existence. The premature death in 1909 of Bulgakov's not yet four-year-old son, Ivashechka, tore the fabric of this father's heart, but it also proved the occasion for a revelation of God's grace that remained with him for the rest of his life. As he wrote in his 1917 work on religious philosophy, *Unfading Light*:

> My holy one, at the sanctuary of your remains, beside your pure body, my fair one, my radiant boy, I found out *how* God speaks, I understood what "God spoke" means! In a new and never-before-known clairvoyance of heart, along with the torment of the cross heavenly joy came down into it, and with the darkness of divine abandonment God reigned in my soul. My heart was opened to the pain and torment of people—hearts until then strange and hence closed were exposed before it with their pain and grief. For the only time in my life I understood what it means to *love* not with a human, self-loving, and mercenary love, but with that divine love with which Christ loves us. It was as if the curtain separating me from others fell and all the gloom, bitterness, offense, animosity, and suffering in their hearts was revealed to me. And in ineffable rapture, frenzy, self-forgetfulness I said then—you will remember this, my fair one—I said: *God spoke to me*, and then hearing you I simply added that *you spoke to me too*. . . . To forget *this* and to doubt *after this* means for me to die spiritually. One can lose one's treasure, be frightened before its defense, but even unworthily cast aside and lost, it is a treasure all the same . . . .[6]

Death revealed a different face to Bulgakov following his operations for throat cancer in 1940. This time it was a traumatic manifestation not of death but of *dying*. Yet any revelation of the border straddling this world and the next cannot but manifest Christ as well, the one who freely shared in the death *and* the dying of the human race. This experience provoked Bulgakov to reflect on the eschatological significance of illness, both in his own life and for all humanity. If Paul could write that Christ's death and resurrection made him the "Lord of both the living and the dead" (Rom 14:9), then in Bulgakov's sophiology of death, Christ becomes the Lord of both the sick and the dying. To touch death in illness is to be in communion with the Christ who "co-suffers" and "co-dies" in and with every human spirit. This point is key to Bulgakov's *sophiology*, his theological system

---

6. Bulgakov, *Unfading Light*, 14–15.

structured around the vision of *Sophia*, Divine Wisdom, presented in the Scriptures and the Church's tradition. For in God's pre-eternal Wisdom, the divine plan for creation, all things are incorporated, even those facets of fallen existence that oppose God's will, such as death (Wis 1:13), because all these aspects of human life God has made his own in Christ.

According to sophiology, *God has no created opposites*; Divine Sophia (Bulgakov's name for the divine essence) is perfectly expressed, though in finite form, in Created Sophia, our creaturely world. Accordingly, the divine Son can assume the lowliness of human flesh in the incarnation of Christ so as to elevate humanity, even while remaining precisely who he is, without any alteration of the divine nature. And this coincidence of the nadir of human weakness with the plenitude of divinity means that even the darkest hours of human existence become an incognito encounter with God in Christ, the "Last Adam" who, as the prototype of eschatological humanity, is also revealed to be the "First Adam." Bulgakov's aim in his writings on personal eschatology is to disclose this oft-unrecognized theophany, to turn our face towards the bruised countenance of the Savior, engraved with divine sorrow for our wounded humanity. Christ appears to us in these moments precisely through the hiddenness of our divine abandonment, just as the Son experienced the infinite distance between himself and the Father on the cross in the absence of the Holy Spirit's consolation.[7] It is in this most universal experience of divine abandonment, experienced in illness, dying, and in death, that each person encounters Christ in the most intimate of meetings.

The social character of Bulgakov's eschatological thought indicates his continuing intellectual struggle against Marxist secularized eschatology, now very much realized in the Soviet Union that had exiled him. Much of his earlier post-conversion writings had focused on what he (rightly) perceived as the coming eschatological crisis of Marxist revolution. In his seminal 1909 essay for the volume *Landmarks*, "Heroism and Asceticism," Bulgakov denounced the Russian revolutionary intelligentsia for its immaturity and proclivity to violent excess in the quest for heroic martyrdom.[8] The lack of self-discipline and maturity in these figures could only lead to the perpetuation of systems of control on the bodies of others, a future Bulgakov accurately predicted in "The Foundational Antinomy of the Christian Philosophy of History." Indeed, as Vladimir Solovyov had remarked just a

---

7. Readers of Hans Urs von Balthasar will hear echoes of his paschal trinitarianism in these lines. This is no accident, for as Jennifer Newsome Martin has shown, Balthasar was greatly influenced by Bulgakov's sophiology. *Hans Urs von Balthasar and the Critical Reception of Russian Religious Thought*.

8. Bulgakov, "Heroism and Asceticism," 17–50.

few years before Russia's great crisis: "[i]t is quite clear to the impartial mind that revolution and spoliation are a bad school in which to learn justice."[9]

This critical perspective on revolutionary socialism never left Bulgakov the theologian, himself now a repentant Marxist. Yet in the later writings of his dogmatic period, such as in "The Soul of Socialism," he softened his tone to some degree when reflecting on this faith of "revolutionism." He contextualized this revolutionism as an inevitable dialectical response both to the Church's political conservatism throughout its history—its rejection of historical tasks in favor of a flight from the world—and to its alignment with unjust political powers. These together pushed those hungering and thirsting for justice to seek other, more violent, means of establishing the kingdom of God on earth. Bulgakov's diagnosis of revolutionary utopianism as a system of disappointed and misguided Christian consciousness reflects his conviction both that the human spirit naturally desires God (who is Justice itself) and that Christian eschatological hope functions as the hidden fountainhead of revolutionary striving, even if in a truncated and perverted form. This genealogical critique, so prevalent in today's theological discourse, was a regular feature of Russian émigré analysis of Marxist thought.

But this critique also pointed to hopeful possibilities for addressing the revolutionism and secularization proceeding apace even in Bulgakov's lifetime. There is room for common cause between socialists and Christians, Bulgakov thinks, even if the atheism propelling revolutionary socialism must be repudiated at every turn. The Church can no longer live in the apocalyptic present of the earliest Christians, ignoring as they did the grave injustices in their midst (such as slavery); it must instead recognize that it possesses a historical destiny, and that this destiny is bound up with the entire human race that Christ assumed in his incarnation. The Church's task is therefore the progressive realization of the ideals of God's kingdom on earth, the "churching" of culture. Connected with this "churching" is that theological commitment that will appear most idiosyncratic to readers of Bulgakov today, namely his chiliasm, or the doctrine of a future thousand-year reign of Christ on earth. As he puts it in chapter twenty of his commentary on John's Apocalypse: "God's Word contains two revelations about the end of history and of the world: the first is immanent and historical, a matter of internal maturation, and the second is transcendent and catastrophic, connected with the Parousia."[10] This means that "the thousand-year reign is a definite era in the history of the Church with a beginning and

9. Vladimir Solovyev, *God, Man, and the Church*, 41.
10. Bulgakov, *The Apocalypse of John: An Essay in Dogmatic Interpretation*, 181.

an end."[11] Whatever one makes of this doctrine, it is well to remember that Bulgakov's championing of the teaching was motivated by the conviction that the Church was to play a central role in bringing history to an organic conclusion and that the synergism between God and humanity on display in Christ's hypostatic union was not to be abolished by a one-sided act of God's omnipotence at the end of time. God's act in the parousia will indeed be divine and unique, a gift to the Church and the world, but it will also be a *response* to the Spirit's mission of making Pentecost a universal reality on earth through human work in history.

This brings us to the apocalyptic side of Bulgakov's eschatology, and especially his *dogmatic* universalism, or affirmation that by saving all rational creatures, God will in the end be "all in all" (1 Cor 15:28), with no remainder. Bulgakov explicitly attaches himself to the tradition of apocatastasis ("universal restoration") first theologically articulated by Origen of Alexandria (AD ca. 184–253) and developed at length by St. Gregory of Nyssa (AD ca. 335–395). This was by no means the dominant tradition in the Orthodoxy of Bulgakov's time, due in large part to the condemnations of Origenist eschatology in a synod connected with, but not properly belonging to, the Second Council of Constantinople in AD 553—a condemnation that in the course of the centuries came to be mistakenly attributed to the fifth ecumenical council.[12] (Gregory of Nyssa's universalist eschatology, by contrast, has never been ecumenically condemned.) Bulgakov's universalism was only one specimen of a growing dissatisfaction with the traditional doctrine of hell understood as eternal conscious torment, a dissatisfaction felt in multiple Christian communions over the last centuries.[13] Yet its more immediate context was the eschatological writing of Russian Silver Age theologians, such Vladimir Solovyov (1853–1900), Nikolai Berdyaev (1874–1948), and Fr. Pavel Florensky (1882–1937). Solovyov's apocalyptic *Short Story of the Anti-Christ* has already been noted. His greatest contribution towards universalist thought, however, is found elsewhere, namely in his sustained Christian arguments against the death penalty, for the logic undergirding capital punishment bears a striking resemblance to the logic supporting the idea of eternal torments. Both, after all, cut off definitively the possibility of repentance for the sinner. Solovyov's arguments against

11. *The Apocalypse of John*, 183.

12. Norman P. Tanner, for example, does not include these anathematizations in his *Decrees of the Ecumenical Councils*, on account of historical scholarship arguing against their attribution to Constantinople II. The scholarly consensus remains that the eschatology in view in these condemnations was not that held by Origen himself but was instead representative of (not always faithful) followers of Origen centuries later.

13. See, for example, Rowell, *Hell and the Victorians*.

the death penalty would reappear in modified form in Bulgakov's universalist eschatology.

Berdyaev's critique of hell was more philosophical than theological (to the degree such distinctions can be made of the writers of the Russian Religious Renaissance) and it focused on the distorted psychology and politics of fear that the doctrine of eternal torments abetted, especially for those with ecclesiastical power.[14] "[T]he idea of hell is torture, and torture may force man to do anything," Berdyaev famously wrote.[15] In his view, disinterested love for God becomes impossible in the face of the possibility of eternal damnation. Bulgakov was sympathetic to this perspective, but it is not a form of argumentation that drives his universalism. More akin to his thought is the theology of his mentor Fr. Pavel Florensky as expressed in the latter's book, *The Pillar and Ground of Truth*. In the chapter "Gehenna," Florensky lays out the fundamental antinomy constraining theological discourse on the eschaton, that between God's omnipotence and love on one side and the freedom of the human person on the other. In a manner very similar to how Bulgakov would later frame the issue, Florensky zeroes in on the question of whether creatures can ultimately thwart God's design for them by refusing His love. If we answer yes, we deprive God of omnipotence and love, and our doctrine of God falls into incoherence. Yet if we say no, God's love for human *freedom* is undermined. The truth of God's love and power leads us to contradictory conclusions.[16] Florensky, while formally abjuring any resolution to this antinomy, does in fact pursue some form of reconciliation. In his eschatological view, sinners can so deface the image of God within them such that in the final purgative separation of wheat from chaff (1 Cor 3:12–15), the image of God within them will remain, though its sinful psychological accruement will be cast off into final darkness to suffer eternal and irreversible torments. In this way God's creation remains unscathed, untouched by human freedom exercised in sin, although the "I" that remains in such a scenario is so different from the psychological ego that Florensky's view is hard to distinguish from the idea that God simply destroys the sinner and creates a new self altogether.

Florensky was writing against the "vulgar Origenism" prevalent in his day. Bulgakov, in his turn, offered a complex biblical, philosophical, and theological argument for Origen's "larger hope" for the salvation of all. Looking back from today, it proved to be the most sophisticated and

14. For similar, more contemporary reflections on the doctrine of hell, see Hart, *That All Shall Be Saved*.

15. Berdyaev, *The Destiny of Man*, 266.

16. There exist significant parallels between Florensky's view and the "hopeful universalism" of Hans Urs von Balthasar.

elaborate in the twentieth century, and indeed perhaps "the most ambitious and systematic attempt *ever* to defend Christian universalism."[17] In his
posthumous work *Truth and Revelation*, Berdyaev linked Bulgakov's legacy
as a theologian with his "decisive and courageous rejection of the eternal
pains of hell."[18] But Bulgakov was not always so forthright with his views
on the eventual reconciliation of all with God. In his first major work of
philosophical theology, *Unfading Light* (1917), Bulgakov hesitates to affirm
universal salvation, even though his thinking clearly tends in this direction.
At this stage, the antinomical thinking of his great tutor, Florensky, still has
its grip on Bulgakov, although the hold is already loosening. By the time
of his posthumously published essay "Augustinianism and Predestination"
(the final excursus to *Bride of the Lamb*), he could write that "[i]t is the business of religious philosophy and theology to unite in a general conceptual
framework both theses—which from the outside sound like contradictions
or at least antinomies (by no means the same thing)—to unite them, therefore, as thesis and antithesis."[19]

  Bulgakov's mature sophiology is just such a conceptual framework,
and its fundamental christological premises receive a brilliant exposition in
the eschatology of *The Bride of the Lamb*. As we have already noted, sophiology emphasizes the *correspondence* (or "co-imaging") between divinity
and humanity based on the reality of Christ's genuine incarnation and on
the image of God binding the Creator and rational creatures. This means,
ultimately, that human freedom cannot function as an "opposite" existing
in true (and not just apparent) tension with God's universal salvific will.
Human freedom in its perfection dazzles us in the "not my will but thine"
of Gethsemane, and it is by that spiritual struggle and its culmination in
Golgotha that Jesus Christ takes Adam's place as the new head of the human
race. The result is that "where sin abounded, grace did much more abound"
(Rom 5:20). Bulgakov's christological maximalism is the foundation of his
universal salvation; in Chalcedonian Christology Bulgakov discovers the
"dogmatic way out of this antinomy of the absolute and the relative, the
divine and the creaturely" ("Apocatastasis and Theodicy").

  In Christ, God takes responsibility for the freedom given to humanity
in its creation, a responsibility whose misuse explains the millennia of evil
the world has known and continues to suffer. Christ is undoubtedly the content of Bulgakov's eschatology, but it is the question of theodicy, of freedom

---

17. McClymond, *The Devil's Redemption*, 1009. He writes this of the *Bride of the Lamb*, but it applies to the entirety of Bulgakov's eschatological oeuvre.

18. Berdyaev, *Truth and Revelation*, 67.

19. See chapter 8 of this volume.

and suffering, which serves as the scaffold for his universalist edifice. In his view, the unending torments of the wicked would appear as an eternal blight upon the character of God, who allowed his creatures to come to such an end. For Bulgakov, it is not simply that a sophiological Christology resolves the antinomy of human freedom and divine will; it is that a truly religious consciousness cannot reconcile itself with anything less. The image of God we express in moral resistance to the doctrine of eternal torments reflects the truth of the divine–human reconciliation visible in God's image made flesh, Christ. And so Bulgakov insists—on the basis of ample scriptural testimony—that God will ensure creation's final, blessed outcome, lest God damn creatures precisely in giving them the freedom He knew they would abuse. Bulgakov's logic here is subtle and liable to misinterpretation, so let me clarify. It is not that God is guilty for the sad history of human sin; rather as the Father and Creator of finite, fallible creation (by virtue of its constitution *ex nihilo*, as St. Athanasius emphasized in *On the Incarnation*), God is ultimately *responsible* for his creatures and whatever choices they might make, whatever consequences they might bring upon themselves and the innocent earth. And this implies, necessarily, a salvation as universal as God's love, for throwing your child into the deep end of the pool may be the only way to guarantee her growth as a swimmer, but to turn your back on her as she drowns is to abdicate parental responsibility and any claim to parental goodness or love.

Yet despite its function as a theodicy, an affirmation of universalism does not change the fact of divine silence in the face of suffering *now*. Only the eyes of faith can perceive God's care and responsibility for his creatures today, since the mysterious working of Providence remains inscrutable to us who are caught *in media res*. As Bulgakov puts it elsewhere, "God is love, but the world is full of malice, struggle and hatred. The world is full of the immeasurable suffering of creatures. Groans and wails are borne to heaven, but heaven remains mute and without answer. Such is the kenosis of the Father's love."[20] To the unbelieving heart, however, this divine kenosis, or God's refusal to interfere with the freedom of humans to destroy themselves, is simply a pious name for divine absence. The protest of Ivan Karamazov in Dostoevsky's *The Brothers Karamazov* still resounds today with its plaintive echoes; it is always possible to "return one's ticket" and refuse the afterlife and its promise of eternal reconciliation if you believe the enormity of earthly suffering was too high a price to pay for universal salvation.

But in the polyphony of Dostoevsky's theological vision, Ivan has neither the only nor the last word. The Elder Zosima also remains, inviting the

20. Bulgakov, *The Comforter*, 385.

Christian to take responsibility for the sins of all, to become a co-worker with God's providence in the space divine kenosis makes possible. In Bulgakov's view, only universalism can render such cooperation with God existentially viable. Only the hope that God's love is such as to seek the last sinner, to the utter limit of damnation, can ground our faith in God's goodness *now*, in our present vale of tears. No amount of brilliant or clever theologizing can substitute for that fundamental act of faith that underlies every utterance of the word *Father* in Christian prayer; yet to believe in the Father's commitment to saving every precious child of earth makes that leap of faith a bit shorter of a distance to cross. This is the heart of Bulgakov's eschatology: the hope, grounded on the Father's character revealed in Christ, that God will in the end truly be all in all. "And hope does not disappoint, for the love of God has been poured into our hearts by the Holy Spirit" (Rom 5:5).

1

The Foundational Antinomy of the Christian Philosophy of History

IN CHRISTIAN CONSCIOUSNESS THERE inevitably struggle against each other two conceptions, two perceptions of history: the optimistic-chiliastic and the pessimistic-eschatological. Both of these have deep roots in Christianity and at the same time are incompatible with each other. Their mutual relationship can be defined as an antinomistic conjugation: here we have a religious antinomy, logically irresolvable but nonetheless psychologically felt. Between them there exists no logical conflict of contradictory claims, but rather an antinomy of judgments, the nature of which Kant illuminated in his *Critique of Pure Reason*, in his analysis of the unavoidable antinomies of pure reason. Such antinomies cannot be and ought not to be reconciled— for they are irreconcilable—but rather they must be understood in their genesis and significance. Then they can, at least, be explained as expressing different sides of or conditions of unified being, which, nonetheless, reason with its current powers is unable to contain and to understand without contradictions. In antinomies there is given experiential, graphic proof of the supra-rational character of being, or, what is the same thing, of the insufficiency of the powers of reason for adequately comprehending it. The presence of antinomies inevitably leads us to the conclusion that the current state of being is transitional, unfinished, and, in this obvious incompleteness, it now reveals openings to different possibilities of consciousness.[1]

---

1. This antinomic nature of consciousness was noted with the striking force of philosophical intuition by Dostoevsky (who would hardly have known Kant) in his materials for *Demons*, first published in the appendix to the eighth volume of its sixth

For non-religious consciousness, life simply *happened*, it is an accident; for religious consciousness, life is *given* and, as given from above, it is
holy, full of mystery, of depth and enduring significance. And life is given
to our consciousness not in the form of an isolated, individual existence,
but rather of the lineal, the historical, the universal, the global; it arises in
the infinite flow of life proceeding from the Fountain of life, the God of the
living [Mark 12:17] who does not know dependence and who created not
death but life [Wis 1:13]. In the face of this universal and cosmic life, and,
therefore, in the face of history, responsibilities are placed on us, along with
the "talents" entrusted to our use [Matt 25:14–30] from the very moment
of our birth. For religious consciousness, history is a holy sacrament, and
one that furthermore possesses meaning, value, and significance in all of its
parts, as was deeply felt in German classical idealism, especially in Hegel.
But at the same time history is also our task, our work; we can and we must
relate to history "pragmatically," as its creators. But human activity cannot
be realized apart from the individual setting of goals, apart from historical
tasks and ideals; they arise in the consciousness of the actor with the same
necessity as that by which we, when looking ahead, see the horizon. We
can, of course, choose not to look ahead at all and therefore never see the
horizon, but, if we lift our eyes, we inevitably have it before us, and even
more than this, we cannot shake the feeling of its attainability, the illusion
that we can reach it; and after our consciousness has become fully sober, we
cannot shake the feeling that it is possible at least to walk towards it. We are
surrounded by historical horizons in which, with more or less clarity, this
or that goal is projected, in which a chiliasm with some content or another
is foreordained.

We may be completely free of Judaistic chiliasm, of hope for a historical miracle as a *deus ex machina*, for the interference of supra-historical and
supernatural forces in history, having recognized that the historical path in
its entire expanse is completely open for man. We may even be thoroughly

---

printing. Stavrogin (the prince) says here in a conversation with Shatov: "I don't understand why you consider the possession of a mind, that is, consciousness, the greatest of
all possible existences? . . . Why do you reject the possibility of a secret? Note also that,
perhaps, unbelief is natural for man, and this precisely because he puts mind above all;
since mind is a property only of the human organism, he thereby neither understands
nor wishes to understand life in another form, that is, life beyond the grave—he does
not believe that *that* life is higher. On the other hand, the sense of despair and wretch-
edness is proper to man by nature, for the human mind is so constituted that at every
moment it doubts itself, is not satisfied with himself, and man is therefore prone to
consider his existence inadequate. We are, clearly, transitory beings and our existence
on earth is, clearly, a process, the uninterrupted existence of a chrysalis transitioning
into a butterfly."

permeated by that pragmatist conviction that history is wholly our domain and that supernatural forces of grace act in history not in a directly miraculous fashion but instead by irrigating or nourishing the roots of the human soul, in those depths where human strivings and decisions ripen. But from the formal-chiliastic perception of the historical horizon, i.e., from the actual faith in the attainability of the ideals of progress, we can never be set free. Granted, in such a perception of history we constantly and consciously substitute only the part for the whole, the phenomena accessible to us for the inaccessible noumena, but we are not in a condition to be freed from this historical phenomenalism—not unless we reject our active-optimistic relationship to history, the striving for historical harmony, for the resolution of dissonance, for progress. The religious perception of history was most strongly manifested of course in the prophets, as the fruit of their enthusiasm and inspiration; it is inseparably bound up with Christianity too, and thus also somehow bound up with it is this entire complex of feelings and ideas.

Granted, if we attempt to consistently think through this complex of ideas imposed on us by the practical character of history, by our practical historical reason, we will be easily convinced that a horizon is nothing more than a necessary optical illusion and is thus for that reason unattainable, and that progress is permitted only through infinite movement, in a bad infinity. We are convinced that before us lies an antinomy, quietly slipping from our hands like a shadow when we want to catch it. We must fall into a self-blinding illusionism, must acknowledge the validity of a Fata Morgana, must reconcile ourselves with a bad infinity, must come to believe in the reality of the horizon in order to become completely comfortable with the theory of progress; we must fall into historical harmonism and, having numbed ourselves to other ideas and perceptions, we must affirm the conditional as the unconditional. This historical chiliasm, torn from its religious roots and reborn in the humanistic theory of progress that is so widespread in our days, leads humanity to a religious hibernation, makes it unable to take flight because it has grown heavy and fully content with itself and the world.

Of course, in these circumstances the only language that can speak in a commanding fashion is that of religious and mystical experience, which authoritatively rouse us from sleep and allow us to feel the other, tragic side of being. The day's din of temporality alternates with night's whisper of eternity, and under the swelter of life, the icy breath of death occasionally blows by, and when this breath enters a soul, even just once, that soul can thereafter hear this silence even in the middle of the din of the market, can feel this cold even under the scorching sun. And he who in his own experience has recognized the real power of evil as the foundation of worldly tragedy loses his erstwhile credulity towards history and life. In the soul, sadness settles deep within, and in the heart there appears an ever-widening crack. Thanks to the reality of evil, life becomes an auto-intoxication, and not only the body but also the soul accept many poisons, in whose face even Metchnikoff[2] with his anti-toxins is powerless. A historical sense of self is colored by a feeling of the tragic in life, in history, in the world, it is freed from its eudaimonistic coloring, it is made deeper, more serious—and darker. The idea of *eudaimonistic* progress with the hope for a final harmony is more and more crowded out by the idea of *tragic* progress. According to this idea, history is the ripening of tragedy and its final act; the last page is marked by an extreme and already unbearable tension; it is the agony followed by death, which lies in wait both for individuals and for humanity as a whole, and only beyond the threshold of death does new life await. Such a sense of the world ceases being chiliastic; it becomes eschatological.

Eschatologism, according to its two-fold character, can be either bright, to the extent that within it there exists a presentiment of otherworldly harmony (the "air of resurrection"), or dark, to the extent that it is colored by a presentiment of the approaching end and of the calamities preceding it. (A similar two-fold character distinguishes personal eschatology as well, our personal relationship to death.) In early Christianity the tones of joyful eschatologism predominated: with fervor they prayed at that time, "come, Lord Jesus," [Rev 22:20] and with impatience they awaited his near advent. In the eschatologism of later Christianity, the dark tones conquer, there predominates the expectation of the Antichrist and of the final trials. But in both these worldviews anti-historicism is equally strong: the feeling of empirical reality and of its immediate demands is dulled, just as when a person who, in preparation for death, loses the taste for and interest in daily affairs and concerns while thought focuses on what is unmoving and eternal. The feeling of the transfiguration of the world, of the implacable battle with its elements, of the contingency of history and of our present life more generally leads the spirit beyond the borders of history and even of the world, and it dulls its sensitivity to the impressions of the latter, makes it not of this world. Sometimes this eschatological worldview comes over the masses (as in our *Raskol* at the time of Peter)[3] like a spiritual epidemic; at other

2. Ilya Ilyich Metchnikoff (1845–1916), a pioneer in immunology, was awarded the Nobel Prize in 1908. —Trans.

3. "Raskol," Russian for "split" or "schism," refers to the most important religious movement of seventeenth-century Russia. It signals the division of the Russian Orthodox Church into two halves, the official Church following the liturgical reforms of Patriarch Nikon in 1653, and the "Old Believers" who worshiped according to the older rites these reforms altered. The anathematization of Old Believers in 1666–67, as well

times it completely abates. The eschatological worldview does battle with the chiliastic, but at the same time it is practically united with it, though in differing proportions. One or the other tone prevails and colors the general mood.

Nevertheless, if we try to make eschatologism the sole guiding principle of history and take it to its natural conclusion, then we will be persuaded that here too we have to do with antinomy. Eschatology denies history for the sake of eternity, the empirical for the sake of the transcendental. But still eschatology does this only within the limits of the temporal and the relative, and thus it inevitably falls under the influence of these limits. To the extent that eschatologism is an intimate mood of the personality, the music of the soul, it remains a living and genuine mystical experience. But convert it into an abstract norm, into a dogmatic idea, and it too turns out to be only a historical program—a violent one at that—which barbarously maims living life, i.e., it becomes an embodied contradiction. It is only this life that is given to us in an unmediated and immanent fashion, and only in it and through it are we able to be born to a new life, outgrowing it only from within it.

Meanwhile, this pseudo-eschatologism turns its squeamish grimace, its cold animosity, precisely towards productive life, raising the denial of history to the level of a historical program that is then implemented by violence, i.e., by the most earthly of means. It is this that defines the dark "medieval," "monastic," "ascetic" relationship to life which provoked against itself, as a natural reaction, that chiliastic humanism that is equally one-sided. This false eschatologism lit the pyres of the Inquisition, raised persecutions against human thought and freedom, justified spiritual despotism, and ultimately incited against itself a hatred that lives to this day. And its falsehood consists primarily in the fact that eschatologism can function only as a personal worldview, as a personal mood, but not as a historical program, which is, furthermore, not even implemented in oneself but time and again imposed instead on the bodies of others. Precisely in this way does there arise the hypocrisy of pseudo-eschatologism so typical of this trend.

And so, the attempt to resolve the problem of a Christian philosophy of history in the light of only the immanent or only the transcendent, the chiliastic or the eschatological, cannot consistently be pursued to its endpoint and thereby reveals the antinomical character of these solutions. This antimony is felt in the experience of every person in accord with the

as official state persecution, increased the apocalyptic fervor of the Old Believers, a significant number of whom practiced self-immolation as a form of social and religious protest. —Trans.

character and the depth of this experience. In the teaching of V. S. Solovyov[4]
we see the classic example of such antinomism. Beginning with the *Lectures on Divine-Humanity*[5] and other works of his early period, he exhibits a
greatly optimistic and harmonious worldview[6] in which abstract principles
predominate and are reconciled in the coming synthesis (under the marked
influence of N. F. Fedorov).[7] He ends, however, full of torment, with the
rending dissonance of "Three Conversations" and "The Tale of the Antichrist" with its radical eschatologism. Such a mood was a turning point for
the author himself too, for after "The Tale of the Antichrist" it was possible
only either to die to the world, hiding himself away in the desert, or simply
to die, and the foreword to "Three Conversations" is full of this presentiment of near death. Solovyov briefly lifted the veil of Isis and looked into
that abyss into which a mortal may not look with impunity, just as it is not
granted to mortal man to know either his own future or the time of his
death, the time of his personal "end of the world." The spiritual biography
of Solovyov in this sense presents an example, unique in recent philosophy philosophy, of the radical exacerbation of the problem of history with
its antinomism. In his spiritual evolution what is revealed is precisely this
antinomism. It is impossible simply to say that Solovyov rejected his former worldview and went over to another; no, both in essence belong to one
and the same Christian worldview which he always confessed, and in fact
he never fully rejected either of them, but in his religious experience both
members of the antinomy were joined at various times in his life with varying psychological force.

---

4. Vladimir Sergeevich Solovyov (1853–1900), a literary critic, ecumenist, theologian, and philosopher, was one of the most oustanding religious thinkers of Russia's
nineteenth century. He is considered the father of the Russian religious renaissance. In
his philosophical and theological work he especially thematized God's wisdom, or "Divine Sophia," as a locus for tying together diverse theological doctrines; his writings in
this vein set the course for the Russian sophiological school, of which Bulgakov became
the premier representative in the twentieth century. —Trans.

5. An English translation can be found under the title, Vladimir Solovyov, *Lectures
on Divine-Humanity*. —Trans.

6. We find the most clear expression of this mood in the recently published letters
(*Russian Thought*, 1910, V) of the philosopher's youth written to Ekaterina Vladimirovna Selevina [Solovyov's maternal cousin —Trans.]. Here we read, among other statements: "The conscious conviction that the present state of man is not as it should be
means for me that it should be changed, transfigured. I do not recognize the existence
of evil as eternal, I do not believe in hell."

7. Nikolai Fedorovich Fedorov (1829–1903), Russian philosopher and futurist who
greatly influenced the Russian Religious Renaissance. —Trans.

Solovyov, however, knew of this antinomy and took it into account. This, unfortunately, cannot be said of Konstantin Leontiev,[8] who expressed the mood of a one-sided, radical eschatologism with an almost complete devaluation of earthly life[9] (neither can it be said of Nikolai Fedorovich Fedorov, who represents the opposite extreme). However, in Leontiev this worldview is complicated byand still enveloped in his aestheticism, in his Nietzscheanism, in the individual particularities of both his taste and even of his literary talent. He does not notice, or he ignores, the antinomical character of the problem, but this very thing is what makes so hateful to him a "rosy" Christianity in which religion is viewed primarily as oil for greasing the wheel of the social mechanism or of the chariot of progress, in which it is valued as a means to achieve extrinsic goals. If the first, for all his seriousness and sincerity, sins through an impious attitude to life, then the second is distinguished by an impermissible lack of seriousness towards the dark side of Christian eschatologism, towards its dualistic-tragic understanding of history. One cannot make the sole guiding motif of life the idea of the inevitability of death, but banishing from thought the memory of the hour of death is the height of religious frivolity. It is necessary to live with full respect for life and concern for it, but to live without forgetting death and by preparing for it in this very life.

I conclude with a comparison. In one of his most significant letters[10] to the late A. N. Schmidt,[11] V. S. Solovyov recounts the following dream that an old dame (A. F. Aksakova[12]) had concerning him: "She saw that she had a letter from me, written in my normal handwriting which she called

8. Konstantin Nikolayevich Leontiev (1831–91), Russian philosopher who predicted apocalyptic catastrophes for Russia in the twentieth century. —Trans.

9. "In the place of Christian beliefs about the afterlife and asceticism there appeared humane utilitarianism; instead of the thought of loving God, of the salvation of the soul, of union with Christ, we have preoccupation about the universal practical good. Contemporary Christianity is no longer seen as divine, as a simultaneously awe-inspiring and dreadful teaching, but instead as infantile prattle, an allegory, a moral tale whose sensible interpretation is economic and moral utilitarianism" (*The East, Russia, and Slavdom*).

10. I have in my possession only a *copy* of this letter, but this, however, was provided to me by A. N. Schmidt herself. It is marked April 23rd, 1900. [On Schmidt see n11 below —Trans.].

11. Anna Nikolaevna Schmidt (1851–1905), a Russian journalist and mystic whose visionary work, *The Third Testament*, made a major impression on many figures of the Russian Religious Renaissance. —Trans.

12. Anna Feodorovna Aksakova (1829–89), a Russian memoirist. She was the daughter of the Russian poet Feodor Tyutchev and the wife of Ivan Aksakov, a prominent Slavophile author. —Trans.

pattes d'araignée.[13] Reading the letter with interest, she noticed that inside was enfolded yet another letter on gorgeous paper. Unfolding it, she discovered a word, written in magnificent handwriting in golden ink, and at that very moment she heard my voice: 'Here is my real letter, but wait to read it,' and right then she saw me enter the room, bent under the weight of an enormous sack of copper money. I drew forth from the sack and threw on the floor a few coins, one after another, saying: 'When all the copper has come out, that's when you'll get to the golden words.'"

Not everyone will have golden words written in his inner letter, but all bear within themselves a certain secret; even if they are not always conscious of it, all possess their own personal apocalypse. But it cannot be disclosed until we have spent all our copper money, until we have rendered to life all that is owed it . . . .

1909–10

---

13. French: *spider legs* (cf. English "chicken scratch"). —Trans.

2

On the Kingdom of God

THE DIVINE LITURGY OF St. John Chrysostom begins with the proclamation, "Blessed is the *Kingdom* of the Father, of the Son, and of the Holy Spirit, now and ever and unto ages of ages." And perhaps there is no other expression more often repeated in Church proclamations than the glorification of God's kingdom, power, and glory. In praising the kingdom of God through her sacraments and religious rites, the Church simultaneously proclaims its coming and expresses her deepest knowledge concerning it. It is in this same sense that must we understand the Church's continual proclamation of the evangelical beatitudes, which are preceded by the prayer, "Remember us in your kingdom, Lord," as well as the unceasing repetition of the Lord's prayer, the very heart of which is, "Thy Kingdom come." In the liturgy of the Great Entrance, in the transference of the prepared gifts from the table of preparation to the altar, a number of different commemorations are pronounced: "Remember in your Kingdom, Lord God." A similar meaning is found in the funeral liturgy's supplications for the gift of the heavenly kingdom, as well as the parting wish often expressed for the departed: "The Heavenly Kingdom for him!"[1] This exclamation expresses a hope and prayerful wish that the salvation of the departed soul might be accomplished.

In all these usages there is contained and taught a whole gamut of different shades of meaning for the kingdom of God, although this very concision makes this teaching almost tacit. In Orthodox doctrine, the question of the kingdom of God has not at all occupied the same place that it has in recent times, primarily in Protestantism, and yet this idea is the very air by

1. I have translated this term literally here; functionally its meaning is equivalent to the English "rest his soul" or "may she rest in peace." —Trans.

which Orthodoxy's life of prayer breathes. In its most profound aspirations, it is permeated by this searching for that "first" spoken of by the Lord: "Seek ye *first* the Kingdom of God, and all these things shall be added unto you" [Matt 6:33].

In the teaching concerning the kingdom of God, perhaps the most important and difficult thing is to separate the kingdom of God from "all these things," with which it is, in some fashion, connected, for it is "added" to it while at the same time being opposed to it. What proves decisive are these shades of meaning—not tones but half-tones, that is, a greater or lesser emphasis on this or that idea. And the difference between the varying tones of the teaching on the kingdom of God relates not so much to the content of the teaching, which is common to the entire Christian world, as to these emphases.

The kingdom of God in the Bible has manifold meanings: historical and eschatological, personal and social, creaturely and divine, sociological and ecclesiological. This is a most universal concept, organically including all these definitions in itself while being exhausted by none of them. But it becomes accessible to our experience only in *personal* life, in spiritual rebirth, which begins subjectively with the transformation of our spiritual world through repentance, *metánoia*: Hence the beginning of the Gospel's preaching: "Repent, for the Kingdom of God is at hand" [Matt 3:2]. Objectively it begins with baptism: "Whoever is not born from above cannot see the Kingdom of God" [John 3:3]. The heart of man is the only throne in creation worthy of the kingdom of God, and God reigns in the heart of man, provided he hand it over to God. As the innermost life of the Christian's heart, as the "life in Christ" (St. John of Kronstadt),[2] the kingdom of God is first of all a spiritual good, a grace-bestowing *eternal life*, according to the Lord's words in John's Gospel: "This is eternal life, that they may know you, the only true God, and the one you have sent, Jesus Christ" (17:3). The human heart is the gate through which the kingdom of God enters; it does not appear apart from this gate, from without, "by observance," for the kingdom of God is within you [Luke 17:21]—in you and through you is it realized.

This is the main opposition between the Jewish understanding of the messianic kingdom and the Gospel's: for the former, the kingdom of God is a historical or metahistorical event accomplished with or *over* people but not within them, whereas for the latter it is an event in the spiritual world, *metánoia*, an address. And the answer to this address is the good news that the kingdom of God is *at hand*, for "The Word was made flesh" [John 1:14],

---

2. A reference to the spiritual journals of St. John of Kronstadt (1829–1909), entitled *My Life in Chirst*. —Trans.

"The King of Heaven out of love for mankind has appeared on earth and lived with men."[3] He himself has become man. The turning of the human heart to God, in all of the pagan world and even in the Old Testament, did not establish the kingdom of God in the human heart, for God remained distant and inaccessible, high and terrible. One could enter into relation with him only on the grounds of his given law, the "Old Testament," which possesses the "shadow of good things to come, but not the very form of these things" (Heb 10:1) and which leaves untouched the veil over the human heart, which is removed only by Christ (2 Cor 3: 13–16). The Old Testament law gave no satisfaction, for it "made nothing perfect" (Heb 7:19), *oudèn eteleíōsen ho nómos*, and by the law no man is justified (Gal 2:11) from among those kept under the law (3:23), *hypò nómon ephrouroúmetha.* "The law was for us a schoolmaster to bring us to Christ" (3:24). Similarly, even the sacrifices offered daily had significance only as a remembrance of sins, but they could not make perfect those offering them (Heb 10:1–4). Therefore these sacrifices, as well as the law, left a dissatisfaction, a certain emptiness, at the bottom of the soul. This cast a deep shadow on the soul of the Jewish people, and as a response to this dissatisfaction were born religious fantasies of the arrival of the messianic kingdom coming by "observance." This was a unique spiritual illness, in a certain sense a natural reaction to religious frustration, a predictable illusion resulting from deceived spiritual vision—an unmet embrace, an unquenched thirst, an unanswered cry. Nature abhors a vacuum, and it fills itself with phantasms through which one can see—even if in a perverted fashion—the coming kingdom of God.

But even more tragic was the spiritual fate of people living in paganism, for the pagans, left for a long time in their infirmity, were incapable of manifesting in purity what "God had revealed to them" (Rom 1:19), but instead "became vain in their imaginations, and their foolish heart was darkened" (Rom 1:21) and "they exchanged the truth of God for a lie and worshiped and served the creature instead of the Creator" (Rom 1:25). The spiritual convulsions of the pagan world, its unceasing efforts in the attempt to outgrow itself, to break through to the other world—in mysteries, ecstasies, in sacrificial offerings—all these were a sort of spiritual still-birth, "the fruitless church of the pagans" (in the words of the ecclesial chant).[4] Paganism sought the kingdom of God and it did not find it, and while never reaching it, it languished in ever-new attempts. It oscillated from faith to faith and ended up as a religious syncretism and altar "to the unknown God" [Acts 17:23], that unanswered question posed to heaven.

3. Dogmatikon, Tone 8. —Trans.

4. Canon of the First Apostle and Evangelist John the Theologian, Chant 3. —Trans.

Neither the pagan nor the Old Testament world reached the kingdom of God, which they both, in their own way, sought: it was not *given* to man, even while it constituted his deepest and most inward spiritual longing. And then there rang out the words of the good news: "The Kingdom of God is *at hand*," and it is "within you," *entòs hymôn*. The ambiguity of this expression—simultaneously indicating here the presence of the King and God among men as well as the new accessibility of the kingdom of God to the human spirit—is not accidental, and it indicates the inner link between these two. Man has received an answer, complete and unconditional, to his questioning of heaven. The kingdom of God ceased to be an unachievable object of searching and became instead a reality revealing itself in response to personal effort. And this answer, this fulfillment, this reality of the kingdom of God, "within, among you," entòs hymôn—this is Jesus Christ, the perfect God-man.

The kingdom of God is *at hand* for man because in Christ, God and man are completely united. And what was accomplished in him is effective for the entire human race as well. The kingdom of God is the incarnation in process, in addition to being its power on display, the realized union of two natures, two wills, two feelings—divine and human.[5] And on this cornerstone, which is Christ, each one builds his edifice from his own material—gold, silver, clay, wood, straw (1 Cor 3:11–12). Christ's humanity, the body of Christ, is the Church of Christ in which he lives and acts by the Holy Spirit; the Church is the very kingdom of God, at hand and in the process of realization. And between the kingdom of God and the Church there is no barrier or difference, just as we find no such distinction in the New Testament either. One of the most remarkable features of this New Testament teaching is that its teaching on the kingdom of God imperceptibly and naturally becomes a teaching on the Church, and not only in the epistles of the apostle Paul and in John's Gospel, where the spiritual side of the kingdom of God is revealed, but also in the Synoptics, and even in their most critical sections (e.g., the words of the Lord to Peter in Matt 16:18). And just as the scope of the concept "Church" is not exhausted by any one meaning alone but instead moves from one to whichidea to the next, so too the kingdom of God proves equally as undefinable and multifaceted as the Church, this abiding incarnation. Is it not this fact the mysterious significance of the Gospel story of the Lord's transfiguration points? This story is preceded by the mysterious words of the Lord to his disciples that some of them "would not taste death until they saw the Kingdom of God"

5. A reference to the christological definition of the Sixth Ecumenical Council. —Trans.

(Luke 9:27) "come in power" (Matt 9:1) or the "Son of Man coming in his kingdom" (Matt 16:28). The typical interpretation of this passage that we find in the holy fathers is that it refers precisely to the transfiguration of the Lord, understood as a certain immediate revelation of the divinity of Christ, the manifestation of his glory or a theophany ("revealing Your glory to Your disciples as far as they could bear it"; "O Christ God, Your disciples beheld Your glory as far as they could see it"—as the Church ode for the day sings).[6] If we accept this interpretation of the Gospel text—and it is difficult *not* to accept it—then coming to know Christ's divinity, beholding his countenance, just *is* the kingdom of God, i.e., eternal life manifesting in the temporal. But when Peter wanted to contain eternal life in time and to restrain it there, "building three tents" [Matt 17:4], the error in this wish was disclosed. Yet the Orthodox Church, as a result of the controversies provoked by the teaching of St. Gregory Palamas in the fourteenth century, established at the Constantinopolitan councils the dogma that the Taboric light seen by the ascetics ("hesychasts") in a state of rapture was a genuine vision of divinity, identical in this sense with the transfiguration. Eternal life, the grace-bestowing vision of the kingdom of God, is available in this world, according to the meaning of this dogma; it is as if a new ascent to Mount Tabor and contemplation of the Lord's glory takes place. The power of the transfiguration is the kingdom of God, and the "some" who did not taste death before they saw the kingdom of God are not only the disciples but all who commune in eternal life and who are expressly honored with the vision of God's glory.

And so, the first and immediate meaning of the kingdom of God for each person is spiritual life, the measure of his ecclesiality, of his communion in the gifts of the Holy Spirit and the fellowship with God in Christ that is given by the Church. This kingdom of God is completely near to us; yet at the same time its acceptance depends on the searching of each, and it is not given apart from this searching ("*seek*" the kingdom of God, the Lord says [Matt 6:33]) and effort ("for the Kingdom of God is taken by force" [Matt 11:12]). The spiritual, graced life that is given in the Church is the kingdom of God being accomplished within us, and we possess an interior self-evidence for this, a self-authentication, "for life has appeared, and we have seen and we testify and announce to you this eternal life" (1 John 1:2, cf. 1 John 2:25). Connected with this are these words from the Theologian:[7] "The anointing which you have received from him abides in you, and you

---

6. From the Troparion and Kontakion of the Feast of the Transfiguration. —Trans.

7. In the Eastern Christian tradition, John the apostle is known as "John the Theologian," one of the only three figures in Christian history to earn this title (Gregory Nazianzen and St. Symeon the New Theologian being the other two). —Trans.

have no need that anyone teach you, but . . . this very anointing teaches all of you, and is true, and is no lie" (1 John 2:27). To the Christian is granted the anointing (*chrîsma*) of the kingdom of God, the royal gift of eternal life. And this gift is both consecration and sanctity. Spiritual life, eternal life in God, consecration and sanctity—all these are different ways of expressing the same gift of the kingdom of God given by the Church, in the Church, and through the Church.

The ascetical writings of the holy fathers are replete with evidence confirming the common idea that *eternal life* is already granted to the Christian now *and* that he must seek after it. Therefore, the entire grace-bestowing life of the Church, with her prayers, liturgies, sacraments—through which the grace of the Holy Spirit is always flowing—belongs to the domain of the kingdom of God, and by living in the Church, we enter into the kingdom, we commune with it. And this must be said especially of the sacraments, in which the grace of the Holy Spirit is continually given, and in the first place and most of all concerning the Eucharist, the sacrament of the incarnation. The Divine Liturgy is the coming kingdom of God, which is essentially the incarnation, and it therefore begins, as we have already noted, with the proclamation, "Blessed is the *kingdom* of the Father, of the Son, and of the Holy Spirit." Communion in the mysteries of Christ is the effectual entrance into the kingdom of God. After the transformation of the holy gifts, the priest prays (secretly): "So that they may be for those who partake of them . . . the fullness of the Kingdom of Heaven."[8] This meaning of the kingdom of God is explicated with particular force in the writings of St. Symeon the New Theologian.[9] As a whole, the entire liturgy, which is stamped with a profound realism, belongs to the domain of the kingdom of God. The liturgy bears the meaning not simply of a remembrance, of a moral teaching or even of prayer; no, in its entire symbolism it also contains the power of

8. Text of the Divine Liturgy of St. John Chrysostom accessed here: << https://www.goarch.org/-/the-divine-liturgy-of-saint-john-chrysostom>>. —Trans.

9. "What are these good things?" asks St. Symeon, concerning those good things which the apostle Paul tasted when he was taken up to the third heaven. "Together with the good things stored up in heaven, these are the Body and Blood of our Lord Jesus Christ which we see every day, and eat, and drink. . . . Do you understand which Kingdom it is that He says we are to seek? The one which is high up in Heaven, which is to be revealed at the resurrection of all the dead? . . . God Who is the Maker, reigns over all things in heaven, and on earth, and beneath the earth. . . . No less does he reign over each one of us in justice and knowledge and truth. Thus it is this reign which Christ tells us to seek, such that . . . God should reign also over us. . . . Thus does God reign in those in whom He did not reign before, . . . through tears and repentance, and these are made perfect through spiritual wisdom and knowledge, . . . and thus no one should be so stupid as to reject Christ who is present everywhere and seeks to reign over us all." (St. Symeon the New Theologian, "Third Ethical Discourse," translation altered).

the holy mystery of the kingdom of God on earth. In the heavenly Jerusalem come down to earth from heaven, the Seer of Mysteries saw no temple, "for the Lord God Almighty is its temple, and the Lamb" (Rev 21:22). But in the present age, until the kingdom of God shall come to pass, we are in need of a temple. The goal of the Christian life is acquiring the Holy Spirit, the venerable Seraphim taught, but that just *is* the kingdom of God, or "truth, peace, and joy in the Holy Spirit" (Rom 14:17). It is for the "sending down of divine grace and the gift of the Holy Spirit" that the Church prays before the consecration of the holy gifts.

And this consecration by the Holy Spirit, this assimilation to him, is in fact the accomplishment of *salvation*, which is why the kingdom of God *is* salvation. But salvation is precisely that anticipatory taste of the life of the age to come, which we experience while still immersed in the waves of time. Eternal life begins here, and whoever does not know it here does not know it at all. Before the general resurrection, one can catch the scent of the age to come, a foretaste of eternal beatitude, albeit in grief, in repentance, in struggle. This combination of the eternal and the temporal is the mystery of the spiritual life that Church writers persistently teach. "The one who hears My word and believes in him who sent me does not enter into judgment but has passed from death into life" (John 5:24). Related to this spiritual good of salvation are all the apostle's texts about the kingdom of God, where the kingdom is depicted as the spiritual achievement of man: Rom 14:17; 1 Cor 4:20; 6:9–11; 14:50; Gal 5:19–23. Such is the direct and immediate, religious, spiritual-mystical, "immanent" meaning of the kingdom of God. It is sanctity. "Be ye holy, for the Lord thy God is holy" [1 Pet 1:16]. And sanctity grants a direct and immediate vision and communion with God, with such a fullness, furthermore, that it is *already* real and present, not simply expected and hoped for. It is eternal life's distinct character to extinguish the sense of temporality, past and future, and thus in it we find quieted that tense expectation inherent to eschatology more generally, for eternal life contains in itself the abiding *now*.

But as such, the kingdom of God is the x sought after in ascesis, it is that value for whose attainment we must give away all other values in exchange. This is the pearl of the Gospel parable [Matt 13:45–46], this is the field with the hidden treasure for whose sake you become estranged from and sacrifice everything. Therefore, to the kingdom of God belongs not just the goal but also the means, all those efforts and struggles that take place on the path of seeking it. Not only salvation itself but also the path of salvation, all ascetical feats undertaken for the sake of the Lord, are the kingdom of God. For in that bi-unity of divine-human life which is the kingdom of God, it is not only the reign itself but also the accession, the effort of the human soul to give itself away; it is the path, the bearing of the cross following after Christ.

This rupture in time opening up to eternity contains in itself the overcoming of time. Time is compressed into a single point, it becomes imperceptible. *From within* the "Kingdom of God is at hand," and the over-whelming power of this accomplished nearness destroys the sense of abiding in time.[10] It is generally known that the earliest Christians expected the immediate second coming of Christ, and for this reason their prayer was the following: "Even so, come, Lord Jesus!" The words: "Children! These are the last days" (1 John 2:18) and "to us, upon whom the ends of the ages have come" (1 Cor 10:11) were understood not simply in the broad ontological sense, as indicating the already accomplished incarnation, but also in the direct sense, that no time remained at all. *History* did not exist for early Christianity as a whole. In order to feel the weight of time and the burden of history, there was required a sort of distancing from God, the extinguishing of the consciousness of God, as it were. But the graced nearness of God at that time was such that it alone became the all-consuming reality. And this nearness revealed two possibilities within man: the joy of the wedding feast of the Lamb [Rev 19:6–9], as well as the trepidation of the creature in the face of the Creator and that of sinners before the judgment of truth. Among its many spiritual gifts, early Christianity possessed this feeling of the near-ness of Christ, paschal joy. By grace this feeling is given to us in Holy Week, when the Risen Lord is found as if in our very midst. The paschal feeling is the joy of resurrection.

But however overwhelming this feeling of eternity and fullness, it nonetheless also leaves room for a sort of inner knowledge that it is not the definitive fullness, for God does not give the Spirit by measure [John 3:34], and we always rise from strength to strength [Ps 84:7]. In other words, the nearness and genuine presence of God and his kingdom in the world reveal to man a spiritual view towards the future: from the kingdom of grace he looks out onto the kingdom of glory, and he awaits its coming. This consti-tutes the eschatological aspect of the kingdom of God. Like eternal life, the kingdom of God (because it is a spiritual good) is a *personal* possession, and without possessing it, it is completely impossible to participate in it. The kingdom of God, coming in power, is received or not received, is internally assimilated or rejected, and depending on this it is, for some, blessed com-munion with God, and for others, the source of hell's torments. In this latter

---

10. This victorious sense of eternity's imminence—which swallows up temporal-ity—permeates the final words of the Apocalypse: "And the Spirit and the Bride says, 'Come!' And let him who hears this say, 'Come!' The one who testifies to these things says, Even so, come quickly! Amen. Even so, come Lord Jesus!" (Rev 22:17, 20).

sense, the kingdom exists for all creation, even for the demons, since even the demons believe and tremble. Demons know its inevitability, and they pray it might leave them for a time: "Jesus, Son of the Most High God! I adjure you by God, do not torment me" (Mark 5:7): "You have come here to torment us before the time" (Matt 8:29). But the kingdom of God—for every person who receives it as a personal possession, as a personal achievement, ascent, and breakthrough—also becomes a *cosmic* or pan-human event. It comes in power, and this its future advent is the kingdom of God as an eschatological value. About this kingdom of God the prophets and Gospels speak in different images. Especially in the Synoptics, in the parables, the kingdom of God is invariably understood as a future event connected with the advent of Christ, with the judgment and the separation of the wheat from the chaff, with the wedding feast, with the encounter with the bridegroom and so forth. These ideas and images are so numerous and expressive that they invite some scholars to view this whole teaching in the light of eschatology and to align Christ's teaching with the Jewish apocalypses. These scholarly interpreters rarely distinguish between Christ and these apocalypses, thereby restricting him within the horizon of the latter. Of course, such a convergence between the Gospel and the apocalypses is possible only if we remove from the New Testament all its fundamental teaching concerning spiritual, eternal life—a move that scholarly hyper-criticism also does not hesitate to make.

The Lord definitively taught concerning his second coming and the beginning of the kingdom of God connected with it; this same teaching is contained both in the apostolic epistles and in the Apocalypse, and it was the foundational possession of the early Christian Church: *Maranatha, even so, come!* [1 Cor 16:22]. The advent of the kingdom of God is an event not only metaphysical but also historical; it takes place not in the inner world of a discrete individual, through *metánoia*, but rather through a change in the relation of God to the *world, parousía*. This change consists in the coming near of God to the world, in which God becomes an immediate and self-evident reality, like the givenness of this world is for us now. How accurately we can define this change—that we cannot know. Its ground is in the incarnation, and its consequence will be that divine truth becomes the only and defining principle of life, its only law. And this, its defining significance, is expressed thus: "goods which the human heart has not conceived but which God has prepared for those who love him" (1 Cor 2:9). And this will be a new act of creation, as it were, "of a new heaven and new earth wherein justice lives" [2 Pet 3:13], the descent of the Heavenly Jerusalem down to earth [Rev 21:10], abiding with Christ and seeing his face, and through him the vision of the Holy Trinity.

When we pray for the departed, that they might be granted the "heavenly kingdom," this of course refers to the same heavenly beatitude of communion with God, which is anticipated already in the afterlife, in the state of disincarnation.[11] Christian faith in the resurrection of the dead is essentially the same faith in the advent of the kingdom of God, and this faith is grounded in the good news of Christ's resurrection. "If Christ be not raised, our faith is in vain" [1 Cor 15:17]. The resurrection of Christ encompasses the resurrection to new life of all of humanity as well as the renewal of the world. Life—this victory over death, the last enemy—is the true moment of Christ's accession. The kingdom of Christ, which in his earthly advent was not of this world, becomes in the universal resurrection triumphant in this world, as Revelation says: "the kingdom of this world has become (the kingdom) of our Lord and his Christ, and he will reign for ever and ever" (11:15, cf. 13:10). This kingdom, along with the universal resurrection of the dead, is also reflected in the transfiguration of earth and heaven and of all creation. But the essence of this kingdom is that "we shall ever be with the Lord" (1 Thess 4:17). It is characteristic of this kingdom, therefore, that between God and creation, between Christ and man, there will be no distance, God will be manifest for creation and will therefore reign over it in a manner evident for all to see. In our current state, exiled from Eden and clothed in garments of skin, the world—and man in it—lives a certain antinomical life, and for this world, God is only an object of faith; by the eyes of faith man himself sees God but does not know his kingdom in the world. It is granted to his freedom to oppose this kingdom and to reject it. In the coming kingdom, this obstacle will be eliminated, as it has already been removed in the accomplished incarnation.

And *this* nearness of the Lord is what constitutes the prayerful sigh of those who love him, and the flame of this love permeates the apocalyptic prayer: *Even so, come, Lord Jesus* [Rev 22:20]. This prayer, as we know, has gone out of use, and from the middle of the second century it began to give way to a prayer that was even opposed to it, the prayer *pro mora finis* [for the delay of the end]. For we who lack faith and whose hearts are hardened, this prayer [i.e., *Even so, come, Lord Jesus*] is difficult and beyond our measure, even terrifying to us. One must not deceive and be deceived in prayer; to pray this prayer, therefore, requires a genuine strength to desire the end, to crave the Lord more than anything else, to be free of attachments to the world, possessing it—in the apostle Paul's words—as if not possessing it [1 Cor 7:29]. Our attitude towards this prayer is the measure of our

---

11. That is, in the post-mortem state in which the spirit is separated from the body and soul. —Trans.

Christian freedom, as well as of our Christian faith and love. Without that special call, without that unique outpouring of grace that marked the early Christian period in history, this prayer is beyond man's capacity, and he does not directly venture it, although in a more general form the prayer is also found in the Lord's Prayer: "Thy kingdom come!" Something similar characterizes our attitude towards our own death, which is indeed also *personal* eschatology: dreadful is the hour of death, and before it every living being trembles. But at the same time, death is joyful for the believing heart, as it was for the apostle Paul: "for me to live is Christ and to die is gain. I have a desire to depart and to be with Christ" (Phil 1:22–23). Such ease and joy with regard to liberation from the world is granted only to God's elect, but the shadow of death is always before us, and only frivolousness forgets this.

Eschatology is the foundational element of Christianity. It contains the answers to all the torments and questionings of the life of this age, to all its ruptures, incomprehensibilities, and tragic difficulties. Those who wish to completely "ethicize" the idea of the kingdom of God, seeing in it only an inner good (like Kant, Tolstoy, and many representatives of the latest Ritschlian theology),[12] do violence both to Christ's gospel and to the Christian soul. For the gospel is the good news of the kingdom of God coming in power and proclaimed to all creation (Mark 16:15), and our souls thirst and wait expectantly for this kingdom coming in power and glory. Eschatology answers the demands of the *entire* human being, unlike metaphysical egoism, which is content solely with an inner coming of God's kingdom. But nevertheless, the kingdom of God, which comes in power, cannot be anticipated, for our consciousness cannot contain it; it constitutes an object of faith. Its concreteness grows in tandem with the intensity of our spiritual life, and it is revealed only to the inner eye. All attempts at externally foreseeing and describing it lead only to crass carnal distortions; such were the Jewish conceptions of the messianic kingdom. Faith in the coming kingdom of God is implied in faith in the Creator and Redeemer: God, who is capable of creating the world through his power and of saving it through his sacrificial love, has revealed the power of the Creator along with the love of the Redeemer in the new creation of the saved and transfigured world. In it, God will be all in all [1 Cor 15:28], and no longer will anything result from the creature's rebellious self-will.

Eschatology leads beyond the world and time, beyond the limits of this age. It swallows up the present with the future, and it depreciates the present

12. Albrecht Ritschl (1822–89), a major German Protestant theologian of the nineteenth century. —Trans.

and to a certain degree robs it of any flavor. As far as we can tell, this was the spiritual orientation of early Christianity, which, having no enduring city on the earth and seeking the one to come [Heb 13:14], failed to notice, as it were, the present, having no interest in it and not believing in its permanence. It remained unresponsive and unaccountable to its age, which it viewed as the domain of the beast and the kingdom of the antichrist. In this sense, early Christianity neither knew nor believed in history. The words of the apostle John, "Children, this is the last hour" [1 John 2:18], have an ontological meaning, but primitive Christianity understood them chronologically, as the straightforward absence of time, as time's end. This was a sort of child's naivete, destined to pass away with time, as well as a spiritual holiday that had to give way to the workday. And with the passage of time, it became clear that, although with the incarnation the fullness of time had already begun, nonetheless time had not ended for humanity, and history goes on, although in its new and most crucial era, namely the history of the Church, Christian history.

The Church faced the question of how she should respond to this new task. In the person of her fathers and teachers, the Church understood this question—and of course, she could not do otherwise—as the same question of the Gospels, "when will the Kingdom of God come" (Luke 17:20), and how does it come, and is Christian history already the beginning of its coming? This question was occasioned not only by the widespread chiliastic belief of Judaism but also by the books of the prophets, Old Testament and even New Testament, which speak of the kingdom of God. It is described in images that can be applied to earthly history: the depiction of the mountain of the Lord, the city of the Lord, as the palpable kingdom of God with his saints. And there is one event in the Gospels that can be symbolically interpreted in this sense: the entrance of the Lord—as the promised lowly king—into Jerusalem before his passion. And in this entrance, as also in those few hours he spent afterwards in Jerusalem, he was the earthly King, "just and having salvation" [Zech 9:9]. The King showed himself to be a king even here, in this world, despite the testimony that his kingdom is not of this world [John 18:36]. This event was a certain symbolic anticipation, evidence that the kingdom of God—for whose advent the Lord prayed unconditionally—could appear even on earth. Similarly, and also in symbolic images, we find evidence for the kingdom of God's reality in history, still within the limits of earthly time, in the mysterious text of Revelation concerning the thousand-year kingdom (22:4–6); although this kingdom remains merely an episode in global history, it gives way to a new and definitive overflow of evil and a final confrontation with the antichrist. These few verses have always attracted the attention of interpreters, and its first interpretations—by

writers the Church recognizes as saints: St. Justin the Philosopher, St. Ire-
naeus, Bishop of Lyons—were quite close to Jewish, carnal chiliasm. In time
there prevailed in the Church the spiritual understanding of this prophecy,
according to which its fulfillment was related directly to the spiritual life
of the Church. Such was Blessed Augustine's interpretation, which became
the dominant—although hardly the only possible—interpretation for the
whole Church. Nonetheless, the acceptance of history as the Church's own
responsibility, and thus also the inclusion of the paths of history in the path
of the kingdom of God, eventually took place.

For Western Christianity, this was dogmatically and practically manifested in the establishment of a direct equivalence between the organization
of the Church, *civitas divina*, and the kingdom of God: this was expressed in
Blessed Augustine's foundational treatise, *de civitate dei* [*The City of God*].
In later developments, this idea found expression in the pretensions of papal
power to possess the "two swords" [Luke 22:38], meaning governance in
matters earthly and heavenly. Papal government strove for expansion without limits, and although it has, in effect, shrunk to the size of the Vatican
Palace, nevertheless in principle this governance has never been rejected by
the pope (see the *Syllabus* [*of Errors*]), and it expresses the same idea seen in
the coronation of emperors and, more generally, in the ideal of holy empire.
All these are only different projections of the same general objective: to realize the kingdom of God, through the effective influence of the Church, in
this world.

But similar, or analogous and even equivalent, was the Eastern
Church's idea of the Orthodox emperor crowned by the Church. If pagan
emperors were depicted in the form of the beast and the dragon, then the
Orthodox emperor Constantine—who put the Roman imperial crown beneath the cross and who erected the *labarum*[13] above the Roman armies—
was glorified by the Church as "equal to the apostles," and thus his historic
accomplishment was taken to possess apostolic significance. The idea of an
Orthodox kingdom has not only a political but primarily a *religious* significance. At first in the Byzantine Church, and then later in the Russian
Church, which inherited this idea, to be "emperor" was seen as a special
sacred rank of royal ministry whose prophetic prototype was already out-
lined in the messianic Psalms 20, 21, and especially 72. This ministry was
understood on the model of Christ's royal ministry, and its mission was the
realization of the kingdom of God on earth. However much historical reality distorted this mission, it remained in force, as the principle expression

13. A Roman vexillum or military banner on which the Christian *chi rho* symbol
was displayed. It was first used by Constantine the Great. —Trans.

of the idea that the Church is called to realize the kingdom of God on earth and so possesses the graced charism of dominion, which it communicates to the emperor and through him to the people. For the emperor is the head and representative of the entire Christian people, for whom and with whom he exercises his ministry. And this dominion knows no borders—it extends to all spheres of life. The Orthodox emperor must be the guide and educator of the people on the way to the kingdom of God, he must serve the Church and do her works in this ministry beyond the walls of the Church. If in Byzantium he was called the "external bishop," then his ministry was exercised as a "liturgy outside the Church," as it were, that is, as the sanctification of the entirety of life. The principle significance of this is that here already we see the overcoming of the confines of individualistic Christianity and a recognition of the tasks of building a Christian society in history. In the sphere of Christian dominion are contained all questions: political, social, and cultural, and there is no sphere of governance not subject to it. The nature of the Christian emperor's power imparts to all forms of rule a sacred character and consequently increases the influence of the Church on all of life. Of course, to focus the entirety of theocratic power on the person of the emperor is to narrow its scope of action, for even hierocracy presupposes and depends on the people's hierocracy, theocratic democracy, so to speak. As an aside, this aspect of the theocratic idea was manifested with particular power and clarity in the Anglican reformation, and especially in the Cromwell era.

In Orthodoxy's consciousness, in its Byzantine-Muscovite era, this tie between the Orthodox Church and sacred imperial power was considered so essential and inviolable that one could hardly imagine the Orthodox Church without the emperor, just as you could not imagine it without the bishop. The work of organizing the earthly kingdom was seen as being, if not equal, then on the same level as the management of heavenly affairs; the rank of emperor was considered as essential for the Church as that of the priestly ministry. And this teaching of the Church, that at his coronation the emperor (and in him and through him, therefore, all of civic ministry) was granted a special grace of the Holy Spirit, was sealed and safeguarded by a special anathematization pronounced—as is customary in the Orthodox Church, on the "week of Orthodoxy" (the first Sunday of Great Lent)—together with the anathematization of Arianism, Macedonianism, and other heresies. And yet imperial power is now a thing of the past, the era of Constantine in the history of the Church has come to an end or, at least, has been paused, but Orthodoxy still abides. How can we understand and dogmatically comprehend this newly arisen situation in the life of the Church? Does it mean that the Church has been deprived of a portion of its gifts of grace? And if it has not, how can these gifts manifest today, and can they at all? Or are we now once again in those eschatological days, beyond history, when the Church must exist in the kingdom of the beast, in the midst of the churning, theomachic elements, while Christian history has already come to an organic end?

Medieval history in both the West and the East sought theocratic power and an ecclesiastical culture; its ideal was the universal "enchurchment" of life, which was conceptualized and implemented by means of a sort of theocratic coercion: *compelle intrare*, "force them to come in."[14] Recent times have severed this tie and proclaimed instead the slogans of "separation of Church from government" and "secularization of culture," the universal deconsecration of life. Meanwhile, the Church comes to represent merely a branch of the broader culture, which itself develops in every sphere with complete autonomy. But does the Church agree to this? *Can* it agree to exist in this position? Of course not. It desires, as before, to remain "all things to all people" [1 Cor 9:22], and, although it takes new forms, the universal "enchurchment" of life still constitutes its mission and aspiration. In response to the universal secularization of life, the Church strives with new strength for the sanctification of life, for life's rebirth in the Church, yet not *from without* but from *within*. The Church must not and cannot strive to once again pick up or possess the sword of government after it was wrested from its hand by the judgment of history. It is a harmful and deceptive utopia to hope to restore the old order, for the clock of history shows that it is already the last hour.

But what was accomplished beforehand through government can now be realized through society—not from above, but from below—and the old, coercive theocracy must give way to freedom. In the Christian world new paths are being sought, and on Orthodoxy's tree new buds are growing. For our generation new tasks arise: to fill the old and abiding ideal of theocracy with new content, to find new paths for it. This search is painful and difficult. It contains the possibility of false substitutes and deviations. The most important and difficult thing for the Church will be to preserve its inner independence and supremacy, not to walk again the path of political accommodation. The Antichrist offers his own "good," which for all its deceptive appearance of good leads away from Christ and conflicts with him. Such is the latest humanistic tendency, which directly or indirectly proclaims man to be god and in the name of man-godhood opposes god-manhood.[15] Such

14. Luke 14:23. The text was in the Church's history used to legitimate the use of governmental violence against heretics; it is particularly associated with St. Augustine's approval of imperial force against the Donatists. —Trans.

15. "Man-godhood" is the diabolical opposite of "Godmanhood" or

is the broadly godless humanism that has sprouted from the soil of materialistic socialism and communism. In the form of Russian communism, it has revealed to the entire world the face of the Antichrist. And this battle with godless, humanistic human good, which in fact is no good at all but rather seductive deception, began already in the days of Christ's earthly life, when the people demanded of him an earthly kingdom with bread and earthly prosperity. Contemporary socialism and communism is a direct continuation of this Jewish chiliasm. These are seductive in their ethical similarity to Christianity, for they desire to do the deeds of love while rejecting love in its fountainhead, that is love of God. That is why this purely external convergence between Christianity and socialism, which sometimes manifests as "Christian socialism," is false and pernicious. We cannot sell our birthright for a bowl of lentils [Heb 12:16] and subordinate the eternal to the temporal, belittling it to make it adaptable. The Church must certainly not remain deaf to the demands of life. It can recognize, in certain spheres, the truth of socialism while never seeking in it a new revelation for itself. The religious promises of eternal life, of a new heaven and new earth, far outstrip even the most daring of socialism's fantasies, rendering the latter merely a narrow philistinism. Socialism without faith is that "kingdom of this world" [John 18:36] that blinded the minds of the Jews of Jesus' time. It is the first temptation in the desert, the temptation of bread, which was rejected and exposed by the Savior. And yet the Lord's Prayer states: "give us this day our daily bread." And although here is meant more than just material bread, it also has in view—and therefore shows to be justified, in a certain sense, concern for—that *economism* of life which distinguishes our times.

There exists not only a negative ethics of economy, consisting in asceticism and in its extreme preaching of voluntary poverty, but also a positive ethics recognizing positive duties in the sphere of economic life. It has sufficient grounding both in the Word of God and in patristic writing. Socialism too can also in some sense enter into the *ethics* of economics, although by no means can it constitute an *eschatology*, which is its current pretension. Humanistic or atheistic socialism in the present day is a religion of economism, while in economy and through economy it desires to resolve all the problems of life and spirit, present and future, promising, so to speak, *salvation* through economy. Such a faith is, of course, incompatible with Christianity, which in opposition to every economism confesses: "man shall not live by bread alone but by every word of God" [Matt 4:4]. The significance of socialism is dreadfully exaggerated these days, since those questions of the

"divine-humanity," the proper way in which God and the human person co-image each other under the example of Christ, the God-man, who lived in humility before the Father. — Trans.

life of the spirit—without which humanity cannot exist—it does not resolve at all. Its usefulness is not so much positive as it is negative, to the degree that it mitigates the burden of the struggle for existence and thereby makes clear the way for purely spiritual needs to arise. But for a Christianity allied with socialism there arises the not minor danger of desacralization, the loss of its own *spiritual* treasures for the sake of external achievements; no matter how great the latter may be, there is nonetheless one pearl and one treasure for whose sake we must give everything away: the kingdom of God and in it, the Lord Jesus Christ himself.

History is not a path of progress, a direct ascent from the darkness of barbarianism to the light of humanism, but rather the tragic conflict of two opposing spiritual powers. And the power of evil, the antichristic principle, is not just the stagnation produced by evil but also the latter's creative power (if such an expression is possible): straightforward deception, fraud, defiance. History is a tragedy, the confrontation of two powers, which by the end of history reaches its fullest intensity and maturity. This is why Christian eschatology—both in the apocalypse of the Gospels, in the Lord's discourses on the end of the world, as well as in St. John's *Apocalypse*—is colored with menacing tones. New Testament prophecies of the last days (for example, 1 Thessalonians) speak to us not of universal harmony but of the manifestation of an individual Antichrist and his servants. And this tragic confrontation and dichotomy runs through every sphere of life, and in the final analysis there must not be anything neutral that lacks some religious coefficient. Seek ye first the kingdom of God and his righteousness and all these things shall be added unto you. These words of the Lord express the spiritual law of the kingdom of God, both in its personal and in its historical and societal realization.

The difficulty of Christianity's historical path of creative work is also connected with the fact that this creativity bears within itself the possibility of going in two directions. In the nature of the Lord Jesus Christ there are joined both a divine and human essence—according to the Chalcedonian dogma, inseparably and unconfusedly (*adiairétōs kaì asynchýtōs*). This dogma was disclosed and confirmed at the Sixth Ecumenical Council with respect to the two wills and energies in the Lord Jesus Christ. The human essence is not suppressed but rather illuminated from within by the divine essence. And this relationship is also the norm for all of Christian life and its historical paths; by it are condemned the practical monophysitism or monothelitism that efface or completely eliminate the action of one principle at the expense of the other. Erroneous, therefore, is that pseudo-ascetic—Manichean rather than Christian—view which takes away Christian responsibility for history while expecting everything to happen by divine activity. In practice this means reconciling with the power of sin and evil in its crassest form, and even worse—consenting to it. This practical mono-physitism has marked those times in Church history when the Church was caught up in the most extreme dependence on the government and thereby left the government free of her own effectual influence, when the Church was as if absent in history, practically denying any responsibility, which, nonetheless, she still bore. But the even greater monophysitism is human-ism, which, for the sake of developing the human element, neglects the one thing needful [Luke 10:42], that which one should seek before all else. The kingdom of God is taken by violence, said the Lord [Matt 11:12], and this effort refers not solely to the graced spiritual domain but also to the human. And everyone in his personal life must in practice seek the kingdom's real-ization—dyophysitism, the union of both paths. In the monasteries, which exist precisely for acquiring spiritual goods, there is introduced—as a neces-sary educational tool—obedience, labor (whether physical or intellectual) for the sake of the Lord. A similar obedience exists for the Christian living beyond the walls of the monastery, but the fulfillment of obedience cannot remain external and formal; it requires a responsible, creative intensity from a person, not in his own name but in the name of the Lord who has sent us into the world.

It is by these creative efforts of man, which are stamped with Holy Spirit's gifts of grace, that the kingdom of God is *realized* in history, ripens in history like a plant grown from a seed, like a vineyard entrusted to the workers, as in the Gospel parable [Matt 20:1–16]. History is not empty time just waiting to be filled, like a long corridor that a definite number of people must pass through on the way to the next life. History is a concretely full time that bears within itself its ripening fruit. It must be brought to a close organically so that the kingdom of God might come. We ourselves cannot integrate this series; the fruit is known only to the planter and owner of the vineyard, but it *is* fruit-bearing, and history cannot come to its external end unless it has concluded organically. History is not only an aggregate, the sum of separate lives, but it is the *common task*[16] of all of humanity, which constitutes one tree, as the Gospel genealogy of Christ the Savior testifies with full clarity. In these genealogies, time is calculated not simply by succession of generations but also (in St. Matthew) by certain periods or cycles of fourteen generations each, and *before* their elapse (just like Daniel's

16. The term "common task" is taken from Nikolai Fedorovich Fedorov (1829–1903; see chapter 1, n7 above), who used it to refer to the common goal of humanity to eradicate physical death and to procure physical resurrection through advances in science. Bulgakov means here simply that the development of history is the corporate task of humanity as a whole, not just of this or that individual. —Trans.

earlier, prophetically pre-determined seventy weeks) the time of Christ's birth could not arrive. But the other times and periods of history are also like this.

This plan of history is known only to the Lord, for it is said of that day that it is known neither by the angels nor by the Son (according to his human nature, of course) but only by the Father [Matt 24:36]. But to the one entrusted with the cultivation of the vineyard, it is granted to his human eye to measure history, to survey its achievements, to set its goals. And it is precisely in *this* sphere of setting goals that human effort is exerted to realize the kingdom of God on earth. Man does not set for himself absolutely unreachable goals, but only reachable ones, even if they cannot be realized completely. It is here that the problem of chiliasm returns for us. When we fix our gaze into the distance, before us stands the horizon that separates us from this distance. We know that this is merely an inevitable illusion, and yet we cannot free ourselves from it.

Likewise, does not the horizon of chiliasm arise as we gaze out onto history, like some sort of defined point of historical achievements, like the goal of progress? Nonetheless, we must introduce in advance a number of restrictions on this idea. Clearly, it cannot change the basic understanding of history as a tragic confrontation that ripens in history with increasing force: the idea of an earthly paradise remains inadmissible. But this does not do away with the Christian hope that even here, on earth, a ray of the transfiguration can shine and that the fullness of the kingdom of God is attainable. And who can say what this fullness and its achievement will be like? If an enervating dreaminess is reprehensible, a *Christian* dream is still admissible, and this dream is given a place in Revelation through the mysterious prophecy of the first resurrection and the kingdom of Christ with the saints for one thousand years, on the eve of the final conflict and the uprising of Gog and Magog [Rev 20]. However we may interpret this prophecy, allegorically or spiritually, it cannot be entirely erased or eliminated. It contains in itself a certain possibility of some sort of *fullness* of the appearance of the kingdom of God on earth. This possibility is realized not by human efforts alone but by the power of Christ.

This kingdom will be visible only to the spiritual and only through spiritual eyes. And those who look on God now already abide in this kingdom—*for themselves*. But this kingdom is not just gazing on the face of eternity through time and in spite of it; it is rather the penetration of this same eternity into time. It is not only assimilated—it enters in. Nonetheless, it will not be visible for the entire world; it remains restricted not only in time (one thousand years) but also in place, because it presupposes the presence of the horde of Gog and Magog beyond it. Yet in it will be manifest the fullness.

This is like the Lord's royal entry into Jerusalem, but on a global-historical scale. One must not become intoxicated with this dream, for then it becomes spiritual deception; one cannot structure one's personal life around it, for each one, in his soul, must break through to his own proper, personal chiliasm. But it is also impermissibleto lose this dream, or at least this is so for the soul in which it was once enkindled. Whether it is realizable in history and to what degree cannot be definitively stated, but in people's souls this star shines with a luster that points the way. And for each person this star becomes visible through his own historical and personal prism.

3

The Soul of Socialism (Part II)

MATERIALISTIC ECONOMISM MUST LOGICALLY lead to passive fatalism, because it is not personhood with its creative strivings but rather the impersonal economic process that determines the paths of history. Here there is no place for good and evil, or for any ideal values at all. But in practice, in complete inconsistency with its doctrine, socialism is developing in this recent era the greatest historical dynamism, namely "revolutionism." Since 1789, the spirit of revolution has been hovering over Europe, penetrating deeper and deeper, absorbing into itself new social material, such that society in our time is beginning to be defined by its relationship to revolution, either for or against it.

Revolution is a fact and a principle. As a *fact*, revolutions take place with an elemental anarchy, they are like the eruption of a volcano, spewing lava and ash, or like an earthquake altering the strata, bringing some materials down and raising others up. The elemental powers are already evil in their irrationality, and even more so when man himself becomes such an element. Beastly savagery and frenzy are aroused, and in the masses there awaken age-old resentment, vengeful malice, and built-up envy—of course, alongside the heroic enthusiasm of individual persons, leaders, or groups. It is not clear but rather filthy and muddy water that the bursting Acheron[1] bears. Historical earthquakes are never "moral idylls which could satisfy school teachers," as even Hegel noted. In the rushing stream of revolution, there comes to the surface, like foam, the baseness of humanity, which is often hidden in the darkness—the worst in man arises so that, I suppose,

---

1. One of the rivers of the underworld in ancient Greek mythology. —Trans.

the best might also be revealed [1 Cor 11:19]. The violence and despotism of the oligarchy, the Red Terror,[2] along with revolutionary hypocrisy, demagoguery, and careerism, reflect the wild and uniquely possessed state of the masses and their "leaders."[3]

As a *principle*, revolution is a fundamental break in the thread of a historical tradition, the wish to begin history again, starting with oneself. The pathos of destruction is here the pathos of creation. Barbarization occurs here not only through the altering of social strata but also as a consequence of the general anti-cultural stance of revolution's relationship to the past, even if in practice it serves the culture of the future. Therefore it is not accidental that nihilistic revolt against historical tradition directs itself against faith as well, that it becomes "militant atheism." One cannot explain this solely by appeal to the sins of ecclesiastical institutions, which are here exposed and punished. Revolution bears within itself a general nihilistic enmity towards values and towards the holy, and it would be incomprehensible if earthly mutiny did not recognize itself as an uprising against heaven too, if it did not cross over into theomachy.

This is all true, but clearly revolution is not the normal state of souls, so when exactly does illness become attractive and catastrophe good? Furthermore, illness has its own sufficient grounds, its causes, which are often very profound and reach far in the past. The executioners here become historical victims too, and those who bear the guilt for them are all who have promoted revolutions, either actively or passively. Revolutions are certainly not made by the revolutionaries themselves, who in this regard fall into a false historical hubris; rather, they themselves (along with the counter-revolutionaries) are made by the revolution. What *is* certain is that there exists a certain *idée-force* of revolution, the explosive that sets in motion inert matter, and this is, in addition to envy, also a special *faith* and a *pathos*. In the idea of revolution what finds expression first of all is a striving towards the future, a thirst for it and a faith in it—*amor futuri*. In it there is contained a certain ideal for the future and, most importantly, a certain vision, a projection of this future from the place of the present; its soul in this sense consists in a *utopia* (*u-"topos"*), something as yet unrealized in any place but that must come to pass (this word "utopia" originates with Thomas More, the confessor and martyr of the Catholic Church in the sixteenth century). Utopias can differ,

2. The Red Terror refers to the period of Bolshevist ("Red") political repression during the Russian Civil War (1918–22) immediately following the 1917 Communist revolution. —Trans.

3. This particular Russian word for leader, *vozhd'*, was used in the immediate postrevolutionary period to indicate revolutionary leaders like Vladimir Lenin and Joseph Stalin. —Trans.

but generally speaking a utopia is the object of social faith, hope, and love, "the substance of things hoped for, the evidence of things not seen."[4]

Utopianism is not necessarily opposed to realism—it can and must be united with it. Here we have a difference between the goal and means, the task and its fulfillment. Utopia in this sense is an "*ideal* with changeable content,"[5] with the former a matter of necessity and the latter of historical teleology. Only by a disturbance in the necessary balance does utopianism intrude into the sphere of realism, with delirium as a result, or realism loses its striving for the ideal and degenerates into a pragmatism emptied of ideals. The Christian ideal of the kingdom of God is realized in a series of changing historical objectives (which in our day consists, among other objectives, in the achievement of social justice united with personal freedom), together with their corresponding necessary practical measures (in this sphere it is possible to have practical disagreements, because Christianity, which is called to establish unity of spirit, cannot identify itself with any one program or party).

In essence, utopianism belongs to Old Testament messianism as much as it does to Christianity, but in recent times it has been effectively monopolized by revolutionary socialism. Although even in Marxism it is considered good form to repudiate "utopian socialism" for the sake of "scientific," that is, realistic socialism, this too is of course no less utopian than other utopias. Utopia is always a fairy tale, a tale about the future, since from the present it is impossible to see the future, but it is also a prophecy about the future, for this future is already contained and anticipated in the present. Utopia is the inner nerve of the dynamism of history. "The heart lives in the future; the present brings dejection" (Pushkin);[6] such is the law of the human heart, its dream. There is indeed a reverie that enervates, yet without a dream man cannot live. History is made not by sober prosaics but by dreamers, people of faith, prophets, "utopians." For them the present "dejection" is only prehistory (*Vorgeschichte*), the prologue to history with its "dialectic," where "*Widerspruch ist Fortleitende*" [conflict moves things forward] in realizing the mind of history—*List der Vernunft* [the cunning of Reason] (Hegel).

4. Hebrews 11:1. This classic chapter explains that faith is victorious religious utopianism. Here are mentioned the just ones of the Old Testament who, "not having received the promises, only saw them afar off and rejoiced" (v. 13), who "by faith conquered kingdoms, wrought justice, obtained promises" (vv. 33ff.), "and all these, having testified in the faith, received not what was promised."

5. Bulgakov quotes here, with slight alteration, the slogan encapsulating the philosophy of law espoused by German thinker Rudolf Stammler (1856–1938): "natural law with changeable content." —Trans.

6. From Aleksandr Sergeyevich Pushkin's poem, "If life deceive you" (*esli zhizn' tebya obmanet*). —Trans.

And this dialectic turns out, by force of events, to be a revolution against a present they will not acknowledge, a present they are ready to sacrifice for the sake of the future—to sacrifice love of one's neighbor in the name of "love for the distant."[7]

But once it has lost its spiritual equilibrium, faith becomes superstition or a fanatical reverie that is animated no longer by a vision of a coming city but by deceptive mirages. Utopianism, which constitutes the soul of revolution, is thus also missing—because of its lack of religious roots—spiritual equilibrium. Its social idealism is found in contradiction to that wingless positivism to which it is bound in the name of an imaginary "science." The utopianism of Marx, like that of other positivists, is completely irrational, full of contradictions and religiously barren. Its ideas on history go no further than *Vorgeschichte*, the epochs of class conflict, but *Geschichte* itself is empty of content. Irreligious utopianism in revolutionary socialism, to the extent that it is not demagoguery, transforms into a feverish delirium, a *Fata Morgana* for the delirious in a waterless desert. But, in the name of love, which "rejoices not in injustice but rejoices with the truth" (1 Cor 13:6), we must even here see an expression of a genuine thirst that does not know, that cannot find the religious font that would quench it; not understanding itself, it cannot recognize its own truth. The break with Christianity, and even with any faith in a personal God, visible in social idealism, in "progress," in this acute recivisim into paganism, can appear definitive and irreversible (and the frenzies of sacrilege in Russia, together with the religious asphyxiation of the people and the antireligious inquisition, might convince us even more than the bacchanalia of the French Revolution did).

Socialist utopianists—wild and frenzied in Russia, sluggish and cold in other countries—make of social revolution a religious idol. But on the opposite side, the people of the Church see this as sufficient grounds for condemning the socialist utopianists and for washing their hands of any personal responsibility. There arise mutual estrangement, deafness, and a lack of understanding. The watershed between Christianity and neo-paganism (imagining itself to be atheism) is certainly not marked by the imaginary line of "science." (In this regard, we should sooner speak of an approaching meeting of faith and knowledge rather than its opposite, and present-day materialism is, generally speaking, as much obscurantism as it is a failure of thought.) The watershed is instead marked by historical dynamism, by the

7. A reference to Friedrich Nietzsche's (1844–1900) *Thus Spoke Zarathustra* (1883). In the famous chapter "Rebellion" from Dostoevsky's *Brothers Karamazov* (1880), Ivan Karamazov confesses to his brother Alyosha that he cannot love his neighbor but only "those who are "distant." Poljakova, "Fyodor Dostoevsky and Friedrich Nietzsche." —Trans.

relationship to what is socially efficacious. One cannot, of course, downplay the ill will and, consequently, the deliberate, conscious enmity towards the holy that is present in "militant atheism," and especially among its ringleaders, the ranking functionaries of the revolution and their *oprichniki*[8] who make a career out of Christ-betrayal and spiritual infanticide. But Satan, besides his genuine and terrifying face, also takes on the appearance of an angel of light [2 Cor 11:14], clothing himself in the garb of social justice, and the atheist movement is animated by the deception of the father of lies who created the false utopia of a godless world with him as its lord. Spiritual sobriety, as well as simple truthfulness, demands a thorough investigation of a position before issuing a definitive verdict and submitting the case, as it were, to a higher court. And where many are prone to see a spiritual confrontation, in which all guilt is found solely on one side, is this not a certain misunderstanding created by intellectual poverty and ill will but also by the presence of guilt on the other side as well?

"Repent—*metanoeîte* (come to your senses, examine yourself), for the Kingdom of God is at hand" [Matt 3:2]. These words from the forerunner, and later from Christ, bear the most extensive meaning and have a particularly social-historical application. Does not this *"repent"* call us to new achievements, and especially to the testing and re-examination of what we are accustomed to consider self-evident and on which we rest complacently? Do the people of the Church seek social justice or the social utopia corresponding to the needs of their era, with its unique dynamism, or do they remain satisfied only with a static conservatism that for them exhaustively sums up "fidelity to tradition"? Does there exist for us a historical future with its new tasks, or is the entirety of Christian historiosophy completely exhausted by the expectation of a global catastrophe in which we can find only the devalorization of all historical values—*alles, was entsteht, ist wert dass es zu Grunde geht?* ["All that comes to be deserves to perish wretchedly"].[9] But there exists a spiritual *horror vacui* [i.e., "nature abhors a vacuum"] and can we be surprised if people, not finding a way to quench the demands of their conscience, go out to seek it in a "far country" [Luke 15:13]. But it was not so from the beginning [Matt 19:8].

No one can say that a sense of history is lacking in the Old Testament, for the Old Testament itself is sacred history wholly striving towards the coming messianic kingdom. And not only that—in its schema the entirety

8. The *oprichniki* were members of the bodyguard corps, the Oprichnina, of Tsar Ivan the Terrible (1530–84). They were known for terrorizing Ivan's political opponents through acts of savage cruelty. In the centuries following, *oprichniki* came to designate any Russian political police force of great brutality. —Trans

9. Mephistopheles to Faust, verses 1339–40. *Goethe's Faust*, 161. —Trans

of global history is also included (we see this already in the book of Genesis, later in the prophets, particularly in that prototype of subsequent apocalypses, the book of Daniel). In Old Testament prophecies, we find such ambitious utopias (in the positive sense of the word, of course) that are completely unparalleled in their audacity. Here we find not only religious historiosophy but also historical tasks inspired by ideals, tasks surpassing even our current historical reality. On that score, the preaching of the prophets (Amos, Isaiah, Hosea) contains, among its many aspects, a social meaning as well. Is it any different in the New Testament? Does it abolish the prophecies of the Old Testament? Neither dogmatically nor historically can this be admitted. Nonetheless the general feeling of life radically changes in the New Testament: into its depths there is introduced an antinomism—with both its wisdom and its difficulty—that the Old Testament man, on account of a certain naiveté, could not accommodate. The kingdom of God is summoned ("thy kingdom come") into the world, but the kingdom itself is not of this world [John 18:36]. It is *entòs hymôn*, that is, first of all "within us" but also "among us" [Luke 17:21]. In relation to the world, a tragic bifurcation thus occurs, of love for the world and simultaneous enmity towards it. Due to the complexity of this relationship in Christianity, there is no room either for the messianic paradise of Jewish apocalyptic or for the earthly paradise of socialism. The question can even arise—does *history* exist at all for Christianity, or is it an inconquerable duration of *empty* time in which there is already nothing left to accomplish, "the *last* days?"

This conclusion would mean that, since the time of the incarnation, everything has already been accomplished on the divine side. But for Christian humanity, these last days also constitute their own aeon, with its own achievements and revelations. The New Testament Apocalypse is a revelation concerning *history*, and not just concerning its end, as it is often interpreted. Here in its symbolic images (which are to some extent typical of the apocalyptic genre in general) there is revealed that struggle of two principles that constitutes the tragedy of history, with alternating victories and defeats; here we see mentioned not only the triumph of the Beast with his False Prophet but also the phenomenon of the thousand-year reign of Christ on earth. Other places in the New Testament fill in the essential details: the preaching of the gospel to all nations (Matt 24:2) and its connection with other events, the conversion of Israel as "life from the dead" (Rom 11:15), the manifestation of the "adversary." All these are borders demarcating historical epochs.

The future in its essence has been heralded by the Holy Spirit (John 16:13), but in its particulars it is kept in the dark, for it a matter of human creative work as well. Therefore history *does exist* within the borders of the "last days"; it is not a bad infinity eternalizing the intermingling of good and evil, as our contemporary paganism thinks, but it possesses an organic end, a *transcensus* to a higher state, which is accomplished by the power of God. This *transcensus* is not itself a simple historical event, for it is transcendent to history, and it does *not* take place in historical time ("and the angel swore that times will be no more" [Rev 10:6]). History with its apocalypse, although intrinsically dependent on eschatology, cannot be extrinsically oriented towards it, for the end lies not within history but beyond it, outside the limits of its horizon, beyond its border. The fact that these two perspectives blend into each other is often abused by those seeking to save themselves from historical panic by a flight into eschatology. The thought of the end should unceasingly ring within the inner man (along with the memory of death and the judgment), but it is forbidden to us to determine the times and seasons [Acts 1:7], to falsely prophesy concerning them. It is not for this reason that revelation of the end was given to us (concerning the general resurrection), but instead for the increase of vigilance ("watch," Matt 24:42) and as a certain guarantee of the victory of good, of a positive outcome to history.

History, religiously experienced, is the apocalypse in the process of accomplishment, apocalypse here understood *not* as eschatology but as historiosophy connected with the feeling of striving towards the future, with the consciousness of pending tasks and continuing historical work. Time is measured not in years but in deeds, and if a person senses that pending tasks and historical possibilities lie before him, he cannot think of the end passively, unless all of history for him represents solely the unending triumph of the Antichrist and constitutes nothing more than a preparation for the latter's personal appearance. Quite the opposite—Christianity calls us to courage, labor, inspiration. Christ praises the "faithful and good" servant who put to use his "talent," and he condemns the "wicked and lazy" servant who buried it [Matt 25:14–30]. Christian historiosophy unveils apocalyptic expanses and distances in the quest from the present city to the coming one, for "the form of this world is passing away" [1 Cor 7:31]. And that is why revolutionary dynamism, which remains blind and elemental in its atheism, is capable here of coming to know itself in its own truth. The real idea of progress, that is, of movement towards a goal, and an absolute goal at that—the kingdom of God—can be accommodated only within Christian historiosophy, which reconciles itself with nothing parochial and limited or with any historical philistinism. This idea was revealed in the days of early Christianity's springtime, when in a world weighed down by the flesh there arose to oppose it a small flock exhibiting a heroic indifference, which (according to Celsus)[10] ate

10. Celsus was a second-century Greek philosopher who wrote the (to our

away at the very foundations of antiquity in its fundamental values, both of government and of culture.[11] But this rejection of the world on their part was tied to their expectation of the end and a resultant detachment from history and its affairs. This is the source of early Christianity's social quietism, on the one hand ("let each one remain in the station in which he was called," 1 Cor 7:20), and its unique conservatism, on the other ("There is no power but from God" [Rom 13:1]), though the latter is often accompanied by the threatening tones of the apocalypse. This was a unique apoliticism that attached importance only to a person's inner state (hence the seeming indifference towards slavery, an institution that was historically undermined from within, of course, precisely through Christianity). The primacy of the internal over the external remains here unaddressed; it is precisely this that serves as the spiritual foundation of the community. Yet this *primacy* does not mean public indifferentism and a lack of values. This public absenteeism, which in early Christianity seemed pragmatically wise and was in fact the only possibility at the time, would become a weakness when Christianity became influential in government and society.

In reality, Christianity served as the spiritual leaven for a new society, for in it was born a new sort of personhood, and its actual influence reached, of course, far beyond the limits of the activities of the Church's own institutions. What is more, it is impossible to deny that Church communities, as is the case with the rest of humanity, rarely ever lived up to the height of their calling. Furthermore, they often became a stronghold of conservatism, or, at all events, of unprogressive attitudes, both externally and internally. The more internal opposition on the part of the Church towards revolutionism (at least of the nihilistic kind) flows simply from her faithfulness to *tradition*, which permeates her entire life. Tradition is the *living memory* of the Church, as opposed to the historical amnesia of those children of revolution, who would date history's beginning with themselves. There exists simple human dignity, which does not reconcile itself with this nihilism's spiritual tastelessness; there exists historical consciousness, which perceives this abolishing of history as a barbarization; and there exists, finally, the *Church's* consciousness, for whom a fundamental break with tradition constitutes the most cruel heresy. Yet at the same time, fidelity to tradition is not equivalent to immobility and it is not tied to what is obsolete and antiquated; *that is not fidelity to tradition* but simply secularized conservatism, not always

---

knowledge) first lengthy critique of Christianity, entitled *True Doctrine*. It is preserved only in the Church father Origen of Alexandria's (ca. 184–ca. 253) response to it, known as the *Contra Celsum*. —Trans.

11. Bulgakov has in mind here the indifference to death exhibited by the early Christian martyrs. —Trans.

sufficiently distinguished from the former. Unfortunately, on account of human weakness, much unecclesial contraband is smuggled in under the banner of the Church, and in its centuries-long journey, many things have stuck to the bottom of the Church's ship that are foreign and at times essentially inimical to it—the very thing that provokes the schadenfreude of the atheists who have skillfully demonstrated this in their exhibitions and museums. The fire of revolution—however painful—proves here to be purifying even for the Church community.

But in any case, the relationship of Christianity to the world and its values can by no means remain only an immanent relationship, as in neo-paganism. When eyes are turned to heaven, then they are blind to what surrounds them, and the call of eternity creates indifference towards the "dreary songs of earth."[12] There exists a Christian freedom from the world (prevalent especially in former ages) that seeks to realize itself in an external flight from the world. But this flight with its disinterest in values could not, practically, be realized fully even in anchoritic monasticism, which carries into the desert worldly passions; moreover, even from the desert, monasticism strives, or rather is *called*, to make an impact on the world. It was precisely in monasteries that there arose, on occasion, Christian utopias that later became driving forces in history ("The Third Rome," holy empire, theocratic government), and one can even say that the more fiery and sincere the spiritual intensity there, the more effective it was in the world (examples: St. Francis and Franciscan spirituality, Luther and the Reformation).

Yet not infrequently this rejection of the world results in conservatism towards the world, and this conservatism then goes even further, becoming something that could hardly be called world-denying, for that matter. One can generally say that in Christianity a search is always ongoing for the guiding idea of the historical development of an epoch, and everyday conservatism cannot be considered here as the normal or sole variety of Christian social consciousness. Of course, between atheist revolution and Christian community a chasm lies. But does this mean that Christianity, by virtue of its "supra-historicity," knows only static conservatism, or can it and must it know dynamic effectiveness too? Is a Christian reformism possible, one animated by the idea of the kingdom of God and possessing its historical utopia, or rather, *utopias*—not, of course, of "paradise on earth," but of victory, or rather, of the victory of good on the path of world-historical tragedy leading to the final separation of light and darkness?

Here we meet the fundamental question of Christian life in our time, namely (in its contemporary formulation): how can we "enchurch the

---

12. From the poem "Angel," by Mikhail Yuryevich Lermontov (1814–41). —Trans.

culture?" Once again the Sphinx of history questions our mind, our heart, and our freedom: yes or no? This question is the historical watershed dividing the waters. The simplest option here is to avoid the question under the pretext of a separation in the individual's soul between the things of Caesar and those of God. This is Protestantism's answer, and it legitimizes the secularization now suffocating the world. Perhaps this answer had a historical justification in the effort to free itself from papal theocracy, but the same separation is not infrequently pronounced in the name of Orthodoxy too. Ascetical rejection of the world, personal pietism, these—in a spirit of world-denying "apoliticism"—are considered here the exhaustive answer, while the vacant battleground is immediately seized by the ruling powers or by purely "political" passions.

The Church is indeed "apolitical," in the sense that her eternal values cannot be identified with any relative goals or historical institutions (in the same way that the party of untrammeled autocracy was considered by us to be the only and truly Orthodox option). The Church must be not a party but the *public conscience* that permits neither political accommodation nor indifferentism under the pretext of humility. Yet she must strive not to isolate herself from society (which results in secularization) but rather to spiritually take hold of society *from within* (this was the ideal of "free theocracy" of the early Solovyov and the late Dostoevsky).

Before our very eyes, the different Christian confessions, each in their own way, together and individually, are taking steps (granted, still hesitant steps) along the path towards a Christian society. On a global scale (unfortunately, without Catholicism),[13] this movement is connected with the name of the Stockholm conference of 1925.[14] Responsibly joining ranks with it were representatives of different Orthodox Churches, who thereby took upon themselves the responsibility of educating the nations in the spirit of social Christianity. One of the weakest sides of this movement is insufficient clarity—to say the least—on the theoretical, or rather, dogmatic foundations of the movement for religiously overcoming secularization. The Church places on its own conscience the burden of society, and this not just in practice, as hitherto been the case, but also on principle, and for this it is necessary to have faith, enthusiasm, vocation. We must comprehend the revelation of God in history as an apocalypse in progress that leads to the fullness of historical achievements and *in this sense* also to the end of history, not just to a simple alternation of events in their pragmatic comprehensibility. And in this task there should be another means of comprehending history: the living sense of

13. The Catholic Church's first official foray into the ecumenical movement was with the 1964 Vatican II *Decree on Ecumenism, Unitatis Redintegratio.* —Trans.

14. The World Conference of Life and Work, a precursor to the formation of the World Council of Churches in 1948. —Trans.

the incompleteness of history (*Vorgeschichte*) that still leaves room for "utopia," for what does not exist but must yet arrive, for an ideal and for hope.

Christianity, in its idea of the kingdom of God, possesses such a universal, boundless ideal, which contains in itself all good human goals and achievements. But it also possesses its own promise, which in the symbolic language of the Apocalypse is designated as the coming of the thousand-year reign of Christ on earth (Rev 20). This symbol, which is the guiding star of history, has already for a long while been locked away due to a one-sided interpretation, such that it is considered almost a specific "heresy" not to accept the prevailing interpretation of it, one that leaves nothing of the symbol's meaning intact. But this maximal manifestation of the kingdom of God on earth symbolized here not only cannot remain just a passively accepted prophecy (or one completely rejected for ideological reasons); it must instead become an active "utopia," a hope. Of course, this symbol by itself is abstract, but it is always being filled in with definite content, as the next step or achievement in history, as a call from the future addressed to the present. Out of panic or spiritual laziness or fatigue, false eschatologism rejects responsibility for history while nonetheless in practice (i.e., in a heathen fashion) it participates in history. But since society is unavoidable, even if only as one's particular fate, then it must make room for seeking the Christian justice of the kingdom of God, and—"seek, and ye shall find" [Matt 7:7]. The gifts of the Church are irrevocable [Rom 11:29], even if we ourselves refuse them and bury them in the ground [Matt 25:14–30]. But whatever fails to find a worthy response from contemporary ecclesiality imperceptibly becomes the possession of forces hostile to the Church. Who knows how many Sauls linger today in the atheist camp, seduced by its dynamism, because they found in us neither an audience for their questionings nor answers to them. It is power and truth that conquer, not evasive and [politically] accommodating apologetics. The tragic experience of our nation, as well as the threats of new clouds gathering above, call us to new paths of thought and life. "*Thy youth shall be renewed like the eagle's*" [Ps 103:5]. Unceasing renewal is the law and condition of spiritual life, as well as of *fidelity to living tradition.*

4

The Problem of "Conditional Immortality"

BROADLY SPEAKING, THE FIELD of eschatology is the least distinguished in terms of movement of theological thought. Even in the West where, beginning with the era of the Reformation, theology got off the ground, and—for good or ill—new life arose in various theological spheres, this applied least of all to eschatology. We could instead speak here of a certain lack of eschatological feeling, which manifests either in the traditional repetition of what is unrepeatable *in that form* or in the easy acceptance of the painless solution of so-called "universalism." Two types of eschatological thinking prevail: a penal codex of complete savagery or an appeasing amnesty that in practical terms shirks all the difficulties of the problem. The first approach is more and more becoming a practical impossibility in our day, for it has lost all interior persuasiveness; the second represents not the overcoming but the simple rejection of the first (not to mention the serious biblical and theological difficulties attending this type of thinking). Faced with these two options—medieval orthodoxy and a humanitarian universalism—there arises the question of another, third approach that, while uniting the advantages of both, would also be free from their weaknesses—a sort of *tertium*.

Thus, from the rejection of the two horns of this eschatological dilemma there arises in the second half of the nineteenth century the theological doctrine calling itself the theory of "conditional immortality" or "conditionalism." At all events, it merits attention simply because it poses with radical acuity the question of immortality and eternal life: the preliminary question for any eschatological doctrine. Some believe that the human being is essentially mortal, like animals, and therefore that death is a kind of anni-hilation; from this there clearly follows a negative eschatology of emptiness. Such is the currently widespread faith of atheistic unbelief (for, of course, unbelief too is only a species of *belief*, since the nature of the question does not allow a rationally demonstrable resolution). *Or* the human person is es-sentially immortal, eternity is proper to him, and eschatological doctrine at-tempts to define the content of this eternity. In the theory of conditionalism we have yet a third alternative: the human person does not possess natural immortality but can acquire it or *not* acquire it. Immortality is conditional: it is *given* or it is *not* given depending on certain conditions. Such is the formulation of the problem of eschatology that we find in "conditionalism." Once this has been accounted for, it cannot be evaded by quietly ignoring it.[1]

The theory of conditionalism as a notable current of theological thought emerges in the second half of the nineteenth century in Europe and America, primarily, of course, and even almost exclusively among Protes-tant theologians not connected with the orthodox tradition. Several emi-nent theologians and philosophers (among the latter, for example, stands Renouvier)[2] are numbered among its proponents. The leading founders here are two Protestant pastors, the Englishman E. White[3] and the Swiss Petavel-Olliff,[4] to whom numerous followers attached themselves. The writ-ings of both, despite a certain theological primitiveness, nonetheless distin-guish themselves by a more than typical force of conviction and therefore also of persuasiveness. They propose conditionalism not only as theological truth, which revelation indicates we should accept, but also as a salvific idea that alone is capable of liberating contemporary Christianity from a scan-dalizing lacks of answers on the question eternal life, for it is from this lack of answers that both Christian life and especially Christian mission suffer. According to the theory of conditional immortality, the destiny of human-ity in eternal life will be paradisical bliss, and by this will be realized the

---

1. In Russian theological literature the sole presentation of the theory of condition-alism is given in passing by Prof. Nikolai Nikanorovich Glubokovsky. *The Preaching of St. Paul*, vol. 1, 571–91. [A theologian and scholar who specialized in the apostle Paul, Glubokovsky (1863–1937) served as Professor of New Testament at the St. Petersburg Theological Academy before the revolution of 1917.—Trans].

2. Charles Bernard Renouvier (1815–1903), a French idealist philosopher. —Trans.

3. Edward White, *Life in Christ (A Study of the Scripture Doctrine of the Nature of Man, the Object of the Divine Incarnation, and the Conditions of Human Immortality)*, 1878. [Bulgakov notes that he is working with the French translation produced in 1880 —Trans.].

4. Emmanuel Pétavel-Olliff, *La fin du mal* [translated into English as *The Struggle for Eternal Life*], 1891; *Le problème de l'immortalité* [*The Problem of Immortality*], 1892.

prophetic word of the apostle that God will be all in all [1 Cor 15:28]. Yet in this beatitude only the just, those worthy of it, will participate. Sinners, on the other hand, resistant to the very end to the will of God, will die; having turned into nothing, they do not receive the destiny of immortality. Such is the basic idea. Let us turn to its theological grounding.

II

Man was created distinct from animals—which possess only *generic* (genus) life ("according to their kinds": Gen 1:21, 24–25)—because he possesses the genus' *personal* energy, which is realized in personal immortality. The human person was not created so as to be mortal by nature—on the contrary, he possesses, *by virtue of his creation*, the possibility of immortality, *posse non mori*.[5] This immortality is proper to the human spirit, which is similar to the incorporeal spirits. Yet man is distinct from the spiritual world through the *complexity* of his composition, namely in that he is not created as an incorporeal spirit who, though existing in the created world, remains nonetheless *above* it. The human person is an *incarnate* spirit connected with the world. The possibility of death lurks in this complexity not from the side of the "immortal soul" but rather from the side of the *whole* human person, for whom death is not a return to non-being but instead a certain disincarnation, a rupture with the world, an ontological catastrophe. The body is by no means the cause of death; it is, on the contrary, the condition for the life of man, given to him by God at creation. By this complexity the human person is distinguished equally from the incorporeal world, which does not know enfleshment, and from the animal world, which does not possess a spirit but only a "living soul" [Gen 2:7], that animal soul which the human person too possesses alongside the animal world. It is this connection between soul and spirit, between supernatural and natural being, which was *given* by God at creation, that the human person ought to have secured by the power of his free and creative spirit through elevating his being to the highest level of positive immortality.

This was linked with his determinate relationship to God (symbolically expressed in the commandment not to partake of the fruit of the tree of the knowledge of good and evil), as well as with his determinate positive

---

5. Catholic doctrine (see Matthias Joseph Scheeben, *Handbuch der Dogmatik* [*Handbook of Catholic Dogmatics*], Book II, section 165) considers *posse non mori [possibility of not dying]* to be not natural but supernatural, a gift of grace, for the body itself naturally contains the principle of death and dissolution—here we have the echoes of Manicheism and Platonism, as well as a harbinger of the future path of conditionalism.

relationship to the world (expressed in partaking of the fruit of the tree of life). The primordial arrangement did not alienate the human person from the world, and renunciation of the world was neither the goal nor the foundation of immortality. On the contrary, a proper connection with the world, included in the proper connection with God, was the necessary condition of the life of man on the path to the positive conquest of the *non posse mori*, although we do not know how it would have been realized. But the fall occurred. The human person lost the unstable ontological equilibrium of his complex being. Into the world entered death, *human* death, which is quite distinct from the death that reigns in the animal world, despite all external similarities. For human death is not death in the strict sense but is instead an ontological rupture of his one being into the two principles that constitute it. Through death the human person becomes, *outwardly*, the equal of the animal world to which he is not an equal, although the carnal side of his existence belongs to it; he becomes the equal of the incorporeal world as well, to which he also does not belong, although he is akin to it through the spiritual side of his existence. Death is not the cessation of human existence but rather the catastrophic "un-humanizing," as it were, of the human person, the loss of his wholeness.

Conditionalism *denies* the root distinction existing between the human person and the animal world, both on biological grounds (here we have the direct influence of Darwinism and of biological evolutionism more generally) and on account of idiosyncratic exegesis. The human person is created, according to conditionalism, "as a living soul," identical with the animals, and the distinction between them is not qualitative but quantitative: the human person has the same living soul as the animals, except this soul possesses certain distinct features. These are, specifically, language, and the moral and religious sense that distinguish the human person from animals. Thus, *life* is identical for the human person and animals, as too is their death or mortality. "In the Old Testament the *soul* and *life* (*nephesh*) ascribed to the human person are often ascribed to animals as well." "We must either share immortality with our neighbors in the animal kingdom or we must sacrifice our own hopes and recognize ourselves as mortals, just as they are."[6] "The image of God in man is not something ontological but rather a 'shadow,' *l'ombre n'est pas la réalité* [a shadow is not a reality]";[7] "*une ombre de ressemblance—l'ombre n'est pas l'identité*" [a shadow is a matter of resemblance, not identity].[8] "The 'image of God' in Adam consists of the

---

6. White, *Life in Christ*, 19, 89.

7. Pétavel-Olliff, *Le problème de l'immortalité*, 399.

8. Pétavel-Olliff, *Le problème de l'immortalité*, 399.

capacity to understand and to emulate his Creator and thereby through this moral path to rise to immortality."[9] Man was not created immortal, but he is instead a "candidate for immortality." Absolute immortality is natural only for God, and *conditional* immortality for man. The power of death is the same for the human person and for animals: it is the annihilation of life, the rupture of a vital unity, the complete and final dissolution of a whole natural complex, the simultaneous destruction of both body and soul, the "annihilation of substance,"[10] the abolition of personhood. The influence of Platonism,[11] with its teaching on the immortality of the soul, namely *l'immortalité inconditionnelle et impie de religions panthéistes* [the unconditional and impious immortality stemming from pantheistic religions], corrupted this straightforward understanding of death as complete annihilation, despite the fact that of the six hundred instances where the soul is mentioned in the Bible, not once is it said that the soul is immortal[12] (though neither does it say in any instance that it is mortal). For this reason, the threat of death for the human person in paradise in the event of his disobedience signified not any sort of "spiritual death" but rather his immediate and complete annihilation. "Death could only mean for Adam too that reality which went by the same name in the animal kingdom." "The original threat foretold unavoidable death."[13]

And so the human person was given conditional immortality. Its condition was the fulfillment of the will of God. This continuation of existence depended on material food, on eating of the fruit of the "Tree of Life"[14] of which man was deprived on account of disobedience. The human person fell, and the consequence of this ought to have been the onset of immediate death, which thereby would have made the existence of the human race impossible, for it would have been cut off with its first ancestor. But this did not occur: the execution of the death sentence was delayed. This occurred through the power of redemption: "at the moment of the fall the

9. White, *Life in Christ*, 87.

10. White, *Life in Christ*, 92–93, 100–101; Pétavel-Olliff, *La fin du mal*, 97: *La suppression totale de tel ou tel individu est une notion qui se laisse très bien concevoir* (!) ["The complete destruction of this or that person is an idea that can be easily imagined." —Trans.]. "God does not tell Adam, 'Your body will die,' but rather, 'you will die'" (103).

11. Pétavel-Olliff, *La fin du mal*, 158.

12. Pétavel-Olliff, *La fin du mal*, 163; *Le problème de l'immortalité*, 147.

13. White, *Life in Christ*, 96, 107.

14. White, *Life in Christ*, 87. The mythological image of the tree of life is here interpreted as the natural-magical means of immortality. Juxtaposed with it in this sense is the apocalyptic tree of life in the New Jerusalem (Rev 22:2, 27).

redemption began."[15] "If the fatal sentence had taken immediate effect, we would have been dead in Adam, or, indeed, we would never have been born at all. Therefore, the very existence of our race is grace."[16] God did not carry out his pedagogical threat, which turned out be a kind of *pia fraus* [pious fraud]. Death was not only delayed, but it even turned out to be not the total death that had been threatened. Namely, instead of the dissolution of personhood, "upon the death of the individual, the spirit is preserved intact so that it may be united with the body on the day of judgment. This survival on the part of the soul we ascribe solely to the redemption,"[17] whose effect, therefore, is anticipated in time. "Redemption is nothing other than the uniting of humanity with divinity, of the creature who broke the law with the supreme Lawgiver."[18]

III

The incarnation, the acceptance by the Son of God, the Logos, of human flesh, has as its goal the redemption and reconciliation of man with God, through the sacrifice of the Sinless One, by his sufferings and death on the cross. "The goal of redemption is to make man immortal."[19] "*Le chemin de l'immortalité passe par Gethsémane et par Golgotha. On cherchait en vain autre route*" [The path to immortality passes through Gethsemane and Golgotha. In vain has any other route been sought].

> According to the predominant dogmatic theology, if the body of man is mortal, then his soul which forms his personhood is, by nature, immortal or eternal. The redemption is not meant to change the nature or duration of this spiritual element. The "resurrection of the flesh" in glory is a circumstance both accidental and secondary in salvation. The grandeur of salvation consists in the deliverance of the soul from the "wrath to come" or eternal torments. A similar deliverance was implied by the divine redemption, the sacrifice of the Lamb of God. All these ideas appear to us to be contrary to Scripture. According to biblical teaching, the redemption has as its direct object the transformation of our nature, our translation not simply from sin to

15. White, *Life in Christ*, 107.
16. White, *Life in Christ*, 110.
17. White, *Life in Christ*, 111.
18. White, *Life in Christ*, 109.
19. White, *Life in Christ*, 193.

holiness but also from *mortality to immortality*, from death to life.[20]

Redemption consists in the forgiveness of the *guilt* of sin, but the *punishment* is not abolished.

> The redemption accomplished by Jesus is not total; Scripture does not speak this way. Each of us through suffering and through dying accomplishes, to a certain degree, his own redemption. But the difference between our act of redemption and that accomplished by Jesus Christ is that He, although innocent, died for the guilty. . . . Only His redemption has the character of representation. The hardened sinner drinks to its dregs the cup of redemption; the ingrained consequences of sin advance to the point of the complete annihilation of his being. Eternal death is the price of his obstinacy: *pour lui, par le fait, Jésus se trouvera n'avoir rien expié* [For such a one, therefore, Jesus' expiation will have accomplished nothing].[21]

Christ was raised from the dead by the Holy Spirit.

> Though He was God, as a man he was undoubtedly "under the law" and died as a sacrifice of reconciliation; as God He was above the law imposed on the creature and was incapable of dying. That is why, when the death sentence was executed on his mortal nature, the Divine Guest Who absorbed the human spirit into His own proper nature, had the power to rebuild his own ruins, the "destroyed temple," to take possession of it and to "raise it up on the third day." . . . He conquered death, yet not as a "son of Adam" but instead as the "Son of the Most High," as the "Lord of Heaven."[22]

The resurrection of Christ is not an immanent-transcendent but rather a wholly transcendent act of God's omnipotence. Our own resurrection from the dead rests on the solemn and infallible promise of the Son of God.

> United with Christ in his sufferings and death, we will go to meet him on that day when our Savior, exercising his omnipotence, will transform our mortal body in accordance with his glorious body. The Father, the Son, and the Holy Spirit are united in accomplishing this glorious deed (Rom 8:11). The omnipotence

---

20. White, *Life in Christ*, 108.
21. Pétavel-Olliff, *La fin du mal*, 141–42.
22. White, *Life in Christ*, 233.

that was manifested in the creation in the world and in the resurrection of Christ will be manifested in the accomplishment of our own resurrection too. If the miracle of the *creation* of man has its own *raison d'être*, then we can count on an even greater *raison d'être* for this *promised* miracle that will grant to the elect the glorious bodies of new life.[23]

The general resurrection, even before its consummation, is preceded by two distinct effects of the incarnation. The first of these we already know—the delay of the death of our ancestors after the fall, a delay that made possible the descendance of the human race from them. Clearly this delay covers all sinful humanity, which, while liable to die because of sin, nonetheless lives, albeit within the confines of a limited, mortal life. The second anticipation of the power of the incarnation, even more striking than the first, consists in that very *immortality* of the soul beyond the grave, against which conditionalists so persistently rebel. They are forced to acknowledge this life of the soul beyond the grave, both by virtue of the indisputable data of revelation and by the logic of their very own system.[24]

> If any element of our nature survives the first death, this should be ascribed solely to the redemption which acts in a supernatural manner to preserve our spiritual being from dissolution, either for judgment or for reward. . . . I am bound to believe the Bible that souls survive death. . . . Here is how one can imagine their state: some sleep, others are completely without consciousness; some think, they perceive, they improve; others find themselves in sorrow or even in torments, some wander the earth as *daimonia*, others are cast into the abyss, others still remain in Hades until the first coming of Christ.[25]

The post-mortem life of the just already possesses the beginning of eternal life and immortality. The life of sinners after death has as its purpose: 1) the establishment of the personal identity of the one who sinned here and who will be awakened there for judgment; 2) torments in Hades (2 Pet 2:9); 3) the healing of their rebellion against God—when this rebellion has an excuse in ignorance—through the preaching to the "spirits in prison"; 4)

23. Pétavel-Olliff, *La fin du mal*, 195.

24. Some conditionalists have accordingly come to completely reject that a soul exists in man in any other sense than it exists in animals, and they claim that the soul disintegrates together with the body at death. Such are the views of Henry Constable, *Hades* [published 1878 —Trans]. The human spirit, according to Constable, is a particle of the divine spirit in the soul which is taken away at death. Man completely dies in death, and his consciousness is awakened only at the resurrection.

25. White, *Life in Christ*, 278–81.

the reception of the greatest, most solemn and terrible punishment: the first death kills the body alone—*to kill the soul* is left to the second death.[26] "The anticipatory suffering is in addition to the torments; in part it signifies punishment, in part persuasion. It leaves room for repentance."[27] This is a kind of purgatory. Generally speaking the post-mortem state does not hold any particular interest for the conditionalists, and it is understood primarily as an intermediate state between death and resurrection.

The resurrection is universal, not only for the good who awaken to the resurrection of life, for eternal life, but also for the wicked who awaken to the resurrection of judgment, for the second and final death, for annihilation. The recognition of this *two-fold* outcome, immortality for some and complete annihilation for others—this is the basic message of conditionalism.

The condition for immortality is not any sort of "ontological or physical change of substance" but rather the moral state of the soul in which Christ has been formed and which thereby attracted to itself the indwelling of the Holy Spirit,[28] the gift of grace. For sinners, on the other hand, there begins the inescapable second death and the final annihilation after a certain indefinable time following the judgment. A general question arises: is this annihilation a death sentence or suicide? Oddly enough, there is no complete clarity on this fundamental question, and individual views vary between these two possibilities. Sometimes it is possible to think that the "second death" is a death sentence that is executed neither immediately nor in a short span of time but instead over the course of the sinner's remaining life, a "mortal life" in the most literal sense.[29]

26. White, *Life in Christ*, 281–82.

27. Pétavel-Olliff, *Le problème de l'immortalité*, 49.

28. White, *Life in Christ*, 254–56.

29. It is in this sense that White develops this idea, *Life in Christ*, 478–90: "The satisfaction or disclosure of the properties of God is the first and final goal of creation and providence. Such is the sound philosophy of liability which, while taking away hope for a universal salvation, establishes the solemn doctrine of retribution. All the unrepentant must answer to their Creator in their flesh and soul, and their fate will be determined by a deadly and definitive sentence. Common goodness will be taken into account. But the one who was obstinate in disobedience cannot hope for a remedy, he will be annihilated 'body and soul in Gehenna.' God will reject all his degenerate and hardened children, since He is faithful to his eternal justice." "His Great Day of vengeance and the vengeance of the Lamb comes." "It is a terrible thing to fall into the hands of the Living God" (Heb 10:31). "I will strike her (Israel's) children with death, and all the Churches will know that I am the one who searches hearts and what is within" (Rev 2:23). "The Lord God is a consuming fire, God is jealous. I swear to you by heaven and earth, that soon you will lose the land, you will not abide long in her but will instead perish" (Deut 4:6). "The anger of God abides on the disobedient" (John 3:36), etc. (note the capriciousness in how conditionalists cite and interpret texts).

Others authors settle, so to speak, on the immanent side of death when describing annihilation. Most importantly, the very idea of resurrection for the new and final "second" death is softened, since it unexpectedly contains in itself the possibility of repentance and reform after resurrection.[30] Instead of an implacable judgment, we find here a sad inevitability and a kind of suicide on the part of the recalcitrant.[31]

"Universalists" put this question to "conditionalists": "if the wicked will finally be annihilated, then for what purpose did the wisdom of God call them into being?" In response, the answer is given to the effect that God did not give being to the *wicked* but to those capable of choosing between good and evil—the valuable yet also dangerous gift of freedom.

> A forced immortality would constrain this freedom. It befits the divine love of freedom (*il est digne du libéralisme de Dieu* [it befits God's liberality]) not to oblige to live eternally those beings who stubbornly reject the rational conditions of existence. . . . Is not the possibility of suicide that God leaves to every person in

30. "The resurrection of the dead can be explained as the final remedy of grace," *"en vue d'épreuve"* [as a test], God does not completely reject the person who is not yet completely spoiled," and "the final annihilation awaits only the most hardened" (Pétavel-Olliff, *Le problème de l'immortalité*, 204). "The varying expressions of the Scriptures permit us to believe that they will be subject to a new testing, and a special preaching will be addressed to them" (Pétavel-Olliff, *Le problème de l'immortalité*, 5).

31. "This is a progressive and unconquerable fall, a growing diminishment of two factors of human existence—sensation and activity (Pétavel-Olliff, *Le problème de l'immortalité*, 4). "Horrible agony, and then night without dawn. This soul is no longer conscious and is not responsive. The soul was, it loved, it lived; it no longer loves, it is dead, it does not exist" (11). "The complete destruction of the human soul will undoubtedly be preceded by suffering in correspondence with the innate intensity of the vitality of this soul. The most grievous torments will be accompanied by agony for the soul most richly endowed, along with the destruction of greatest mass of vital powers. In this sense, 'to him who receives more, more will be required'" (13). "Suffering will certainly play a role in the future torments, but this is only the preliminary phase. The highest punishment will put an end to the individual only in the painful perdition in post-mortem existence. According to the scientific law of continuity, the unrepentant sinner will fall prey to a long and sorrowful marasmus. Afterwards, for the most rebellious, there comes a woeful silence, which Scripture speaks of as 'the second death.'" "They ask us—how then do we understand annihilation (*aneantissement*)? We answer: the gradual diminution of capabilities available to the individual I, and at the very end the extinguishing of this foundational capability, thanks to which we possesses other capabilities. "In dieser Durchdringung des ganzen Seyns vom Tode geht die Persönlichkeit (Luke 9:25) im Sterben auf (*apóleia*); es ist nicht absolutes Nicht-Sein, aber absolute Passivität und Todes-unmacht und Todes-jammer" [In this complete penetration of all of Being by death (*apóleia*), personality (Luke 9:25) is undone in the process of dying; it is not absolute non-being but rather absolute passivity and the impotence and misery of death.] (Johann Tobias Beck, [*Umriss der biblischen Seelenlehre*, 1871]) (Pétavel-Olliff, *Le problème de l'immortalité*, 16–17, n3).

this world an analogy that enables us to understand the suicide
of the soul and conditional immortality ... Of course, the wicked were not created for destruction, but both their destruction
and in an indirect manner even their original creation will serve
some purpose. The memory of their final destiny (by whom and
when?) will stand as a terrifying barrier against the abuse of
freedom in the future life.[32]

And so, strangely, the final punishment by death proves to be the solemn
triumph of created freedom: *"une immortalité absolue porterait une grave
atteinte à la liberté humaine"* [an absolute immortality would be a grave in-
fringement of human liberty].[33] *"Il est au sens tragique dans lequel l'homme
nanti d'une liberté véritablement sérieuse, peut être plus fort que Dieu, plus
fort que son Sauveur"* [It is in a tragic sense that man is endowed with a
liberty that is *truly serious*, stronger perhaps than God, stronger than his
Savior].[34] "The sinner himself brings about his own annihilation."[35]

IV

Conditionalists seek confirmation for their ideas in the Church's tradition,
specifically in the patristic tradition. In one particular chapter, Petavel-Olliff
(following White) cites a number of early Church authors, predominantly
apostolic and post-apostolic fathers, in whose work he finds traces of a more
or less clear conditionalism. Here he refers to: Barnabas, St. Clement of
Rome, St. Ignatius Theophorus, Hermas, Clement of Alexandria, Arnobius,
Lactantius, St. Athanasius the Great (*de incarnatione*), and Nemesius. The
majority the texts cited are distinguished by the naive moralism particular to
that era, and, of course, the problematic of conditionalism—whose definite
expression we find only in Arnobius—is foreign to these authors. When the
eschatological problem does arise, we see in the early Church (up to the fifth
century) two main streams, which proceed equally from the recognition
of the immortality of the soul: the universalist stream (headed by Origen
and St. Gregory of Nyssa) and the anti-Origenist stream with its acceptance
of "eternal torments," represented in the West by Blessed Augustine and in
the East by Justinian's anti-Origenism. The confession of conditional immortality is peculiar to Judaism, both in orthodox Judaism in the influential

32. Pétavel-Olliff, *Le problème de l'immortalité*, 120–21.
33. Pétavel-Olliff, *Le problème de l'immortalité*, 151.
34. Pétavel-Olliff, *Le problème de l'immortalité*, 346.
35. Pétavel-Olliff, *Le problème de l'immortalité*, 410.

streams of the Talmud and in the mystical stream, in Kabbalah, as well as in the philosophical stream of Maimonides (and in Spinoza too).

Thus conditionalism can find certain footholds for itself even in the tradition. But its main strength—no small strength, it must be said—lies in its *exegesis*, in its ability and persistent wish to find confirmation for its views in the Holy Scriptures of the Old and New Testaments. In this regard, its proponents have done a great work, and their biblical argumentation demands more attentive consideration than it has received up until now,[36] both with regard to their study of the texts themselves as well as to their theological exegesis of the same. In the present essay we will limit ourselves only to the necessary minimum.

Conditionalists first of all compile the statistics for those texts of both the Old and New Testaments that speak broadly of annihilation, perdition, and death: in one hundred Old and New Testament texts it is said that sinners will be exterminated. In the Hebrew language there exist fifty lexical roots signifying the annihilation of living beings.[37] Petavel-Olliff compiled an entire synoptic chart of the various phrases in the Bible, in both Hebrew and Greek, for expressing the *notion d'une destruction complète* [notion of complete destruction].[38] In addition to this summary,[39] our two authors cite a broad collection of Old and New Testament texts that speak of the final perdition of sinners and more generally of those opposed to God's will. The great majority of these texts are found in the Old Testament, of course, in the Psalms and prophets. Nevertheless, even a superficial familiarity with these texts convinces us that, however generous the psalmists and prophets may be with these threats, more often than not the threats are of a relative and, so to speak, figurative character,[40] and only with difficulty do they lend

36. Glubokovsky, *The Preaching of St. Paul.* Stewart D. F. Salmond. *The Christian Doctrine of Immortality,* 1895.

37. Pétavel-Olliff, *La fin du mal,* 105; Pétavel-Olliff, *Le problème de l'immortalité,* 150.

38. Pétavel-Olliff, *Le fin du Mal* 1:349–56; also 546, 552.

39. White compares such expressions as *apóllymi, ólethros,* and the like, in their meaning in Plato's *Phaedo,* where in context they straightforwardly mean annihilation, as well as in the LXX and the New Testament, in order to apply to them also his exegesis of Plato's use of the words(this, of course, is completely unjustified).

40. A few examples: Ps 73:19, 27: "For behold, those separating themselves from you *perish,* you *annihilate* all who fall away from you." Isa 1:28: "But all who fall away and all sinners will perish, and those forsaking the Lord will be *annihilated.*" Nah 1:15: "Celebrate, Judea, your festival, for the wicked man will no longer walk among you: he is completely annihilated." (But see Isa 48:9: "For the sake of My name I will set aside My anger, and for the sake of My glory will I restrain myself from annihilating evil") . . . Overall, in the psalms and in the prophets, we find a remarkable number of texts concerning the perdition of the wicked, but this often, if not always, has in view not so

themselves to an eschatological interpretation.[41] Much more important are those texts from the New Testament writers.[42]

Here is a broad list of New Testament phrases concerning the fate of sinners:[43]

Dying: "If you live according to the flesh, then you will die." (Rom 8:13)

Death: "For the wages of sin is death." (Rom 6:23)

Perdition: "Wide is the door and broad is the path leading to perdition." (Matt. 7:13)

Eternal perdition: "They will be subject to punishment, to eternal perdition away from the Lord from the glory of his might." (2 Thess 1:9)

Corruption: "The one who sows to his own flesh will reap corruption." (Gal 6:8). "They are like irrational animals . . . born to be caught and exterminated . . . in their corruption they are exterminated." (2 Pet 2:12)

Extermination: "And it will come to pass that every soul . . . is exterminated from its own people." (Acts 3:35)

Death: "And I will strike her [Jezebel's] children with death." (Rev 2:23), etc.[44]

much eschatological as historical perdition.

41. See White, *Life in Christ*, 158–62. Edward White proves that nowhere in the Old Testament, and particularly in Genesis, are there any examples of the immortality of man, but instead only of the death of his complex composition. Furthermore, after the fall of Adam, man is spared death solely through the anticipatory power of the future incarnation, the medicine of immortality [omitted here is a large number of biblical texts —Trans.] These texts are meant to demonstrate that man is not immortal, that immortality is a property of God (1 Tim 6:16); that death in its literal sense is a consequence of the fall, but immortality is a gift only for the just, that it is conditional; that the Bible nowhere speaks of the immortality of the soul; that unrepentant sinners are often threatened with death, and that they are spoken of as those who have been annihilated, and that death means that the soul and body are *not* immortal (824). The entire question is concentrated on the understanding of the biblical expression "death."

42. Citations from the New Testament indicating that the lot of sinners is death in the sense of annihilation (White, *Life in Christ*, 378ff): Matt 3:12; 5:25; 10:28; 16:25; (Luke 9:25; 17:23; John 12:25). Luke 9:56; 13:1–5; 20:18, 35; John 8:34–36; 8:51; 10:10, 27; 11:49–50; Acts 3:22–3; 8:20; 20:26; Rom 1:32; 2:6–7; 8:13; 1 Cor 3:14; Gal 6:8; 1 Tim 6:9; Heb 10:26–31; 2 Pet 2:12; 1 John 2:17; Jude 5:7; Rev 2:7; 3:5; 21:8. Compare the table of corresponding words and expressions: ibid., 387–90.

43 White, *Life in Christ*, 324–25.

44. In Pétavel-Olliff, we find an even more massive report of biblical texts with differing content on the theme of immortality: *La fin du mal*, 368–92. Of course, in such a massive report one encounters cases where this or that text is arbitrarily excluded.

In twelve places in the New Testament, the location of unrepentant sinners is named Gehenna. In one hundred places in the Old and New Testaments, the Scriptures teach that the wicked will be completely annihilated. Proponents of conditional immortality collect all the texts where life and death only appear in their mutual relation.[45] We will limit ourselves only to a few of the most difficult texts.[46] *Rom 1:32*: "The heathen know the just (judgment) of God, that those who do (such things) *are worthy of death.*" *Rom 6:23*: "For the wages of sin is *death*, but the gift of God is eternal life in Jesus Christ our Lord." *Rom 8:13*: "For if you live in the flesh, you *will die*; but if by the spirit you put to death the flesh, then you will live." *Gal 6:8*: "The one who sows to his own flesh will reap *corruption*, but the one sowing to the spirit will from the spirit reap eternal life." *2 Tim 6:9*: "lusts . . . will plunge people into *calamity* and *destruction.*" *Heb 10:26–31*: ". . . the dreadful expectation of judgment and the raging of *the fire prepared to devour* enemies." *2 Pet 2:12*: ". . . they, like irrational animals . . . born to be caught and exterminated . . . *in their corruption they are exterminated.*" *Jude 5:7*: ". . . Sodom and Gomorrah, subject to the *punishment of eternal fire*, have been set as an example."

But to these and similar texts, where death and perdition are spoken of in a more or less undefined sense, one may juxtapose other texts where death and perdition are, without a doubt, spoken of *not* in terms of annihilation: *Rom 7:9–11*: "*I died*, and in this manner the law, given to me for life, served for *death* because sin, having found occasion from the law, seduced me and *killed me* by it." "Sin was for me the cause of *death*" (See Gal 2:19; Eph 2:1, 5; Col 2:13; Jas 5:20; 1 John 3:14; 1 Tim 5:6: being alive, she is dead—*zôsa tethnēke*).

But these same collectors of texts must reckon with the existence of verses that are not favorable towards conditionalism. Such are those that speak of eternal torments (Matt 25:41, 46; Mark 3:29; Rev 14:9–11; 19:20; 20:10) or those that speak of divine mercy and of the salvation of the world and of humanity (such are, according to White, 416–18, the following texts: John 3:17; 1:29; 12:32; Rom 5:15, 18; 1 Cor 15:18; Eph 1:10; Phil 2: 9–11; Col 1:19; 1 Tim 2:4–6; 4:10; Titus 2:10; 1 John 2:2; 1 Cor 15:22; 2 Cor 4:13;

45. "Twenty times St. Paul tells us that death is the wages of sin," "*la mort sans phrases*" [death without any qualifications]. (Pétavel-Olliff, *La fin du mal*, 16).

46. It is interesting to observe how they deal with those texts that are awkward for conditionalism. One such indisputable text is 1 Cor 3:13–15: "the one whose works will burn will suffer loss; however, he himself will be saved, though as if by fire." White in this regard insists (*Life in Christ*, 350) that there is nothing awkward about the text: the sinner, if he does not wish to be separated from his works, will also burn.

Rev 4:13). Of course, conditionalists subject these meddlesome texts to an interpretation favorable to their system.

V

And so, sinful and God-defying humanity dies and becomes nothing, *is forgotten*. It no longer exists, as if it had never been. It is just as forgotten in God's memory as it is in human memory (and in the memory of the spiritual world too, apparently—something that conditionalists more or less forget in their own theology). Only the freedom of the creature remains inviolable, the freedom to determining itself either for life in God or for a return to pre-created nothingness. The surviving remnant of humanity (and there is no reason to think it will be the majority) receives eternal blessedness and becomes the justification for creation. Of this surviving part of humanity it will be possible to say, "God will be all in all" [1 Cor 15:28]. It is this perforated world with its sifted humanity that constitutes the final goal of creation, which is its theodicy. Abolished here is the presence of an eternal Hades, to which it is difficult to apply the text that God will be all in all, except in the sense of a scorching fire. Here we are given almost a clear, mathematical, rational answer to the problem of eternal life: the Creator consents to admit to a mistake in his creation, namely the presence of rooms vacant for all eternity, just like humanity consents to its selfish forgetting of the executed suicides. It is impossible to deny the simplicity and perspicacity of such a solution despite its total paradoxicality. It is impossible to deny both the radicalism of thought and the audacity in the formulation of the question, which in another instance might give rise only to timid silence. But in the case at hand, this eschatological heresy, just like other heresies, awakens dogmatic thought. Nevertheless, we must say that the theory of conditional immortality is a true heresy that contains in itself a number of dogmatic errors, and it is this that we must now demonstrate.

We must begin with what nonetheless constitutes the strongest aspect of conditionalism, namely with a critique of its biblical-exegetical argumentation. As we have seen, conditionalists have succeeded in collecting a vast number of biblical texts that speak of annihilation, perdition, and death. It is impossible to deny that this collection of texts—although its individual items are all well-known to attentive readers of God's Word—produces a rather strong impression and can confound, if not incline, readers to affirm conditional immortality or, what is the same thing, the natural mortality of the human person. But this first and, so to speak, outward impression should give way to a more attentive penetration both into the context and into the concrete meaning of each individual text. God's Word does not, in fact, speak of an immortal soul: this philosophical formula is not characteristic of Christian dogma anyway. The latter does not by any means teach the immortality of the soul outside of its relationship to the body; rather, it teaches the immortality of the person who even in death does not completely die and who is raised with his body by the power of Christ's resurrection. In addition, and no less importantly, the Bible never speaks of the death of the person as an annihilation.

In general, the Bible does not speak in philosophical terms, but rather in the language of images that demand in every instance special clarification, with the very same expressions functioning in an indeterminate and ambiguous manner. For this reason, these expressions demand exegesis, at least in those places where there is no obvious meaning. And this exegesis is in a certain sense determined by the whole sum of apperceiving ideas,[47] or dogmatic presuppositions, i.e., tradition, which contains in itself the witness of the Church concerning the understanding of the Bible. Biblical literalism is mistaken, for "the letter kills but the Spirit gives life" [2 Cor 3:6], and often such literalism is even impossible. And it is especially the language of eschatological texts that is the least susceptible to a literal understanding, insofar as its imagery is brightly colored by the language of apocalyptic writing with its fantasy and syncretism, as is clear to anyone who has dealt with eschatological texts. Of course, eschatological language is sharply distinguished from that of parenetic texts, from the apostolic spiritual exhortations that primarily have to do with ideas of moral order. In addition, the difficult task of eschatological exegesis consists in distinguishing in eschatological images the various levels and perspectives that are stacked on top of each another, like a mountain chain in perspective. Consequently, the literal interpretation of texts is often simply impossible, and the dogmatic exegesis that conditionalists give them is by no means indisputable and certainly not the only possibility. It is conditioned by definite theological presuppositions that must be highlighted and verified in the light of more foundational and general dogmatic truths that have already been established by the Church.

Specifically, the foundational concepts by which the theory of conditional immortality operates—life, death, perdition, extermination, destruction, and so on—are not univocal but instead multivalent. In particular, the meaning of the concepts *death* and *life*—the starting point for conditionalism—are by no means self-evident. This is clear simply from the fact that, before conditionalism, no one had understood them in the way conditionalism

47. A reference to the theory of apperception, popular in nineteenth-century psychology, which held that our perceptions of reality are shaped by pre-existing ideas in our minds, the "apperceiving mass" through which reality is filtered. —Trans.

does. Conditionalism simplifies the concepts *life* and *death* to the point of a simple biological juxtaposition. Zoological biologism is the general scheme of this theology. Here life and death are identical for the human person and for the animal. The human being is an animal that is distinguished from the animal world solely by certain characteristics, and not by the fact that he inherently possesses conditional immortality, which is merely granted to him by God. (This somewhat resembles the Catholic scheme: *natura and donum supernaturale* [nature and the supernatural gift].) At first it is granted to him by partaking of the fruit of the tree of life, i.e., through physical means, and later it is restored by the equally physical union of God with humanity in the incarnation, which assumes the same biological significance. The incarnation grants physical immortality, and this exhausts its significance, such that there is no question of the transfiguration, divinization, and glorification of humanity. From this point of view it even becomes unintelligible why the incarnation was accomplished specifically in man (since the man is not distinct from the animal world) and not in some other animal, if the incarnation is understood solely as the physical medicine of immortality. Equally inexplicable is that *anticipatory* effect that the incarnation provides before the latter's accomplishment, namely the preservation of the life of man on earth and beyond the grave. Needless to say, post-mortem existence loses here any independent meaning in the destiny of the human person and represents merely an *intermediate* state between death and resurrection. Here we find a critical gap in the eschatology of conditionalism.

For conditionalism, man is *one* of the living beings in this world that possesses a *relative* life. With this foundational definition it becomes completely apparent that the theology of conditionalism lacks both an anthropology and a cosmology, which in this case are one and the same. For conditionalism, man is not a created god, and he is not the center and lord of the world. This superficial interpretation of the *image* of God in the human person is characteristic of this theology. They do not recognize its ontological significance, as divine likeness and participation in Divinity. They also undervalue the fact that God created man in the fulfillment of his pre-eternal counsel in the Holy Trinity, "*in Our Image*" (Gen 1), and, in making man from the earth, *with his own breath*, i.e., from his very self, did God breathe into man the "living soul" that conditionalists identify with the "living soul" of animals. Conditionalists rightly say that the man does not have, as a *special* principle, an immortal soul that is temporarily enclosed in a mortal body, as if in a dungeon or sheath from which it awaits its liberation. Such is the Eastern-Platonist doctrine. The human person has a spirit predestined for immortal life *in the body*, and that life, although disrupted to some extent by death owing to sin, will be restored in the resurrection.

Yet conditionalists draw from this the mistaken conclusion that the human person certainly does not possess in himself an immortal divine principle, and they even consider the acknowledgement of this fact to be the heresy of pantheism.[48] But we have the word of revelation, that God *breathed* into man, *from himself*, the breath of life. This means that the human person has *in his spirit* an uncreated principle of Divinity that nonetheless possesses for itself a hypostasis created by God according to his image.[49] Consequently, man possesses in himself an uncreated-created principle, he pertains to the eternity of the divine world,[50] though he receives a self-existent personal being only in his creaturehood. We must add to this that the human person, as the center of creation, is intended to rule over it, to participate through his spiritual nature in the divine Sophia. But in the world, the created Sophia, he is a microcosm, and the "joy" of divine Wisdom is "in the sons of man" [Prov 8:31]. Through this, the human person stands in the center of the world, but also above the world. Belonging to the created-animal world, he is at the same time a god by grace.[51] And there is no fear of pantheism here, as is often made out to be the case especially on this point. Pantheism in its bad sense signifies the *identity* of the world with God, and not merely its participation in Divinity. If man co-images God, then that means that

48. Curiously, they find a predecessor here in their main antagonist, Blessed Augustine, who puts forward as Church teaching the position that the spirit (soul-*anima*) of the human person was created by God from nothing. (*De anima et eius origine* [*On the Soul and Its Origin*], books III–V). Noli ergo credere, noli docere, quod non de nihilo, sed de sua natura fecit animam Deus, si vis esse catholicum [Therefore, if you wish to be Catholic, do not believe, do not teach, that it was not from nothing but rather from his nature that God created the soul]. In this, Bl. Augustine is in direct contradiction to the Bible, which testifies that God, having made the body of the human person from the earth, breathed, from himself, the breath of life into humanity.

49. In Pétavel-Olliff (*La fin du mal*, 171) we find the following incomprehensible definition of spirit: "L'esprit est exclusivement l'origine (!!) qui perçoit le divin, c'est le sens moral et religieux, ce qu'on pourrait appeler en un seul mot spiritualiste. . . . Dans le plan divin l'esprit de l'homme en communion vivante avec l'Esprit de Dieu devait pénétrer l'âme, et par elle régner sur le corps et sur tous ses organes" [The spirit is exclusively the origin that perceives the divine, it is the moral and religious sense that one could describe in a word as *spiritual*. . . . In the divine plan, the spirit of man in living communion with the Spirit of God was meant to penetrate the soul and through it to rule over body and all its members].

50. On the contrary, in conditionalism we have the following conclusion with respect to the image of God in the human person: Il portait en lui un fragile miroir de la divinité, le miroir est brisé, et l'homme n'est plus que l'enfant de la poudre. Tiré de la terre, le premier homme n'était que poussière, dit l'apôtre [Man bore within himself a fragile mirror of divinity, the mirror has shattered, and now he is only a child of the dirt. Born of the earth, the first man was nothing but dust, says the apostle] (Pétavel-Olliff, *La fin du mal*, 164).

51. For the development of all these thoughts, see my *Lamb of God*.

God too co-images man. Divine-humanity unites man and God; there is a divine-humanity that is eternal, heavenly, just as there is a divine-humanity that is created. Only on the foundation of this *co-imaging* of God and man can the incarnation be understood ontologically, as the adoption by the Logos of a human nature, the uniting in one hypostasis of two natures or two wills, one divine and one human. In the Christology of conditionalism, the incarnation takes on the character of an ontological absurdity: God assumes . . . the animal nature of man, while possessing no ontological connection with this nature. The absence of an anthropology in conditionalism necessarily leads to the absence of a Christology.

And so there belongs to man, on account of his divine procession, a natural immortality. "God alone has immortality" (1 Tim 6:16), but man possesses immortality in God. One cannot but give credit to conditionalists for their critique of the rational proofs for the immortality of the soul, beginning with the Plato's *Phaedo* (a critique already made earlier by Kant),[52] for immortality is truly proper only to God, but also to one who *participates in God*, as man does.

This paradoxical, antinomic concept of the living image of God as a created god is precisely what characterizes man. As a creature, man must accomplish the task inherent in him by virtue of his participation in God and in that sense by virtue of his uncreated nature; *this* is the power of immortality. This immortality in his created nature is, at first, a *potential* immortality, which begins with the *posse non mori* [possibility of not dying]. This *de facto* immortality is disrupted, as a consequence of the fall, by death, although not by an absolute but only a relative death; yet in the resurrection of Christ it is already restored as the *non posse mori* [impossibility of dying], as the positive power of immortality. This was *granted* by the God-man, but it could only be *received* by man, who co-images him.

The fullness of the image of God in man is his *personhood* living in its own nature, participating in the created Sophia, included in the world, in the fullness of creation. Personhood, understood in this fullness of life, is the *ens realissimum* [the truest reality] in creation. The fullness of the image of God in man, rooted in his personhood, *transcends* his personality as a monad to the level of the multi-unity of all humanity. One can say that the fullness of the image of God does not even belong to man in his individuality but rather to humanity in its *sobornost'*,[53] in love, in the image of the consubstantial triunity of God.

52. See the essay by Prof. S. N. Trubetskoy, "The Immortality of the Soul." [Sergei Nikolaevich Trubetskoy (1862–1905) was a Russian religious philosopher; in his work he developed the thought of Vladimir Solovyov. —Trans.].

53. This word contains a rich storehouse of meaning comprised of such distinct

Here is that primordial participation of man in God, which, making him uncreated-created, also contains in itself the power of immortality, in the supratemporality or immortality of human personhood, the consciousness of which is granted to personhood in the immediate act of self-consciousness: *I am I.* As such, I myself belong to myself, I posit myself, although at the same time, being a created "I," I myself am also given to myself. And this is not pantheism, but it is, of course, the *panentheism* to which the apostle testifies: "for all things are from him, through him, and to him" (Rom 11:36).

VI

To conditionalism belongs the indisputable merit of giving, in accord with its main theme, a more attentive formulation of the question of life and death than is regularly given. We are too *accustomed* to the mortality of life, such that we have ceased to feel the genuine *mystery* of both life and death. Meanwhile this mystery exists already in the animal world to which man is connected, so to speak, through his phylogenesis, as well as in his life as the lord of creation. Every life proceeds from the fountain of Life, the life-creating Spirit, and of all creation it is said: "You take away their spirit and they die, and they return to their dust. You send your spirit and they are created, and you renew the face of the earth" (Ps 103:29–30). The inexhaustible fountain of life in the animal world is the ceaseless miracle of the creation of the world, which philosophy already since ancient times has comprehended as hylozoism, capacity for life inherent in all matter. The life of animals, and the Wisdom both living and acting within them, shook the human soul with a philosophical and religious jolt, and this mystery of animal life found expression in animal cults. Egypt was permeated by this mystery of the life of the animal world in its relation to humanity and divinity, and it memorialized this "wonder" in the zoo-anthropomorphic images of its gods. The life of animals remains transcendent to us in its *limitedness*, on account of their lack of a spirit, but it is also transcendent in its zoological sophianicity, in the "instinct" of the world soul.

Their death too remains transcendent to us because of the limitation inherent in their life, owing both to the absence of immortal personhood

---

concepts as "communal," "conciliar," "catholic." The word is used in the Russian translation of the Nicene Creed ("one holy, *sobornal*, apostolic Church") but it became a mainstay of Russian religious thought with Alexei Stepanovich Khomyakov (1804–60), who used it to distinguish Orthodox ecclesiology from Protestantism and Roman Catholicism. From ecclesiology it moved to anthropology, where the word came to indicate (as here) the inherently communal existence of humanity. —Trans.

and to the fullness of their dying. Death in a certain sense is natural for the animal world. But even animals know most intimately the horror of the violent and untimely death that fills the world, and "all creation together suffers and is in torment up to the present time" (Rom 8:22). In this world there reigns the struggle for existence: animals eat each other, yet they are all eaten up by death. Animals do not possess personhood, only individuality, but this is enough for them to fear death. To the animal is granted the immortality of the genus, according to their kind (the well-known theory of [August] Weismann, which explains death as a factor in the adaptation of life in the struggle for existence, patches up this hole in the world easily enough for this professor in his ivory tower). And nonetheless, even in the animal world we find nothing like this "natural death" as a painless falling asleep. Whoever has experienced the death of animals, those friends of man, knows the anguish of an animal before death, as well as particular crying out for life which sounds like an unwitting reproach against man: "are you not called to give immortality to animal life, and are you not to blame for this anguish of death?" But, if the death of animals is now so excruciating, then, in principle, it could instead be simply the painless extinguishing of a finished life, insofar as animals do not possess in themselves the foundation for immorality. And it is as though the exorbitant profligacy of nature seen in animal reproduction witnesses to the fact that here what is of greater value is the existence of the species and not the individual.

Nevertheless, a number of questions remain open here in what represents a "theological zoology," so to speak: how can we comprehend the creation of *mortal life*, inasmuch as animals, living beings, were created *mortal*?[54] And if "God did not create death" (Wis 1:31), then how exactly can we reconcile this with the creation of the entire animal world only *according to their kind* [Gen 1:25]? We must note that when the animal world is created, what is mentioned is *not* death but rather "a living soul" (Gen 1:20, 24). Perhaps the time has not yet come for humanity to answer these questions, and it is vain to occupy oneself with empty "disputations" [1 Cor 1:20]. We can do no more than acknowledge that death throughout the animal world had already been known to humanity as the annihilation of an individual together with the simultaneous preservation of the species; this represents both the impersonal immortality of life and its frailty with regard to the individual. But for man, the death of animals cannot remain anything other than foreign, since in himself he cannot help but know his immortal spirit in its supratemporal self-consciousness. That is why, despite

54. Bulgakov's point here depends on a juxtaposition of concepts impossible to render elegantly in English, insofar as the Russian word for animal (*zhivotnyj*) means literally "living thing." —Trans.

the claims of the annihilationists, the commandment not to partake of the fruit of the tree of good and evil did not sound to man like the threat of annihilation but instead like a certain mysterious, unfathomed destiny, insofar as it consisted not in that natural death that reigned in the entire animal world but rather in a certain unnatural paralysis of life in concert with the temporary breakdown of man's composition. And even after the divine sentencing, Adam did not believe in death as the annihilation of life. This is seen in the fact that the very moment after the judgment of God, Adam gave to his wife the name *Eve*, that is, *life*, for she became "the mother of all the living" (Gen 3:20). The claim that the death sentence for our ancestors was postponed, despite the verdict, due to the as yet unaccomplished redemption, is a baseless one and represents a completely unbiblical, speculative supposition opposed to the facts of the matter. But the facts are these: Adam and Eve felt their death sentence not as a threat to their human life, which had only just begun in its creative work, but instead only as a grave mystery concerning human life. They understood death, which God did not create, not as annihilation but as an act included in human life. In a word, between death in the animal world and in the human there existed a clear *dividing line* in the consciousness of our ancestors.

It is especially worth noting that in fallen man we see a heightening of the consciousness of his divinity and immortality—an evil spirituality— with greater force than *before* the fall, when man in his creaturely humility lived in God, not yet aware of himself, of his own proper divine likeness. With the fall commences that Luciferian narcissism, self-admiration, which drove Lucifer to his fall in the spiritual world and, after him, man too. With this practical un-deifying of human life, "man-godhood"[55] begins, representing, of course, one particular form of man's spiritual life (the lowest aspect of which leads man towards animality, to the state of "flesh"). Such is the meaning of God's words concerning fallen man: "See, Adam has become like one of us, knowing good and evil (that is, in fallen, Luciferian self-consciousness, in man-godhood); and now, so that he may not stretch out his hand and take also from the tree of life, and taste, and begin to live eternally" (Gen 3:22). Immortality would have been the final assertion of man-godhood (just as in Lucifer it became angelo-godhood). And in the paths of human salvation it was necessary first of all to leave man to his own fate, that is, to *mortal* life. The first death that the world witnessed, the murder of Abel by Cain, was experienced as a great shock, a convulsion of life.

---

55. "Man-godhood" is the diabolical opposite of "Godmanhood" or "divine-humanity," the proper way in which God and the human person co-image each other under the example of Christ, the God-man, who lived in humility before the Father. —Trans.

God said to Cain: "What have you done? And now you are cursed from the earth that opened its mouth to receive the blood of your brother from your hand" (Gen 4:10). Although death was not the creation of God, it came into the world despite God's will as a consequence of the spiritual weakening of man, who had changed his *posse non mori* into the *non posse non mori*.

And yet, since it was included in the plan of the divine providence through the divine verdict, death received its proper place in human life as a disincarnation. This disincarnation, although unnatural, is nonetheless fruitful for the human person, insofar as through it man undergoes that special, so to speak, experience that had become otherwise inaccessible to him, namely a compulsory experience of his spiritual nature, alongside the experience of contact with the spiritual world. In the theory of conditionalism, the post-mortem state has meaning solely as an intermediate time before the resurrection, a time that conditionalists do not know how to fill out, and so the simplest option would be to fill it out with an unconscious state, soul-sleep. However, the post-mortem state in its disincarnateness is an essential part of human life on the way to resurrection, the latter being impossible without it. What is important here is that in its meaning, the death of man is still life, albeit defective with respect to the fullness of man's composition. One need only remember the fact of "the preaching of Christ in Hades" [1 Peter 3:18-20] in order to understand this significance. And so, in the relationship between life and death in the human person, we have here something that, though related, is nevertheless qualitatively different than what we find in the life of the animal world. Specifically, what occurs here is not an annihilation but rather the *awakening* of life, in a sense. The fullness of life, which had been lost in death, is restored in Christ's *universal* resurrection, which has its ontological foundation in Christ's *personal* resurrection. Christ assumed the *whole* Adam, all human nature, and in his resurrection he granted it immortality. For the theory of conditional immortality it would, of course, be more convenient simply to accept that not all of humanity is resurrected but instead only the part of it that is worthy of immortality. But it does not go this far; on the one hand, because of the impossibility of directly contradicting revelation, and on the other hand, due to the demand to make allowance for the agony of dying and to satisfy the feeling of punishment. Fundamentally, however, this renewal of life for the purpose of annihilation, this resurrection for death, is ontologically unjustified.

When considering the future life in the resurrection, we can postulate various possibilities that do not at this moment constitute the subject of our examination. We should note that it is peculiar to conditionalism to demonstrate with great emphasis the presence of the *tragic* side of eschatology insofar as this is expressed in the numerous texts concerning perdition and death in the future life. Although it is impossible to interpret these texts together with the conditionalists in the sense of a complete annihilation of life, we must, consequently, accept them as definitions of one possible *state of life*, and moreover explicitly *not* as that state's exhaustive content. This is because death and perdition do not annihilate the power of life but are rather contained within it and, most importantly, are *combined* with the positive potency of life. Eschatological prophecies must be understood not only statically but also dynamically. Various and contradictory powers and states are compatible in the human spirit's *one life*—inscrutable in its depths—on the paths of eternity. There is no space here to speak of this in depth, but the problematic of conditionalism makes more visible the necessity of a *concrete* understanding of life in its depths.[56] Life, and immortality in particular, cannot be understood as a concrete state of, so to speak, two dimensions; it has three or more dimensions, even if their multi-unity is not subject to rationalistic definition. Therefore, the possibility arises of a simultaneous and equally justified union of two or more differing or contrary determinations: life and death, perdition and salvation, eternal life and unconsciousness. And can we really say that even in our day man knows, that he has conscious access to, the actual reality of the spirit in all its depth, in the subconscious and supraconscious spheres?

Of course, it is an ontological absurdity to postulate the extinction of the soul, its transformation into non-being, its self-disintegration. But today we see with our very eyes the known fact that spirit can be submerged into potency, that it can fail to realize itself in conscious life. Materialists, who deny the existence of the spirit and who reduce life to various "canine reflexes," testify with complete sincerity to the poverty of their own personal self-consciousness, "for they are flesh" [Gen 6:3], "psychical people, lacking

---

56. This merit of conditionalism was recognized by a thinker as far from its conclusions as Baron von Hügel. *The Mystical Element of Religion as Studied in Catherine of Genoa and Her Friends*, Vol. II (1923), 228–30. Baron von Hügel expresses himself relatively gently when he speaks of conditional immortality as possessing "many undeniable advantages over every kind of Origenism." This is not the annihilation *by the Almighty* of the naturally immortal souls of grave sinners, but it means that the human soul "begins with capacity of acquiring, with the help of God's Spirit, a *spiritual personality*, built up out of the mere possibilities and partial tendencies of their highly mixed natures, which, if left uncultivated and untranscended, become definitely fixed at the first, phenomenal, and merely individual level—so that spiritual personality alone deserves to live on and does so, whilst this animal personality does not deserve to and does not so. The soul is thus not simply born as, but can become more and more that 'inner man' who alone persists, indeed who is 'renewed day by day, even though our outward men perish' (2 Cor 4:16)" (228–29).

spirit" (Jude 19).[57] "The psychical man does not receive what is from the Spirit of God because he considers it foolish, and he cannot comprehend it, because it must be spiritually discerned" (1 Cor 2:14). Such a person finds himself in a state of spiritual death, although he happens to be alive. A spiritual resurrection still awaits him.

Generally speaking, both life and death are *intensive* values possessing an infinite quantity of diverse, complex, and fluctuating spectra—from a fading extinguishing (which is not, however, equal to non-existence) up to new birth (which does not, however, violate the continuity and identity of personality). The divine fire of life that burns in the human spirit is inextinguishable, but its light, having been entrusted to a limited creature weakend by sin, flickers and begins to die down, although it is capable of once again blazing forth with a brightly illuminating flame. Its intensity possesses infinite dimensions, and in this lies the foundational, suprarational mystery of eschatology. Conditionalism—albeit in a negative mode—allows us to get a sense of the mystery of concrete immortality.

Incidentally, it is typical of conditionalists that they exhibit great restraint in making judgments—if they make any at all—concerning the immortality of the light and especially the dark incorporeal spirits. First of all, there arises the question of what death could mean here in the absence of a body. However, natural immortality, it would seem, is ruled out here as well, since God alone possesses immortality. Due to the inevitability of recognizing the life of the fallen spirits that are active in the world, conditionalism does not broach this delicate question, thereby avoiding a straightforward conflict with the Scriptures. Meanwhile, nowhere is the conditionalist judgment concerning the possibility of suicide more applicable than here, with respect to Satan and his angels who find themselves in persistent and conscious resistance to God. Why has Satan not already died, together with his hosts? This question remains unanswered from the point of view of the logic of conditionalism while at the same time raising a problem for it. Generally speaking, conditionalism does not introduce into its eschatology the question of the fate of the fallen spirits, although this question was posed already in Origenism. This question remains unanswered in conditionalism, just like the question concerning conditional immortality

57. The Russian *dushevnye* translates the Greek *psychikoí*, whose modern English rendering presents the translator numerous possibilities, all problematic ("sensual man," "natural man," "soulish man"). I have settled on "psychical" following David Bentley Hart's own translation of the word (see *The New Testament: A Translation*, 410) because the contrast Bulgakov intends is between materialists who see only the life-principle ("soul") in humanity and those who recognize the existence of a spirit whose life, in its origin and destiny, transcends the phenomenal and natural plane. —Trans.

itself: in what manner is it possible for naturally mortal human nature to become immortal through union with divine nature? How can such a union be accomplished? Here conditionalism unwittingly falls into a mechanical, purely naturalistic understanding both of the incarnation and of immortality. But man can become immortal only by virtue of his natural immortality, which is merely renewed through the incarnation. Nature is the receptacle of grace. *Humanum capax divini* [humanity has the capacity for divinity].

VII

Here we must examine the conditionalist argument of greatest acuity, although not one entirely free from a certain demagoguery, namely the argument from *freedom*. Life is accompanied by a consciousness of freedom, even if this freedom should direct itself toward self-annihilation. The human person has the freedom to turn himself into the nothing from which he was called into being. God does not do violence to man's freedom by imposing on him a life he finds hateful, a life that he himself is able to destroy, if he so pleases. *To be or not to be* is a matter of man's free choice. For man, metaphysical suicide is possible, a transformation of the self to the pre-creation or even a sort of post-creation "nothing," the complete *destruction* of the creation of God. True, this set of ideas in conditionalism remains undifferentiated from another set with which it is constantly confused and interchanged, namely the annihilation of the fallen spirits by God's omnipotence, by a metaphysical death penalty through which God himself destroys his own creation. Nevertheless, we must distinguish and separately examine these two sets of ideas.

And so, does man possess, in relation to his own proper being, the *freedom* that constitutes the necessary ontological condition of self-annihilation? This question is tantamount to another, more general question: is man *his own creator*, is it by his own freedom that he came from nothing and possesses the authority to return to that nothing? Is man's own being something belonging to him? But if this were true, then man would not be distinct from God who exists by his own power, by the freedom of an act of absolute self-positing, with freedom here representing a completely transparent necessity that excludes any external facticity and that accomplishes its self-existence. For this absolute self-existence (*aseitas*) in God there exists no ontologically external boundary, no *nothing*, which would be ontologically out of place in this all-fullness of the free existential act: "I am who I will be, I am the existing one, Jehovah" (Exod 3:14), a self-enclosed actual infinity.

Man, on the contrary, is a creature, he himself is given to *himself, created* such that he is *defined* for himself. But insofar as *omnis definitio est negatio* [every definition is a negation], he is limited not only positively but also negatively, not only by being but also by non-being, by the gaping chasm separating *nothing* and *something*. Such an existence, of course, cannot be understood as posited by *freedom*, by an absolute ontological act. Nevertheless, it is posited, if not by freedom then *in* freedom. Because it is not a "thing," creaturely being possesses in itself the divine likeness of spirit; although it depends for its being on God's Wisdom, Omnipotence, and Love, it is nonetheless given over to belong to itself, it is left to its own disposal. There arises a *created freedom* distinct from the absolute freedom of the Creator and yet still reflective of it. This created freedom must be called a *modal freedom* in distinction to absolute freedom. It is the form of the being of a *creature* that is *given* to itself in its creaturehood but free in its existence and that, therefore, possesses a *creative* relationship to its own life. It freely acts and lives out the creaturely life given to it. While not free in respect to life's *theme* or *content*, the creature is free in life's realization. The dialectic of the image and likeness of God in the human person, of freedom and creaturehood, of givenness and mission, of createdness and creativity, defines the character of human life in its absolute-relativity: in the absolute of the self-consciousness of freedom and in the relativity of its created act, with a constant reflection on itself, on its own self-being, which, as givenness, is also altero-being. By virtue of this, man is not a thing, but neither is he simply an act; he is simultaneously fact and act in his active facticity and his factual activity. In the sinful condition of internal dissension, in the opposition to his own nature, what prevails is the facticity by which man *is* a *slave* to his own elemental nature and is powerless to subdue it to his self-will. By contrast, when in harmony with his nature, in the health of chastity, in free fidelity to his own norm, man does not know his facticity and is free in the authenticity of his being: "You will know the truth and the truth will make you free" (John 8:32).

The modality of creaturely freedom has as its consequence the fact that it is realized only *within the limits of created being*, in the latter's presuppositions, which possess the force of fact and givenness. Created freedom is *not* free of any preconditions. It looks to the givenness of being and exists only in relation to it and within its limits, beyond which ontologically it cannot go. *What is new*, without which there would be absolutely no creativity, comes to pass here only within the limits of its givenness, precisely "out of" something or "in" something. Sophia defines the entire content of the created world, this content being sophianic in its infinite diversity and in the relative novelty of this sophianic creativity. But out of nothing man can create nothing, not even a small bug, as Dostoevsky wrote, having in view the bug's participation in the fullness of being: "a bug is a mystery." Man belongs to creation, to its fullness, from which flows the fullness of life and creativity, since life and creativity are synonyms.

The opposite conclusion too must also be recognized, that, as surely as man cannot create something from nothing, so too he cannot plunge any being into non-being, dissolve it into nothingness—not even one atom of the universe; the universe is God's, and it is only given, entrusted to man's lordship. "My arm established the earth, and My right hand spread out the heavens" (Isa 48:13). "The Lord, who spread out the heavens and established the earth and formed the spirit of man within him" (Zech 12:1). Of course, humanity can transform the *modes* of being and destroy its given *forms*, and in this sense the destructive energy of man is empirically *not* limited. But ontologically this energy remains powerless: the world is upheld by God in its being and it cannot be returned by man to the abyss of non-being, to the darkness of nothing; it is indestructible.

But if man is powerless to annihilate even one ontological atom, does he then possess the power to infringe upon his own being, and thus to that extent to destroy God's creation, at least in this particular corner of it? Is man capable of entering into one-to-one combat with his Creator and de-creating what he has created? This question itself contains a self-evident ontological absurdity and is only a subtle form of man-godhood or atheism. The idea of a metaphysical suicide of the world has been promulgated by the militant preachers of atheism, by the philosophers of pessimism Schopenhauer and Hartmann, in the form of the extinguishing of the will to live.

VIII

This question, however, cannot be definitively resolved solely on the basis of general remarks concerning the indestructibility of creation. Freedom is also an indestructible fact of creation, albeit within its proper limits and in its proper nature. And it is to freedom that there is given that same consciousness of self-existence, of self-possession, of self-positing, outside of which freedom simply does not exist. The paradox of created freedom consists precisely in this, that while it is created, on account of its connection with the givenness of being, it also carries within itself the self-consciousness of its uncreatedness, of self-positing, and it cannot be disconnected from this without a disintegrating ontological self-contradiction. Freedom is *opposed* to givenness, in freedom the consciousness of man's divine likeness borders on dangerous man-godhood. We must understand this paradox of the self-consciousness of created freedom. It gives evidence of what holds sway in the bowels of being, in the very depths of creation. God creates the human spirit out of his very self, breathing into him a "living soul" and by the creative act calling into being a free individuality, a created "I" that is nevertheless a "co-I" with the triune divine "I" and that bears within itself the image of the latter's freedom. God's very act of creating remains transcendent for the creature, for this creation constitutes the condition of the very being and consciousness of the creature; it ontologically precedes it, remaining "behind the scenes" of being, so to speak. But there also exists in the creature a depth to which the created spirit penetrates through its self-consciousness, finding that it is also a condition of its own being, its precondition. This is the act of created, aboriginal self-positing as a free participation in God's self-positing in the very act of God's creation.[58] A free spirit cannot be created by a one-sided act of God's omnipotence as the entire visible world was created, that is, as a thing (in the ontological sense), for the spirit is personhood, possessing freedom and self-consciousness in this freedom. If it is said that "the soul of a man is more valuable than the world, and what will a man give in exchange for his soul" (Matt 16:26), then this also has an ontological meaning with respect to the special nature of the soul in comparison with all creation.

We cannot know this primordial act of self-positing, which takes place on the borders of creation and on the borders of time, but we feel its consequences in all our being. We possess the memory of it in a certain obscure anamnesis that can be expressed only in the language of ontological myth. And so, we can say that at the creation of the created-uncreated, created-divine spirit, its own created freedom was consulted, and so it also played a part. In the creative "Let there be" addressed to every created person, there is included both God's *question* concerning a person's agreement, concerning his will to be and to live, as well as the *response* in the form of a certain absolute self-positing. Its absoluteness is defined not only by its supra-temporality but also by its inclusion in the absoluteness of God's creative act. In the language of ontological myth, one can simply say that it was not only God who created the human (as well as the angelic) spirit, but that spirit itself determined itself to be (by virtue of its inclusion in God's creation, of course).

---

58. In the preceding reflections and in what immediately follows, Bulgakov adopts and adapts some major themes of the German idealist philosopher Johann Gottlieb Fichte (1762–1814) and his *Ich-Philosophie*. For more on Bulgakov's engagement—both positive and negative—with Fichte, see the "Excursus on Fichte" in Bulgakov, *The Tragedy of Philosophy*. For more from Bulgakov on the supratemporality of spiritual consciousness, see Bulgakov, *The Bride of the Lamb*, 83–88.

It is impossible to further comprehend and to explain this act of creation in freedom and the participation of created freedom in its own creation (which conditionalists have addressed so crudely) without falling into unnecessary mythologizing. But it is possible to establish on the basis of the evidences of our proper self-knowledge that man, and created spirit more generally, in the act of its creation by God, also posits itself with an absolute positing possessing the eternality and indestructability proper to the power of God's creation. God in his love for the creature and in his condescension towards it allows it to co-participate in creation, and to the divine question concerning the will to be there is given in response the indestructible "yes" of the creature. And this "yes" resounds in our soul as the evidence of the "immortality" of the soul, of the uncreated eternality of the spirit. But this is an act standing outside of time, on the very borders of time, defining the entire temporality of being; it is its silent yet indestructible foretaste. Freedom agreed to be, it manifested its will to live, and this life became as indestructible as all the rest of God's creation.

For this reason it is naive to think that within time – even within the time of post-mortem existence, or more generally in the temporal discursivity of life— this act of self-creation could be canceled or weakened. Metaphysical suicide is absolutely impossible, for it is contradictory: it can only be thought as an act of life, presupposing the living subject himself. Regular suicide is a clear manifestation of a will to live expressing itself in the rejection solely of the present condition of life; it is, so to speak, a particular protest in the general process of life, an act of the will's self-assertion. Schopenhauer understood this well when he preached exactly this metaphysical suicide as the extinguishing of the will to live, that is, the weakening of that self-creative act that he imagined as the blind activity of the caprice of an irrational will. Of course, this too is a utopia as delirious as the metaphysical suicide that follows Hades' torments in the theory of conditionalism. Life's spasms and convulsions, of whatever quality they may be—whether striving to defend oneself against or to liberate oneself from a certain condition of life—are an act of life, its self-assertion. The fiery wheel of life cannot be stopped or reversed by human freedom in its discursivity, for this freedom has already been determined for all time. And this self-determination is: to be and to live.[59]

59. A particular application of this general idea occurs in its application to the teaching on original sin (see my book *The Burning Bush*). The spirit, created by God, determines itself to be in the fallen world, and thus accepts for itself the burden of original sin, which otherwise can only be understood as a heredity disease and not as *sin*. Original sin, like the infection of death, plays a central role for conditionalists, although practically it possesses here only the meaning of an inherited disease. In this

IX

Man is a person, and as such he possesses in himself pre-eternally the reposing love of God. He is a ray on the spectrum of Divine Sophia, he belongs
to the Fullness and is included in it. He is necessary for God precisely in his
personhood, as an *other* for God, as God's friend through predestination.
And the memory of God is a *memory eternal* that preserves and does not
forget his friends, and we witness to this "eternal memory" of God in the
prayer for those departing to the other world.[60] Personhood, on the one
hand, belongs to the human multi-unity and in this sense is *one of many*, but
it is nonetheless *the only one* in its unrepeatability and irreplaceability for
man and for God; the soul of man is more valuable than the entire world. It
is a strange act of spiritual self-blinding, this supposition that the theory of
conditionalism makes, that the human personality can perish in the sense
of complete self-annihilation, that it can flee from eternity, can escape it.
And this idea is even stranger with respect to the love of God and and its
correlative, the memory of God, which allegedly forgets its creations. This
very thought is blasphemy against the Creator who created man in his image. And, finally, this appears even stranger as a theodicy—the justification
of the world in God and God in the world. This justification, the victory of
God in the world, is bought at the price of the annihilation of *the greater
half* of creation (for according to their understanding of the Bible, conditionalists are forced to admit—following Blessed Augustine again—that the
saved will be the smaller portion). The quantity, however, is insignificant
in principle, because in a certain sense it is equally difficult to accept the
annihilation of even just one soul. The apotheosis of the world will be expressed in the fact that God will all in all,[61] but only in "all" who survive. To
God is ascribed here a sort of admission of his own mistake in creation, a
mistake that he corrects through the annihilation of the failed creation. He
resembles a schoolboy who rips up his old notebooks when he no longer has
need of them, in this case the notebooks being living persons. Of course,
this is a defamation of the Wisdom of the Creator and of creation, of Divine Sophia and created Sophia. God's lawyers wanted to find a rationally
respectable conclusion with their position, one that would avoid an eternal
hell, which they consider incompatible with divine omniscience, while also

---

they unexpectedly agree with Blessed Augustine.

60. "Memory eternal!" is exclaimed at the conclusion of a Byzantine Rite funeral
service. —Trans.

61. "All" is interpreted by conditionalists either in the sense of "all who remain" or
in the sense of the "aggregate," but not in the sense of "fullness"—an exegetical trick to
weaken the straightforward promise. And in this they agree with Augustine.

fully acknowledging the punishment of sinners. But it is still necessary to remark that this forgetting of the annihilated is ascribed to all the survivors too: those people whom they once loved fall into the void, are annihilated, and it proves a deed of "saved" virtue to forget them forever, as quickly and as decently as possible. How dissimilar all this is to the great apostle who "himself wished to be cut off from Christ for the sake of his brethren according to the flesh" (Rom 9:3) although they were dead spiritually. It is clear that, under the assumption of annihilationism, the concept of the *whole* humanity is abolished. It is turned into an aggregate, a herd of individuals who just barely notice each other, for in the complacency of "being saved" they are quite easily reconciled with the perdition of their fellows. A round "zero," at least with respect to a *part*, is creation's final outcome, for God and for man. That is a *satanic nightmare*, even if inspired by good intentions and eschatological fear.

But no. Man is a son of eternity, he is created for eternity and he has an eternal destiny. Indestructible is God's creation. In fear and trembling, but also in full, self-kindling clarity, let man—every man, with no exceptions whatsoever—recognize his *eternity*, created eternity (*aeviternitas*) born of God's eternity (*aeternitas*). There is no *end* for God's creation.

X

Affirming conditional immortality, as something arising from the conditional mortality of man, is impossible. But there arises another question: are all individuals belonging to biological humanity persons in the spiritual sense? And if not, then it is precisely *these* who are subject not to conditionality immortality but rather to an unconditional mortality, which is absolutely identical to the death of animals; they are, of course, alien to the resurrection as well. This question, naturally occurring in the face of the huge difference of spiritual level that differentiates the representatives of humanity, boils down to this: do all people possess a spirit? Do there not exist among these representatives some who are actually hominid apes—exactly what so many of our contemporaries, in a Darwinian rapture, consider themselves and even wish to be, denying any spiritual principle in themselves?[62] Man,

62. In the following section, Bulgakov broaches a question central to nineteenth- and twentieth-century discussions in biological anthropology and its attendant discourse of eugenics: are all who appear to be human worthy of the name and dignity of "human"? In discussing this question, Bulgakov has reason to mention the mentally handicapped, and in so doing he employs the crass and unacceptable language for them typical of his day. The reader should be aware, however, that Bulgakov's intention in this passage is not to denigrate the handicapped but rather to argue that the Christian's duty

together with the animal world, possesses a body and an animal soul ("in
the blood is the soul of animals"),[63] and he differs from that world by a
higher, guiding, *third* part of his composition, the spirit. And so, can those
individual members of *homo sapiens* who so desire do without this third element that is so disagreeable to them? Could there exist humanoid animals
who possess an earthly mind, animal cunning, and that uniquely bestial
cruelty, but who lack the very humanity of man, the divine principle of
spirit? This idea incessantly knocks on the door of our consciousness in the
face of universally known contemporary experiences.[64] It would be vastly
easier and simpler to straightforwardly class all these animal-like beings as
animals, and not even as higher animals, for that matter, but instead as the
lowest, for they are degenerates. Is not the idea the same in relation to the
most degraded savages, those who are born idiots, and so forth? A mystical
writer of the end of the nineteenth century[65] claimed that in 1848 there had
appeared a new race of people without souls, those humanoid apes, or, more
precisely, "unhuman humans" produced by intentional bestiality.[66] Could
she have been correct in her intuition?

   This question has not been posed in theology, and no direct answer
for it exists. There are, of course, certain orienting texts. What, for example,
is the meaning of God's words concerning the antediluvian giants: "for they
are flesh" (Gen 6:3)? It is true that in the testimony of 1 Pet 3:20 concerning
the preaching of Christ in Hades, there is mention of imprisoned spirits who
did not repent in the days of Noah. Nonetheless, there is no straightforward
indication here that this means antediluvian humanity *as a whole*. What
can these words of the apostle Jude mean: "psychical people, lacking spirit
(*psychikoí, pneûma mě échontes*) (v. 19)" or the comparable words of 1 Cor
2:14: "the psychical (*psychikòs*) man does not receive what is of the Spirit of
God because he considers it foolish, and he cannot comprehend it, because

---

is to treat *all* in a humane fashion, with dignity. —Trans.

   63. An inexact quotation of Lev 17:11. —Trans.

   64. Bulgakov has in mind the horrors of the First World War.

   65. Anna Nikolaevna Schmidt (1851–1905), a Russian journalist and mystic. Bulgakov and his mentor Fr. Pavel Florensky were responsible for printing Schmidt's account
of her mystical vision, *The Third Testament*, after Schmidt's death. Initially much taken
by Schmidt's mystical visions, Bulgakov later distanced himself from her speculations
in the realm of dogma. —Trans.

   66. Apparently, in order to persuade themselves that they are animals, people are
attempting to have apes mate with humans in order to receive indisputable proof of
the animality of the human person. And indeed the question arises of how we ought
to understand these artificial offspring of militant godlessness. This idea was already
known to Moses, for we read: "Everyone who engages in bestiality will be handed over
to death" (Exod 22:19).

it must be judged (necessarily) in a spiritual manner." Does what is spoken of here, especially in the apostle Jude, concern only the absence of spirituality or the absence of spirit itself? The text leaves open both possibilities.

Of course, even in their ensoulment humans are distinct from animals, which, although possessing the wisdom of instinct, do not possess the capacity for *hereditary* reason which allows the *accumulation* of knowledge or progress, at least in the technology of life. But can it be that, since they are distributed among the common life of humanity, these humanoid beings in some cases simply go extinct, like the savages, due to contact with civilization, while in other cases they flourish and even reach the position of recognized and "dear leaders"[67] of the human flock? We have no categorical answer here, and the possibility of the existence of people "lacking spirit" is something we cannot deny. But what is of greater practical importance for us is that we are *not meant* to differentiate such beings or even to single out these non-humans from humanity; in any case, just their conviction alone that they are apes in human guise is not determinative for us. On the contrary, we have the commandment to see in every person our "neighbor," that is to relate to him humanely, like a person. More specifically, we must preach the Christian faith to all heathens, as much to Papuans as to communists, not doubting or suspecting their humanity. The absence of this principle is capable of engendering in us such a veritable zoological racism, such a *differentiation* of humanity into the pure and the impure, the noble and the ignoble, that any variety of class or national racism blanch. We must therefore ascetically overcome and tame in ourselves those feelings which provoke our suspicion whether this or that character in history is really a human—Attila the Hun, for example, or others from among our contemporary "leaders." The Lord has concealed in an unknowable mystery the humanity of every human being, and this mystery will be revealed to us only when at the judgment appear "all nations" [Matt 25:32], all humanity in its fullness. But those to whom it was given to be the "scourge of God"[68] in human guise will not appear at the judgment, for they will die just as all animals do, and in their number will be counted those fierce animals who caused humanity much disaster and suffering. However, death of this kind would differ substantially from that spiritual self-annihilation beloved of adherents to the theory of "conditional immortality," even if it indirectly inspired the latter.

67. Bulgakov's reference to "dear leaders" alludes to titles for Soviet leaders like Vladimir Lenin and Joseph Stalin. —Trans.

68. An early Christian title for Attila the Hun. —Trans.

XI

Let us summarize. The theory of conditional immortality is distinguished by an excessive naturalistic biologism. It understands life as a certain general property or quality of the world; with special force it both feels and confesses this vital power of the world, making conditional immortality a *hylozoism*. In this perception of the world there is share of truth, both philosophically—insofar as *life* and the *living being* represent a foundational and primary category of being that is often not included in the table of philosophy's categories—and religiously, for in the world the power of the life-creating Spirit flows to all beings equally. Nonetheless, we must distinguish with much greater force the different *degrees* of life, from its lowest organic forms up to spiritual-incorporeal angels. And human life is not simply "life," merely in the biological sense, but it is still more a special spiritual quality of life, "eternal life," supernatural and supra-biological. Due to this failure to distinguish, the power of the incarnation is understood by conditionalist in an excessively biological fashion. To mortal man the "medicine of immortality" is offered through the union of divine nature with human nature. The renewal of the lost power of life—not its transfiguration, but a new life in a resurrected, glorified body—is offered to humanity as divinization, as the life of the sons of God and friends of God by grace. The theory of conditionalism therefore suffers from an excessive cosmism and immanentism. Although incarnation is confessed here with full force, it is nonetheless understood only in relation to death and not as the disclosure of the full power of divine-humanity, as the unity of divine and human life in the New Adam, in Christ—in him and so in all humanity. In the general framework of conditionalism, there is no place for the Chalcedonian dogma or for the dogma of the Sixth Council.[69]

But this immanentism constitutes not just a weakness but also a unique power as an eschatological motif. Namely, it introduces into eschatology's domain that one-sided transcendentalism that that is broadly typical of eschatology, in which final destinies are too often understood as an external sentence or activity *upon* a person and to a lesser degree as the state of that person himself. In its one-sidedness, conditionalism stops at what happens or does not happen with man himself, by which a person's various destinies are decided due to his own state, understood as his *work*. Specifically, this refers to the spiritual self-determination of man himself. Man possesses a spirit, it is given to him, but it is given to him as a creative task and struggle,

69. The Third Council of Constantinople (AD 680–81), which defined that Christ, as both fully God and fully human, possessed two wills and two energies, divine and human. —Trans.

his own life's work. Whoever does not desire a spiritual life also does not recognize it in himself; he lacks spirit even while possessing it. And precisely that dying of the spirit in a being who is by nature spiritual, as the result of his own self-determination, is the state of spiritual death—not in the sense of annihilation but rather in the sense of unrealization, of the reduction to potency of that which by its own nature should be actual. Without addressing here to what extent this self-determination could possibly be permanent and final, we find in conditionalism an expression of that valuable idea that, *in a certain sense*, the final destiny of humanity is the immanent disclosure of its own human being, of its will and its creative work, apart from which and without which nothing can be given to it, or rather, received. Here is disclosed that truth of the Gospel, that for him who hath little, even that little shall be taken away, and for the one that hath much, to him much shall be given and he shall have abundance [Matt 25:29]. Even in his final destiny, man is not deprived of creative participation, positive or negative: "Life and death I place before you, a blessing and a curse; choose life that you and your descendants may live" (Deut 30:19).

5

On the Question of the Apocatastasis of the Fallen Spirits (in Connection with the Teaching of Gregory of Nyssa)

THERE EXISTS A CERTAIN theological postulate that concerns the lengthy and multi-stage yet ultimate overcoming of satanism,[1] precisely by virtue of Satan's creaturehood. The spiritual world does not have its own nature. It exists by participation[2] in the divine nature. Nevertheless, being created, it also contains in itself the principle of creaturehood. Angelic "fleshlessness" (which is also a synonym for "worldlessness") is nevertheless united with a certain creaturely *ensoulment*.[3] The spiritual nature of angels proceeds from God and to that extent represents in them an uncreated principle that, however, serves as the foundation of the limited and individual being proper to their creaturehood. Man consists of three principles: spirit, which proceeds from God, and soul and body created "from nothing." Angels, on the other hand, possess their own two principles: the spirit proceeding from God, and the soul, also created *ex nihilo* (although worldless), as the form or cover for the personal angelic spirit and by which angelic manifestations occur. (In

---

1. "Satanism" here refers not to the contemporary religious practice of worshiping Satan, but rather to the principled rejection of God which constitutes Satan's life. —Trans.

2. See *Jacob's Ladder, passim*.

3. Use of the terms "soul" and "psychic" in this text is connected with the threefold distinction Bulgakov employs regularly: body (*telo*), soul (*dusha*), and spirit (*dukh*). Humans possess all three, whereas the angelic constitution comprises only the latter two. —Trans.

man the soul functions similarly, as the cover for the spirit, essential to him and at death inseparable from him.) Through this creaturely form angels have a vital knowledge of their creaturehood, albeit in different manner than humans do. The fleshlessness of angels grants them a consciousness manifesting greater spirituality, as it were, than man's. But it also deprives them of the consciousness of ontological originality manifested in the possession of one's own world, which is proper to man (see Heb 2:5–8).

From this relative simplicity of angelic nature flows their immortality along with the freedom from bodily needs, particularly the need for food, although they are not free of the need for *spiritual* food, the "bread of angels" (Ps 78:25–26; Wis 16:20) in spiritual communion.[4] By this they are granted that peculiar spiritual lightness proper to angelic substance relative to humanity's vested heaviness of flesh. Incorporeality grants a peculiar, unhuman feeling of freedom from the flesh, and the existence of a soul not tied to a body is experienced completely otherwise than the existence of a human embodied soul. (The state of the human soul in separation from the body after death approximates in a certain sense angelic fleshlessness, but it also substantially differs from it through the feeling of defectiveness flowing from the painful rupture—unnatural for man—with the body in death. We can say that in the state of harmony and obedience to God, the covering of the soul for the angelic spirit is completely transparent to participation in the divine nature, and in this sense the holy angels are created gods: "God stands among the gods, among the gods he gives judgment" (Ps 82:1; cf. also 96:7 in the Russian translation), and this in a *different* sense than humans are. The latter, of course, are gods in the fullness of their divine-humanity, even more fully, albeit differently, than angels are. Creaturely ensoulment gives angelic spirits the feeling of their own reality, namely of their creaturehood, which is why this knowledge is the source of their special joy of being, as this is poured out in the praise of diverse forms of created being, beginning precisely with angelic being (Ps 149:2–12; Dan 3:55–88 LXX).

But things are completely different in the world of the fallen spirits with Lucifer at their head. The latter lost his spiritual equilibrium, having proved unable to endure that greatest of heights to which he was raised by the Creator, the heights of the "anointed cherubim," of the "son of the dawn" (Isa 14:9–5; Ezek 28:12–15). He was seduced by these heights, and being the first "in the assembly of the gods," he desired to become "like the Most High," while in actuality he remained in his creaturehood together with those spirits who followed after him and were seduced (as to the nature

4. *Jacob's Ladder*, 105–6 [page numbers for the English translation by Boris Jakim— Eerdmans, 2010].

of their fall, revelation remains silent). For them two paths of temptation opened up. The first led to their unnatural intrusion into the fleshly life of human beings (beginning with the antediluvian mixing of the "sons of God" with the daughters of men, however we might interpret this event: Gen 6:1–4). The fallen spirits became "demons," intruding into human life by direct violence (Luke 13:16) or temptation. Cast out from heaven (this is communicated to us in Rev 12:7–11, in the mysterious narrative of the "war in heaven" between Michael and his angels and the "dragon and his angels," ending with the latter being cast down to the earth), they became "evil spirits of the heavens" and the "rulers of this age" (Eph 6:12); it is as demons that the Holy Gospel knows them. The second and main temptation for Satan and his hosts came from their own self-divinization in their revolt against God.

But the demons, along with the prince of this world [John 14:30], will be banished from the world, both from the earth and from "the sphere of heavenly wickedness" [Eph 6:12], and they will find themselves in their own emptiness, captives to their own subjectivity. What will be the life and destiny of the fallen spirits in this state of exile? The knowledge of his creaturehood is hateful to Lucifer, and he wishes to extinguish it within himself by his pretension to become equal to God or even higher than him. The insanity of this pretension cannot reconcile itself, obviously, with that consciousness within himself of his creaturely *ensoulment*, which speaks to him with full clarity, "you are not God, for you are created, and therefore you ought to bend the knee to your Creator." This makes the one exiled from his kingdom and deprived of his pretended throne as the "prince of this world" furious with impotent pride and malice.

Yet at the same time, this same consciousness introduces an unbearable, rending *contradiction* into the very depths of Satan's being, instilling in him an unconquerable anxiety and a struggle with his very self; it creates the need for incessantly assuring himself (in spite of self-evident testimony to the contrary) of that in which there is not and cannot be any assurance. The living out of this contradiction constitutes the only and exhaustive content of the life of the prince of this world in his exile from this world. Can this struggle extend for an infinite (and in this sense "eternal") duration, a bad infinity, or, having been weakened by the struggle, must he at some point in exhaustion lay down his arms? Is his strength inexhaustible for this hopeless and endless struggle with what is self-evident, such that it can fill the ages of ages, or is even such a supposition impossible because . . . Satan, in point of fact, is a creature and only a creature, making his strength and his capabilities limited? What can save him in this situation is precisely that same creaturehood he rejects as a reality outstripping his creaturely freedom. He can grow exhausted in this unequal struggle—rather, he cannot *not* grow exhausted from it, in the end capitulating before reality and acknowledging that not he himself, but rather God, is his creator, and this means: falling down and worshipping him. Then will there occur an ontological coercion on the part of reality, by force of fact.

But contained in this force of fact is the mystery of the existence of every being, the mystery that Satan hides from himself while nonetheless knowing it in his depths. The mystery is this, that all that exists does so by virtue of divine love, *is* love: "and nothing in nature would there be except love upon it breathe."[5] And it is by virtue of divine love that Satan himself also exists, the erstwhile supreme archangel, the anointed cherubim. He cannot, of course, ever lose that once-acquired knowledge, although he would like to forget it, to trample it down, to annihilate it in his hatred, which is what envy towards an unalterable reality becomes. But a love once recognized cannot but be loved with a responding love: it becomes a sort of fate even for Satan, who, like all creation, was created by the love of God, possesses a divine theme in the foundation of his being, and is, in this sense, sophianic, even if also sophiamachic. He himself knows his own sophianicity, which just is participation in divine love. And see what this revelation concerning the demons means, a revelation communicated by the seer of mysteries, St. Isaac the Syrian: the agonies of Hades are the torments of love, the love of Satan for his Creator.[6] And that love is jealous and envious, unwaveringly focused on its object.

It is this love that, already in the Old Testament, surveys all the works of God's love towards creation. Satan says to God: "I have traversed the earth, and I have walked its entire face" (Job 1:7; 2:2) and he asks permission from the Creator to tempt the righteous one in his faithfulness and in the disinterestedness of his love for God. And this request was not motivated solely by Satan's malice; at least, this is not stated directly in the book of Job, and indeed in that sense it would be difficult to understand God's permitting Satan to tempt Job, a permission granted Satan when he was still in that form allowing him access to the throne of God together with the other sons of God [Job 1:6]. Satan is permitted to complete the trial of love, the testing of goodness, which is necessary not only for Job but also for the tempter himself, in order to extinguish within him his tormenting doubt. But this

5. Poem from Alexei Constantinovitch Tolstoy—poet, dramatist, and writer of the nineteenth century. —Trans.

6. Otherwise known as St. Isaac of Nineveh, this saint, venerated in both the Catholic and Orthodox Churches, lived in the seventh century. His *Ascetical Homilies* included meditations on the purgative nature of hell and the eventual reconciliation of all creatures with God. —Trans.

love that puts to the test—for this is nonetheless still love, albeit already thoroughly poisoned by doubt—ascends from a prototype to the Prototype, from the temptation of Job to the temptation of the very Son of God, first in the desert and afterwards in Gethsemane and on Golgotha.

In the story of the temptation in the desert there are two participants: the tempter and the tempted One who rejects the tempter—"Get thee behind me, Satan" (Luke 4:8), thereby overcoming the temptation. But this temptation too concerns not only the tempted one, before whom the impotence of temptation is exposed, but it concerns in the first place the very tempter himself, as a continuation of his temptation of Job. In order to understand what is happening here with Satan, it is necessary to take this not only *in malam partem* [in the bad sense] in relation to Satan's falsehood and malice, but also *in bonam partem* [in the good sense] as a temptation for Satan himself. Satan, by his tempting, tested not only the identity of the tempted one—who he is—but also the power of his work: "*If* you are the Son of God, then . . ." do this and that. Contained here was the entire fullness of temptation possible for Satan ("*having completed all* temptation," Luke 4:13). "All temptation," insofar as it concerned the tempter himself, was essentially about love, namely God's love for the world expressed in the fact that God handed over his only-begotten Son for its salvation, as well as the love of the Son of God for the Father and his faithfulness in this love.

This temptation could not have been anything but a great shock for the tempter himself, who not only did not receive the desired confirmation of his own path but also suffered failure and shame in this effort. But even this could not yet influence him so as to bring him back to the path of repentance towards God. Rather the opposite: Satan was affirmed even more in his obduracy, as the following Gospel narratives sufficiently testify, along with the corroborating witnesses from the other New Testament epistles and explicitly from the book of Revelation. The plan of tempting Christ, and also of simultaneously seeking self-confirmation, was not abandoned by Satan but only delayed: "And having completed all temptation, he left him *until the time should come*" (Luke 4:13), *áchri kairoû*—until the appointed time. This time came at the mortal languor of Christ in Gethsemane and Golgotha, when the words of Satan's temptation were repeated almost verbatim—under Satan's inspiration—by the high priests, scribes, elders, and Pharisees, as well as by mere passersby and soldiers (Matt 27:39–43; Mark 15:29–33; Luke 23:35–37). Yet neither did this final temptation achieve its goal, for it proved incapable of shaking either the Son's attachment to the Father, his submissiveness to his will, or the God-man's love for the world in handing over his life for the salvation of many. But this constituted just one more temptation for the tempter himself who, with the death of the

Son of God, becomes even more hardened in his pretension to become the prince of this world. One would think that the resurrection and ascension of Christ would have been capable of abolishing this pretension, yet Satan was blinded by the power he achieved in the world following the true King of Glory's departure from it [Ps 24:10]. Only in Christ's second coming will Satan and his hosts be effectively banished from this world, which event will itself constitute the final and decisive temptation for the tempter himself. Of course, this banishment may be experienced by Satan not as an isolated incident but as the culmination of a series of events that, in their sum total, place Satan—who by his embezzlement imagines himself the prince of this world—before the face of the true King of creation, who has redeemed it by his self-denying love. Through his imposture, Satan constantly stands before Christ and unwittingly seeks in him self-validation, a comprehension of his own proper image. Both the hatred and envy born of an impotent rivalry become the increasing scourge and torment of love, according to the insight of the venerable Isaac the Syrian. And so it will be until the fullness of this torment is accomplished.

***

Here we must add something not directly mentioned in the Gospel but that is nonetheless silently implied and even indirectly attested to in the twelfth chapter of Revelation. Precisely there do we find mention of a great sign, the appearance of the woman clothed with the sun. In this image it is natural to see the Church in the personal appearance of the Ever-Virgin. And opposite her stands a great red dragon seeking to devour her offspring—that is, Satan. It is impossible not to see in this fact that the dragon stands opposite her the deliberate, focused straining of Satan against the woman. In Church writings we also repeatedly find witness to a special defeat of Satan by the woman,[7] which in turn confirms our understanding of this exclusive focus of the temper's attention here. And truly, if with his prophetic, albeit evil and malicious, eye he foresees a new offspring from the Virgin and attempts to become a tempter for him (and in so doing becomes the tempted as well) then was it ever possible that his attention—truly frightening and yet so self-important—would not also be drawn to the image of the *New* Eve, so

---

7. "Rejoice, wound bitterly lamented by demons"; "Rejoice, deposer of the inhuman tormenter from his rule" (Akathist Hymn [accessed: <<https://www.goarch.org/-/the-akathist-hymn-and-small-compline>>] —Trans.); "intimidation of demons" ("Prayer to the Most Holy Mother of God" [from the Akathist to the Most Holy Mother of God in Honor of Her Dormition —Trans.]).

distinct in comparison with the one who in paradise once fell for his temptation through her naive inexperience and feminine helplessness? Did not
this appearance of the New Eve have to become for him something agitating, alluring, frightening—a *temptation* of sorts in connection with Satan's
designs, just as the appearance of the New Adam also was? And for the temper himself, furthermore, are not the two temptations united into one, even
inseparable temptation?[8] Satan succeeded in violating the feminine nature
of Eve through the provocation of the lust of the eyes and the flesh, and that
was his general victory over man, because in the person of Eve Adam too
proved conquered [1 John 2:16]. Now feminine nature appears before him
again, the New Eve — in her complete purity and holiness already beyond
temptation[9] —and in her is fulfilled God's decree concerning the seed of
the woman who would strike the head of the serpent [Gen 3:15]. The very
existence of this woman could not but become an agitating temptation for
the tempter himself. The green eyes of the serpent malevolently, relentlessly
watched the New Eve, who was already beyond the impotent provocation
of the lust of the flesh. The appearance of the woman clothed with the sun,
in all her sophianicity, simultaneously attracted him, as a reminder of lost
paradise, while also frightening and repulsing him due to its total inacces-
sibility and its incompatibility with the darkness of satanic depths. In the
events of the life of the Mother of God, in which she accomplished her unceasing cross-bearing, one can also discern the participation of the tempter,
or, at least, the presence of his dark shadow, although he does not openly
act here like he did in the temptation in the desert. By tempting he himself
is tempted, asking himself just what it is that he sees before him in this appearance of the New Eve.

In the entirety of its content, the cross of the Mother of God also
includes this temptation directed against her, beginning with the birth of
Christ, which took place not only in heavenly glory but also in his earthly
squalor and persecution: the slaughter of the innocents by Herod and the
flight to Egypt, Simeon's prophecy concerning the sword; the loss of the
boy on the way, who was found in the temple after searching and only after
three days. "And his Mother said to him: Child, what have you done to us?
See your father and I have been searching for you in great distress. And he
said in response: why were you searching for me?" (Luke 2:48–49). This

8. As is his penchant, Bulgakov here liberally employs the adverbs of the Chalcedonian formula (AD 451) ("unconfusedly, unchangeably, indivisibly, inseparably") to
describe other theological realities. —Trans.

9. To affirm this truth, it is by no means necessary to resort to the mental contriv-
ance of the Catholic doctrine of the immaculate conception of the Most Holy Mother
of God.

was, of course, a new trial and temptation for divine-motherhood. And later on his ministry begins, which visibly and invisibly, explicitly and implicitly, conceals in itself new trials and temptations for the Mother of God. Only in exceptional situations does this become openly manifest, as in the narratives of Matt 12:47–50; Mark 3:31–35; Luke 8:19–31. Here we find described how the Mother of Jesus and his brothers came to call him to return home, but "they were not able to reach him on account of the people"—and it was communicated to him: "Your Mother and brothers are standing outside, wishing to see you." But he did not go out to them, and instead answered them, so to speak, in the third person, "My Mother and my brothers are those who listen to the Word of God and do it" (Luke 8:19–21) and so he, as it were, rejected physical kinship in favor of spiritual kinship (although, of course, not at all thereby diminishing the former). But this was only the beginning of the trials and temptations of the Mother of God in her cross-bearing, which she shared with Christ. And all the events of her earthly ministry were oriented toward the sword that would pierce her heart, especially in the days of Christ's passion, of the final station of the cross: his death on the cross and his burial.[10] But in all these events Satan is put to shame, both inwardly and outwardly, through the impotence of his temptation; he is left defeated equally in relation Christ and to the Mother of God, who is completely removed from his kingdom through her own ascension and resurrection, as is her Son. And thus is accomplished in the life of the Mother of God that "much-bewailed defeat of demons."[11]

***

Here we approach that revolution within Lucifer that is completely inaccessible to human experience and can only be postulated by theological speculation: the obstinacy of resistance is resolved into humility; love fettered by hate is freed from its shackles through recognition of the truth: "you shall know the truth, and the truth shall make you free" (John 8:32). And the truth is the way and the life of love for the Creator and his creation. But with this epiphany and spiritual liberation begins a completely new epoch in the life of Satan, just as it does in the life of the world connected with him. Up to this point he had remained banished from the world, in the outer darkness and its torments [Matt. 25:30]: "The devil . . . was cast into the lake of fire and sulfur, where the beast and the false prophet are, and they will suffer day

10. All these separate features are collected together in the essay, "The Cross of the Mother of God" (*Theological Thought*, Paris, 1942).

11. From Oikos 2 of the Akathist to the Most Holy Mother of God. —Trans.

and night for ages and ages" (Rev 20:10). "And death and hell were cast into the lake of fire. This is the second death. And whoever was not written in the book of life was cast into the lake of fire" (Rev 20:14–15). This torment resulting from the "second" death becomes a part of life, its sole content, such that this dying fills it up completely, being equivalent to the expulsion from the world. This is not even "hell" in the strict sense of the word, insofar as hell is still a condition of life and for that matter always exists only in some sort of union with paradise, both quantitatively and qualitatively.

What we may call Satan's return to life is necessarily connected with the beginning of his repentance. Alongside his liberation from the bonds of his envious hatred, and together with the first thawing of the ice of his un-love, the true torments of hell are just beginning for Satan and his angels in their repentance for all the sins of the world—not just for those for which he was the constant inspiration but also for the most dreadful deed that, against his will and knowledge, served for the salvation of the world. This is the handing over of Christ to death by means of the betrayal of Judas, "into whom Satan had entered" (John 13:27); this was Satan's doing. This deicide was the focal point of the sins of the whole world and of all people, sins both willed and unwilled—in every sin, even if executed with the cooperation of men, it is still the provocation of Satan that is at work. Satan is the one who inspires all human evil and the one guilty for all the sins of the world, which sins the one Sinless Redeemer took upon himself. Hence the immeasurable weight of this sin of the whole world lies on the repentant Satan to the extent that new life stirs within in him; it is a sort of redemption for the tempter himself. And this torment resulting from the repentance of the fleshless spirits—inaccessible to human knowledge—fills up "the ages of ages," a time immeasurable for humanity. Of course, this is not a chronologically uniform time, so to speak, but is instead the aggregate of qualitatively different times of distinct intensity and content; these are measured by a "qualitative quantity" proper only to the spiritual world and unknown to man. Nevertheless even these ages of ages are still time and no more than time, albeit time whose very content is contact with eternity, eternal life, yet precisely in the form of "eternal torments." But this time remains nonetheless limited in extension, possesses its own fullness, and it comes to an end with the conclusion of the torments of the fully repentant Satan, who in the course of these "ages" returns to that for which he was created. And to be the highest archangel, Lucifer—that is why the Creator called him into being.

Nevertheless it is clear that just as salvation, together with the forgiveness of the satanically inspired sins of the whole world, is not brought about by a one-sided act, neither, a fortiori, is this true of the restoration—the apocatastasis. It is not accomplished by creaturely power alone, which was impossible for man who stands in need of the redemptive help of God, which he received through the incarnation in the Son of God's death on the cross. Thus, there inevitably arises the question that was so persistently put forward by the two (and essentially the only) theologians of the apocatastasis, Origen and St. Gregory of Nyssa, a question they answered in the affirmative: are even the demons covered by the universal power of the redemptive sacrifice offered "on behalf of all and for all"?[12] Or must we acknowledge that its power is limited since it manifests only in relation to the earthly human world? But, clearly, to admit any kind of limit to the power of the redemptive sacrifice is impossible, as the Word of God proclaims on this matter with direct and indubitable witness: at the name of Jesus shall bow "every knee on heaven, on earth, and under the earth—*katachthonīon* (i.e., angels, humans, and demons), and *every tongue* confess that Jesus Christ is Lord to the glory of God the Father" (Phil 2:10–11), and "God will be all in all" (1 Cor 15:28).

This puts us before the general question: what meaning does the incarnation have for the angelic world?[13] Although it does not *directly* relate to the world of fleshless spirits, nevertheless it indirectly has a definitive significance in accord with that world's connection to the human world through its co-humanity. We know from the Word of God, and first of all from the Gospel, the full measure of the participation of the angels in the events of the incarnation; in particular, both at the end of the age[14] and more generally in that battle for the "lost sheep" [Luke 15:7] in which the holy angels participate so actively; this comes to an end only in the parousia. Also connected with this is their participation in the Glory in which the Son of God comes,[15] and in the life of the age to come. But we may ask: is this replenishing of the ranks of angelic co-humanity, which is the consequence of human salvation through the incarnation, only a reflected effect of the latter, or does it possess a foundation in angelic nature proper, which is fleshless but nonetheless created? We must give this question an affirmative answer insofar as the angels possess created ensoulment. This is the potency

12. Spoken by the priest during the Divine Liturgy of St. John Chrysostom, in reference to the Eucharistic gifts offered in the Anaphora. —Trans.

13. *Jacob's Ladder*, chapter 8: "The Angelic World and Divine Incarnation."

14. "So will it be at the end of the age: the angels will come forth and will separate the evil from the midst of the just and will cast them into the burning furnace" (Matt 13:49).

15. "Whoever is ashamed of me and my words, of him the Son of Man will also be ashamed, when he comes in the his glory and that of the Father (i.e., in the Holy Spirit) and of the holy angels" (Luke 9:26). Here in an exceedingly clear fashion the Holy Spirit is indicated as the hypostatic Glory of the Father and the Son that is communicated to the glorified world in the person of the holy angels.

of their life, realized to a greater or lesser degree precisely in relation to man and his humanity. In Christ, through the incarnation, this potency reaches its fullness which is revealed in the co-angelicity of humans as much as in the co-humanity of angels. Through this the angelic world too becomes a participant in the glorification of the God-man at the parousia, in which he comes into the world not alone but with all the holy angels with him (as the Gospel testifies, Matt 25:31). Thus the holy angels have their share of participation in the saving power of the redemptive sacrifice (as is liturgically attested by their participation at the offering of the eucharistic sacrifice and their spiritual co-communion with us: "now the powers of heaven do serve invisibly with us"[16]).[17]

In relation to the fallen angelic world, the power of the redemptive sacrifice is realized chiefly in its restoration, through rebirth, of angelic creaturely nature, namely its ensoulment. Here we have an analogy with redemption's salvific action on human nature, albeit together with an unavoidable difference: namely that for the human person the renewal is related to his *entire* creaturely psycho-corporeal constitution, but for the fleshless spirits it relates only to their ensouled nature in its lack of corporeality. Nevertheless the action of the redemptive sacrifice cannot be limited here solely to the restoration of the spirits to their original constitution through their liberation from the darkness of sin. The entire past life of the world with its sin—insofar as the tempter and his hosts are guilty for it—separates them from this original constitution, which was proper to the fallen spirits even before the fall. That it was darkened by the black deeds of the tempter is not this world's only truth; in this world was also accomplished the incarnation, through which the world became other than it was in comparison to the time of its creation. It became the kingdom of Christ, and in it there no longer exists any other principle of being. For this reason the fullness of the apocatastasis presupposes not only the abolition of this worldly "minus" that was introduced by Satan but also the participation of all creation in this new being.

Parallel to the abolition of the worldly failure created by Satan, the latter's ascent to his prototype is not simply a passive reception of forgiveness but also an active ascent, a movement towards Christ by the one who possessed in himself the entirety of antichristic power. This movement, concerning which we can know nothing apart from this general theological postulate, requires yet another new time in which to achieve its purpose.

16. From the entrance hymn of the Divine Liturgy of the Pre-sanctified Gifts in the Byzantine Rite. —Trans.

17. See my essay, "The Eucharistic Sacrifice" (in manuscript). [English translation by Mark Roosien available from University of Notre Dame Press, 2021— Trans.]

The following "ages of ages" must therefore be dedicated to this overcoming of satanism in Satan himself. We must remember, however, that this will be accomplished not by individual fallen spirits in their isolation but rather together with the entire world now liberated from the violent dominion of the "prince of this world." And it is especially important to keep in mind the fact that all the holy angels—with Michael and his hosts at their head—who once cast down Satan from heaven, and who also did not spare their souls even unto death [Rev 12:11], will drag Satan back up to the heaven of heavens, to his former place of heavenly glory. God's Word, which limits its revelation only to the life of this age, is silent concerning this event, but it necessarily follows from the general prophecies of universal divinization and apocatastasis, "God will be all in all" [1 Cor 15:28]. And of course the salvation and glorification of Satan is necessarily included in this "all in all." But here we meet another, further question.

The place of Lucifer in his absence from heaven was occupied by the angel-man, John the Forerunner of the Lord, who, together with the All-Pure One, stands closest of all (in the Deisis)[18] before the Lord of Glory, higher than the angels and the greatest of those born of women [Matt 11:11; Luke 7:28].[19] But is this not an act of self-love, to expel's one's rival? Or, on the contrary, is there not being prepared here a new possibility for a deed of self-renunciation, of self-annihilation, of self-"decreasing" (John 3:30) love? And does not John here—the angel-man in ministry but still a man in natural essence—manifest the power of love to one who possesses angelic nature by virtue of creation but who also, on account of his nature, is destined for co-humanity, and to the greatest degree, to boot? Would it therefore not be natural if in this meeting it should prove that the highest of the angelic thrones, namely the angelic-human one, is the destiny not of one but of two, with the higher and holier of the two offering a helping hand to the other, once fallen and now restored? On this note, it is necessary, furthermore, to remember that this help can be given and offered only through the reception and assimilation of the redemptive sacrifice of Christ, not only by all the angelic world with Michael and his hosts at their head (who at one time led the war in heaven and cast Lucifer down from there) but also by Lucifer himself. This new event in heaven will be accomplished in the presence of the angel-man as well. We have no conception at all of how this will take place, but there is no doubt whatsoever that it must occur. And what is more, this help cannot but be offered by the entire Church as

18. A traditional Eastern Christian artistic representation of Christ flanked by Mary his mother and John the Baptist. —Trans.

19. For more on Bulgakov's unique theology of John the Baptist, see in English the second volume of his "minor trilogy," *The Friend of the Bridegroom*.

well: not only the heavenly but also the earthly Church, those glorified holy people who have the gift of a "merciful heart," of the flaring up of universal love to which St. Isaac the Syrian has testified (serving in this case as the spokesperson for all the saints). And finally, in the heavens, and even above the heavens, this help will appear through the All-Pure and Most-Blessed One, the one more honored than all the holy angels, the one whose merciful heart is the seat of the Holy Spirit, of hypostatic love itself. The power of Pentecost that was communicated to the entire world, the tongues of fire that have ignited all creation, will ignite the souls of dead but rising fallen spirits, and their salvation will become manifest. All this will constitute even more ages of ages, which for us are unknown and inaccessible. Nevertheless, what *is* known to us is the love of God for creation and the promise of that love, that "the Lord has enclosed all in disobedience so that he might have mercy on all. . . . For from him, through him, and to him is everything. To him be the glory forever and ever. Amen" (Rom 11:32, 36).

∗∗∗

Let us summarize. The eternity of torments—understood in the sense of their infinity, together with the eternal perdition of Satan and the other fallen spirits, as well as that of those rejected humans condemned to hell—contradicts the wisdom and grace of God. In this view there is ascribed to evil (as was shown with particular force and persuasiveness by St. Gregory Nyssen and before him by Origen) a depth equal to goodness, to hell a depth equal to paradise. But evil is only an ontological "minus" that does not even exist in itself and by itself but is instead extinguished when separated from being; and the partisans of eternal evil are not themselves aware of what they are affirming, falling into Manicheism and admitting alongside the being of God the independent being of evil. Evil has no depths. It is exhaustible and it exhausts itself, and at a determinate stage of the maturation of being its final impotence inevitably appears; evil becomes fatigued and disillusioned with itself. A static state in the spiritual world, in "eternal life," does not exist, and the endless success of evil—its progress in eternity, as this is defined by the defenders of eternal impenitence and of eternal torments for the rejected and condemned—is an ontological absurdity and a truly satanic blasphemy against God's creation. Furthermore, even if we were to take the penal point of view and were to seek justifications for eternal torments, then we would find an obvious incongruity between the crime—which, however great it may be, is limited in time—and the punishment, which extends into eternity; it is difficult to see the goodness in such an incongruity. Even in earthly criminal law the death penalty is inadmissible insofar as it annihilates not the offense but the offender himself. Similarly here, spiritual death, which is what eternal torments are, also presupposes the annihilation of the sinner's life, the only remainder being a subject suffering in emptiness, with no content of life. Eternal life in the beatitude of communion with God may be understood as a reward for *temporal* deeds, inasmuch as the Lord is "generous and merciful" [Ps 103:8], and he repays the eternal for the temporal, "much" for "little" (Matt 25:21, 23).[20] But is it possible to draw the opposite conclusion concerning repayment in torments—paying back much for little and the eternal for the temporal?

In connection with this dynamic understanding of eternal life, which is opposed to the static, we must completely eliminate the understanding of eternity and eternal life as immobility and immutability; on the contrary, we must think of it as movement and therefore as change, which is, generally speaking, proper to creaturely life. Once again it must be said that there exist not one but two eternities: divine and creaturely. Only divine eternity in its absoluteness is immutable and in this sense immobile, immobility here being identical with eternal life (in distinction from creaturely life, for which immobility would mean precisely the absence of life). Creaturely eternity (*aeviternitas*), on the other hand, realizing divinization in itself through participation in the divine life, is a *process* in which fullness is realized by an ascent from measure to measure. In this sense, temporality or *history* is always proper to creaturely being, and not just in the present aeon, which concludes with the parousia and the resurrection of the dead, but also on the other side of this border, in those ages of ages about which revelation's testimony says little. Therefore "eternity," when applied to creaturely being, by no means signifies the negation of temporality together with creaturely mutability but instead presupposes diverse ages or stages, "ages of ages"; it is a qualitative determination, specifically in relation to divine eternity.

Nevertheless, duration, and in this sense the temporality and mutability of creaturely being, possesses a *principle* that proceeds from God: "by him all things were made" (John 1:3), "all things are from him, by him, and to him" (Rom 11:36). And this principle serves not only as the *first* time of being but also more generally as its primary and supra-temporal determination of state, a touch by the right hand of God, a procession from divine eternity, the divine creative act, the spark of God in creaturely being.

---

20. True, in this Parable of the Talents it speaks not just of taking away from the one who has none as well as from the one who had but did not multiply (v. 29), but afterwards this too is added: "cast out the unfit servant to the outer darkness, where there will be weeping and gnashing of teeth" (v. 30). But is it right to read eternal life into this saying from a parable that concerns remedial punishment?

Thereby is creaturely being given its ontological foundation, which it can
never lose. The creature always retains in itself the ontological memory of
this foundation, it bears it within itself and it knows it as a sort of holy
anamnesis and simultaneously as a pledge of salvation through the power
of God's predestination—it knows it as a divine promise concerning itself.
It is extremely important to understand this promise as accompanying man
not only in this life but also in the future, and at the "Dread Judgment"
this ontological foundation of individual being will be revealed in all the
forms of its temporal realization. This anamnesis is salvific and renovating,
and it can never completely fade away in creation, for it is concealed in the
depths of being inaccessible to empirical mutability—it *is* this being itself in
its ontological foundation. And this is especially important to remember for
the "salvation" of Satan, for this anamnesis in all its indestructibility is also
proper to him: he *remembers*—ontologically remembers—his state *before*
his fall, when he was Lucifer, the highest of cherubim, and this memory
burns him. This memory maddens him in his diabolism, it is the main
source of his demonism, a rabid fight with his very own nature, a wish to
reject it and forget it, replacing it with . . . what, exactly? With emptiness.
And it is this anamnesis, strange to say, that makes of him both the tempter
and . . . the tempted one. He cannot remain indifferent, calmly and disdain-
fully contemplating the appearance in the world of Christ and the Mother
of God and even of holy angels and people; he loves them with hate, for hate
is a language of love . . . until such time when hate will become its true self
in the invincibility and indestructibility of love for what is higher than itself.
And this anamnesis is the helping hand of the Creator, which can never be
removed, even from a creation in revolt.

But to what extent is it proper that this final fulfillment of salvation be
called apocatastasis, that is, renewal, both with respect to the fallen spirits
and rejected humanity? It is obvious that this definition is imprecise, or even
completely wrong. It would be unfitting if in the history of the world nothing had occurred.[21] But in history there has occurred, first and foremost,
the divinization of creation through divine-humanity, that is, through the
incarnation and Pentecost. There occurred the entire history of the world
and humanity, both as a whole and in the destinies of every individual person. Therefore, if we can speak of apocatastasis, then this is only in the sense
of ontological anamnesis—in the sense of the beginning, not of the end. In
the world nothing is lost and nothing is annihilated except evil, conquered

---

21. In the word's philosophical history, "apocatastasis" ("restoration") had meant
the periodical restoration of all things to their beginning following the world's destruction (as in ancient Stoicism, for example). It is this definition of apocatastasis that Bulgakov here rejects. —Trans.

by the power of God and thereby exposed in its non-being. But the history of the world, which is also the history of the Church, is the building up of the kingdom of God, the City of God. And this can be called apocatastasis only in the sense of the universal salvation whose foundation was already laid when all that exists was created.

6

Apocatastasis and Theodicy

IN THE APOCATASTASIS, THE final destinies of creation are realized—both in the world of spirits and in the human world—and its final goal is divinization, *God all in all* [1 Cor 15:28]. What is revealed is the love and the goodness of God, manifested in creation. In the apocatastasis, the eternal plan of God is completed, Wisdom is justified in her deeds (Matt 11:19, "by all her children," Luke 7:35), "theodicy" is unveiled. In the face of this world "lying in evil," there unavoidably arises the question of how to justify this evil or how to understand its status, the question of its admittance into the paths and destinies of the world. Human consciousness can reconcile itself neither with the self-sufficiency of evil nor with its finality and unconquerability expressed in the failure to fully eradicate evil, which is what the allowance of eternal perdition would represent. If evil does in fact have a place in creation, then this can be only as a relative and thus transitional principle, as a path and a means, but not as the final completion and much less as the primordial state. That is why this state is understood as one of innocence and sinlessness alone, both in relation to the world of spirits and the world of humans; the *Manichean* confession of the primordiality of evil would represent a satanic blasphemy against the Creator.

But neither does religious consciousness reconcile itself with the invincibility, and in this sense the "eternality," of evil as included in the general plan of the world's creation, insofar as in this plan the guilt and responsibility for the final perdition of creation—in the persons of Satan and the fallen spirits, together with fallen humanity—falls on the Creator himself, who, while not having created evil, has nonetheless permitted it for eternity. The world could only be created, of course, if it contained freedom (for a world of mannequins would be unworthy of the Creator), yet this freedom is only *creaturely* freedom. And creaturely freedom encompasses either the inevitability or at least the possibility of a fall. To admit the first option is obviously not possible because it would mean blaspheming the Creator, to whom would be ascribed the desire to create the world precisely as fallen, or at least to create a world predestined for a fall. But it is equally impossible to admit the creation of a world in which the fall, although only *possible*, would nonetheless be final and irremediable, for this would indicate the world's absolute self-determination for evil despite the complete relativity and limitation of its created existence. Similarly, admitting an absolute confirmation in evil, given the relativity of the very foundation of created being, contains in itself an ontological contradiction, yet this hardly troubles those defenders of "eternal" torments who also thereby defend the eternality of evil. But at the same time this view imputes to the Creator the creation of a world in which no longer just the possibility but rather the inevitability of evil is actualized, insofar as the latter takes on not just relativity but absoluteness and "eternality" as well.[1]

God creates the supreme archangel, Lucifer, endows him with the very highest of his gifts, making him the anointed cherubim, the "seal of perfection, the fullness of wisdom and the crown of beauty" (Ezek 28:12), places him on the "holy mountain of God" (v. 14), and he is "perfect in his ways from the day of his creation, until lawlessness was found in him" (v. 15). Is his very own perfection, given to Lucifer by God, a temptation that is

1. The biblical expressions "eternal" and "ages of ages," next to the words "hell," "fire," and "perdition," allow the possibility of various interpretations and can by no means be claimed to be unambiguous or precise. Nonetheless, these expressions are often thought to have only one meaning, which in practice is taken to mean a certain creaturely absoluteness that has no end, though it does have a beginning. A religio-philosophical analysis of the concept of creaturely eternity or absoluteness has not been undertaken. Such an analysis would inevitably uncover the complete groundlessness of this absolutizing of the temporal and the relative, together with the complete incoherence of the notions of "eternal torments" or eternal perdition as an absolute minus in creation. Infinity, which in this context is often considered tantamount to *eternity*, is in fact, of course, not tantamount to it insofar as the latter has neither beginning nor end, but only intensity and depth, and is in no way a quantitative or temporal definition, instead only a qualitative one. Infinity is in any case an imaginary notion, as it contains in itself an explicit logical contradiction. Namely, it contains the negation of its own positive content: without-"end" [*finis*], no-"end"; it is a general "no": a minus, zero reality. And in this sense the positive word "end" here can be replaced by any other word (like "beginning," or "middle," etc.), insofar as the negator "no" equally absorbs it into itself and destroys any positive content it may have. The interpretation, then, of infinity as eternality is thus in principle incongruous and arbitrary, equivalent to substituting the "minus" of some content for the "plus." As a whole, the imagistic language of the Word of God does not lend itself to literal and rationalistic interpretation.

manageable and conquerable for him, or does his very fall become his in-exorable fate? Furthermore, if this fall is also irremediable and the evil from it remains forever, do we not then arrive at this conclusion: that in the origi-nal plan for creation such an error was permitted, which, of course, could not have been concealed from the Creator, and for which he is therefore responsible? And this same conclusion applies as well to the fates of both the fallen angels and the humans who proved powerless in the face of satanic temptations and assaults. Are they not at the dread judgment condemned to eternal torments and, seeing as they are powerless to resist these tempta-tions, are they not also, as it were, *pre*-condemned by virtue of the very plan of creation itself? Those who in the name of pious obedience are so easily reconciled with such a definition of the Creator attest rather to their blind and slavish submissiveness, motivated not by love and reverence but by fear.

Here we see repeated what we find in the book of Job—in that pro-totype of the "problem of theodicy"—concerning the justification of evil and suffering in the world. The laments of Job are met only with pious con-demnation from his friends, and these laments remain unanswered (and, of course, they are not answered in the epilogue of Job, which narrates the new wives,[2] children, flocks, and so forth given to the innocent sufferer in replacement for those he lost). It is clear that evil and suffering in the world are inexplicable except as *conditions* for the highest good, and for that reason they are temporary and relative. Of such a kind—though representing the most extreme instance—are Christ's suffering and death on the cross. They were accepted by him for the salvation of the entire world and for universal resurrection, and by no means for the beatitude of just the few and elect, a beatitude accompanied by the abandonment of the greater part of humanity to the state of "eternal" torments and rejection in the depths of an absolutely unconquerable evil. Such an outcome for creation cannot and must not be recognized as "the justification of wisdom" in her deeds and paths. For all his humility and obedience to the will of God, man does not have the right to and must not—it is a sin against his conscience—accept this outcome as the highest truth about the world and, what is in this case immeasurably more important, as the highest truth about his Creator.

Some may say: "but are we not encroaching here on terrain that is con-cealed from us in holy mystery? With respect to this mystery we can only hold fast in trembling obedience to what has been given to us in revelation." But here we must not dissemble. If what we have been given on this matter is in fact *revelation*, then that presupposes that our reason and conscience

---

2. The standard text of Job 41 gives no indication that Job received a new wife, much less multiple ones. —Trans.

can be satisfied with this revelation. Yet these people cannot accept this fact, despite their own conscience, since they abide in a state of intimidation. The holy mystery retains all its force, as the apostle says, "O the depth of the riches of the wisdom and power of God! How inscrutable the destinies he has allotted, and how unknowable his paths!" (Rom 11:33). But this inscrutability and unknowability apply not to the *what* but to the *how*, only to the means, not to the goal. For revelation indicates the existence of only one goal: "God enclosed all in disobedience in order to have mercy on all" (v. 32). Therefore, although we may recognize the powerlessness of human philosophizing with respect to the paths by which the Lord leads all human beings and incorporeal spirits to salvation, what we are *not* permitted to doubt is the goal and final fulfillment realized on this path: "God all in all" [1 Cor 15:28], universal pan-en-theosis.

It cannot be gainsaid that the proper comprehension of this point is not only hard but also dangerous, insofar as it opens an abyss on both sides: the oversimplification and vulgarization endemic to a penal worldview, and the cheap libertinism seeking a salvation that is universal and without cost. But the answer to this problem is the general principle that, although salvation is a gift of grace, there is nothing free about it, nothing that is not spiritually hard-won. The forgiveness and mercy of God are in this sense *not* an amnesty that simply ignores sin, closing its eyes to it, as the senseless "pitiers" would so desire (*misericordes*, as Blessed Augustine had already named these proponents of irresponsibility). Such indifference taken as mercy is a seduction born of craftiness and deception, and the answer to it is found in the wrathful words of the just Judge: "Depart from me, you cursed ones, into the eternal fire" (Matt 25:41). But would it be zeal for the Lord's justice if in a senseless literalism we ascribe to that justice a punishment that is eternal and immeasurable—absolute, as it were—for temporal and limited, that is *creaturely*, faults? and will this be acceptable to our conscience both in this life and in the age to come? And must we not therefore seek a dogmatic way out of this antinomy of the absolute and the relative, the divine and the creaturely, "eternal torments" predestined for creaturely being that is immersed in temporality? Can—and *should*—our faith accept this as the final truth about God-Creator,[3] that he created a world in part (however small or great that part may be) predestined for eternal perdition or rejection, given over to the fate of absolute evil, to be rejected by its very Creator?

Evil is temporary and relative, accepted by the Creator on the paths of creaturely being in its history, as a fact of anthropology and cosmology, but

3. This is one of Bulgakov's preferred names for God when speaking about God under the aspect of his relationship with the world. The corollary and contrastive term would be "God-Absolute," or God as he is in himself in trinitarian life. —Trans.

it suffers failure in the end; it is not in fact evil but rather goodness insofar as it turns out to lead to a good end. Let us grant that evil possesses no natural necessity of its own on the paths of created being and that it arises only as a possibility of the latter. Still, evil is in any case connected with creaturely freedom as one of its modes, and freedom is the most great and inalienable gift of God; it is also the very foundation of created being, its royal privilege, and its value, however we may appraise it, cannot be overestimated. At the same time, freedom does not exist in an ontological contradiction with the divine plan of creation, which, obviously, cannot encompass an eternal perdition predestined even for just a portion of creation. To allow this would effectively mean the failure of creation, and not just in part, but as a whole, and we must not reconcile ourselves with this loss as easily as the partisans of eternal hell do.

One may further ask: in these two possibilities, these different paths of creation—one of which includes the absence of evil and a fall away from God (albeit temporary and partial) and the other of which presupposes it—is there a certain equivalence and, therefore, in the final analysis, an equality of value? Or is even this comparison itself improper? The logic of creation demands a *positive* answer to this question, however paradoxical it may seem. Both 1) the path of a good without sin and 2) the path of a sinful departure from good, coupled with sin's eventual overcoming, turn out, despite their differences, to be equivalent. The difference pertains only to the path but not to its outcome. The latter cannot ultimately be wrested from the hands of God, as it were, and wholly surrendered to the decision of the creature on whom the final determination of the destinies of creation would therefore completely depend. To assume this would be to ascribe to creation the power to truly alter the destinies given by God. This is , of course, as impossible as the admission of the (even partial) failure of creation, for eternal torments and eternal perdition for even a part of creation cannot be counted as creation's success, even by the most fanatical of the doctrine's proponents. It remains for us to accept that the *final* destinies of the world on the paths of God remain independent of created freedom despite that freedom's ineradicability on the paths of their accomplishment. There occurs here a certain *free necessity*: the simultaneous ontological immutability of the foundation alongside the modal diversity of freedom in its emergence in life. But in what sense and to what extent can *difference* here be recognized as equivalence? Is not the power of this difference so great that created freedom turns out to be not only modal but also ontological? This latter supposition, however, is already inadmissible on account of its incommensurability with the power of determination inhering in both divine creation and created reality, insofar as the former establishes the *what* and the latter the *how*. It is in the face of precisely *this* ontological law that we must therefore recognize the equivalence of the difference and thus also the ultimate goodness of evil insofar as it turns into good.

But what exactly follows from this? That there is no difference in the eyes of God between Lucifer's abiding in "the garden of God" and his being cast down from heaven? Between the apostleship of Judas and his betrayal? Or, more broadly, between all worldly and historical evil permitted in creation and the primordial and unalloyed "very good" of creation? Of course, such an absurdity cannot be affirmed in the static sense if one considers the content of the historical process, in its separate acts and conditions, in which evil stands opposed to good. Nonetheless it is fully possible and even unavoidable to acknowledge this in a dynamic sense, as the diversity of the paths by which one and the same outcome is achieved. "The Lord reigns . . . for he has established the universe and it shall not be moved" (Pss 93:1; 96:10). Difference here is united with equality of value. It is not granted to created freedom in its instability to shake God's ramparts to their foundations, although these ramparts are permitted to be moved *by* freedom before they receive their final confirmation *in* freedom.

The creature is incapable of weighing and determining that an unalloyed standing in the good and the evil that has been eradicated are spiritual *equivalents*. Here we have only the insistent word of the Gospel that the "tax collectors and prostitutes precede you in entering the kingdom of God" (Matt 21:31) and the word about the "lost sheep" for which the owner "rejoices more than he does for the ninety-nine who are not lost" (Matt 18:13). Let us also recall the special attention the Lord shows to the sinful woman who anointed the Lord with oil, Mary Magdalene, from whom the Lord cast out seven demons and, once he was resurrected, to whom he appeared and called by the name "Maria"[4] (related to this are those figures from hagiography like Mary of Egypt[5] and others). So too in the common and final destinies of the world: who can factor the paths and take stock of individual destinies and accomplishments? Of course, no one can say the sinful woman should have sinned, that it was better that she sin rather than walk the just path, but nonetheless it was precisely the path of sin that proved salvific for her. This path of sin was an act of her creaturely freedom that in its self-determination was capable both of sinning and of falling into error. But sin, of course, remains sin and error remains error. The Lord does

---

4. This unsubstantiated conflation of Mary Magdalene with the "sinful woman" of Luke 7:36–50 goes as far back as Pope Gregory I in the sixth century. —Trans.

5. Mary of Egypt, a fourth-fifth century saint who, according to the hagiography, lived a promiscuous life before her conversion. —Trans.

not prohibit creaturely freedom's self-determination in sin; rather he only knows and oversees its final outcome.

To admit the irrevocable and final falling away of Satan—who, since he is a creature of God, preserves in his very being his divine foundation—would be to introduce a logical contradiction into the very foundation of being, thereby showing that foundation to be simultaneously divine and satanic. Such a contradictory conclusion would be ascribable either to the impotence or to the error of the Creator. According to this view, Satan was created such as to have in himself both the potential and the power to definitively fall away, yet at the same time he was placed in God's paradise at such a height—an unbearable temptation for any created being—by which he could not but be seduced. But in such a scenario the final guilt does not rest on the one who fell into this temptation; this is instead the result of a mistake, as it were, in the plan of creation, a lack of correspondence between the task assigned and the power to complete it. And of course, it is necessary to repeat the very same thing with respect to the other fallen spirits and to fallen man as well, who is sent to the eternal fire "prepared for the devil and his angels" [Matt 25:41] (and if Scripture speaks here of destiny, this is definitively never, by any means, an irremediable destiny).

In *this* interpretation what is at issue is an incorrigible mistake in creation that must be paid for by those incapable of overcoming this mistake and coping with temptation, and this all the more so since the chief tempter himself was not only not kept away from the world and from humanity but was instead presented with the full possibility of tempting Adam and Eve and of taking possession of the entire human race through deception—presented, that is, with the possibility of becoming the prince of this world. This entire complex of ideas leads unavoidably to a conclusion incompatible with theodicy, incompatible with the relative justification of evil in the world. It leads rather to the opposite conclusion, namely to laying the responsibility for all worldly evil and suffering on the Creator of the world, who proved, as it were, incapable of managing his own creation. Such is the inevitable conclusion, as long as we stop halfway at the *first* part of eschatology, at judgment and separation, and if we take this as the final determination, exhaustive in its immobility and completeness. Do we not find here, on the contrary, a test for faith in the mystery of God's love, of that faith that is the announcement of things hoped for and the manifesting of things unseen [Heb 11:1]?

7

The Redemption and Apocatastasis

OFTENTIMES IN THEOLOGY THE redemption and apocatastasis are examined independently. Thus it happens that the universality of redemption is understood such that it implies in no way the universality of salvation, and the "It is accomplished" [John 19:30] from the cross is thus taken in a limited sense: salvation is accomplished *not* for all but only for the elect, while the proportion of all humanity comprising the latter is determined differently, at each person's discretion. Many, following Blessed Augustine, determine this portion to be the minority of humanity and most certainly *not* the majority. If, however, the power of the redemptive sacrifice is defined in our liturgical exclamation as "in behalf of all and for all,"[1] then it is thereby interpreted in a contrary fashion, as free from any exceptions, as universal. But is it not also defined similarly in the relevant sacred texts of both the Old and New Testaments? From the former category the first place belongs to the 53rd chapter of the Old Testament Evangelist Second Isaiah,[2] a chapter

---

1. This is the expression found in the Slavonic text, at least, which in this case alters somewhat the Greek *dià pántēn* [*sic*] *kaì katà pántōn* [for all and in all], with its indefiniteness and ambiguity. But this expression takes for granted—on the foundation of the previous mysterious prayer—"all that was accomplished for us"—in the saving accomplishment of Christ. [I reproduce Bulgakov's Greek text exactly; the text should read *katà pánta kaì dià pánta*. Greek text of the Liturgy of St. John Chrysostom accessed here: << https://www.goarch.org/-/the-divine-liturgy-of-saint-john chrysostom?_101_ INSTANCE_ulcNzWPdScz6_languageId=el_GR>>. —Trans.

2. Bulgakov here refers to the scholarly convention (established since the turn of the twentieth century) of understanding the biblical book of Isaiah as a composite text including three major contributions by different hands, the second of which is known as "Deutero" or "Second" Isaiah. —Trans.

dedicated to the salvific feat of the Messiah (vv. 2–12): "The Lord laid on him the sins of us all" (v. 6), through "his knowledge (his feat) he will justify *many* (here of course not in the limited but in the expansive sense: *all*) and their sins he will take upon himself" (v. 11). And the New Testament texts testify in agreement to the universal significance of the redemptive sacrifice, of Christ's blood. "We have redemption through his blood, the forgiveness of sins according to the riches of his grace" (Eph 1:7); "He handed himself over for us as an offering and sacrifice to God" (Eph 5:2); "In whom we have redemption ("by his blood"—only in the Slavonic and Russian text, missing in the Greek) and the forgiveness of sins" (Col 1:14); "having handed himself over for the redemption of all" (1 Tim 2:6); "reconciliation with the people by his blood" (Col 1:19);[3] "All have sinned and are deprived of the justice of God, and we are justified by grace according to the gift of redemption in Jesus Christ whom God gave as a sacrifice of propitiation in his blood through faith" (Rom 3:23–25); "As by the transgression of one man there came judgment for all people, so also the justice of one man brought about the justification of life for all people. For as the disobedience of one man made many sinners, so also the obedience of one man made many just" (Rom 5:18–[19]); "Christ died for all so that those who live might no longer live for themselves but for the one who died for them and rose again," "God in Christ reconciled the world to himself" (2 Cor 5:15 [2 Cor 5:19]);[4] "Not knowing sin, he became for our sake a sacrifice for sin so that we might in him become just before God" (2 Cor 5:21); "Not by perishable silver or gold are we redeemed . . . but by the precious blood of Christ, as from a spotless and pure lamb, predestined even before the creation of the world but having appeared in these last days" (1 Pet 1:18–20; cf. Rev 5:9–13). (On the predestination of the Lamb before the creation of the world according to the definite counsel and foreknowledge of God, see 1 Cor 2:7; Eph 3:9–11: "The economy of the mystery hidden from eternity in God who created all things by Jesus Christ according to his pre-eternal decree." Cf. Acts 2:23; 4:27–28; Rev 13:18; Eph 1:3).

The general idea expressed here and in similar texts is this: the sacrifice of redemption has power for and pertains to *all* of creation and most certainly to all of humanity, since it was predestined in God's eternity "before the creation of the world." Nowhere is it implied that it was limited in its universality, in either power or intent. Salvation is accomplished for all people and for all of creation, "for the dispensation of the fullness of time, in

3. A mistaken citation, typical of Bulgakov when he cites from memory. The verse seems to be a pastiche of various Pauline phrases drawn from texts like Rom 5:10 and 2 Cor 5:18–21. —Trans.

4. The first verse quoted here is 2 Cor 5:15, the second 2 Cor 5:19. —Trans.

order to unite all things in earth and in heaven under Christ the head" (Eph 1:10). "For all things were created by him, things in heaven and on earth, visible or invisible; whether thrones, dominions, principalities, powers—all were created by him and for him, and he is before all, and in him all things subsist" (Col 1:16–17). And "it pleased him (the Father) that in him [Christ] all justice should dwell and through him to *reconcile to himself* all things, both in heaven and on earth, having made peace through him, by the blood of his cross" (Col 1:19–20),[5] "that at the name of Christ should every knee should bow in heaven, on earth, and under the earth" (Phil 2:10).

But alongside this general and foundational definition of *universal* salvation we have the no less firm biblical teaching concerning the judgment and its resultant separation of the saved sheep and damned goats (Matt 25): "each one was judged according to his works, and death and Hades were cast into the lake of fire. This is the second death. And whoever was not written in the book of life was thrown into the lake of fire" (Rev 20:13–15). If we stop at an understanding of this and similar texts, such that this is the last and final, now unchangeable and irreversible, destiny of not only the saved but also the damned, then we must see here—between the former texts testifying to a general and universal redemption and therefore also to universal salvation, and the latter texts pertaining to perdition and separation—not only an obvious disagreement but even a direct contradiction, which is often either not noticed or not resolved in various interpretations. But if one recognizes the complete insufficiency and general flimsiness of both these interpretive options, then one must inevitably attribute the divergent and as it were mutually contradictory definitions to different worldly aeons that allow the possibility of a transition from death to life, from perdition to salvation, albeit by means of "eternal torments," of a progressive "apocatastasis," or more precisely, a universal salvation, and one without any limitations or exceptions but only with diverse forms and multiple stages. It is precisely such an understanding of the question that we set out here. But for now it is still necessary to theologically comprehend and to confirm such an understanding in connection with the teaching on the incarnation and redemption.

It would be superfluous to demonstrate that, in the absence of Adam's original sin and the infirmity of all of creation bound up with it, it would have been the incarnation itself that would have resulted in the universal deification of man and together with him of all of creation, resulting as well in their universal salvation, progressing from strength to strength [Ps 84:7]:

5. The Slavonic and Russian translations read: "that all *fullness* should dwell." —Trans.

"God will be all in all" (1 Cor 15:28). But precisely in order to eliminate this idea, despite its self-evident inner logic, those denying the final universality of salvation prefer to completely reject the very possibility of the incarnation in the absence of its redemptive necessity. They are prepared thereby to admit a division between Creator and creation for the ages of ages—a division that entails the contradiction of "God will be all in all."[6] The incarnation is admitted exclusively as a means of salvation from sin, though only salvation for some accompanied by condemnation for others and the perdition of many. But in such a case the very work of salvation and its fruit take on a limited character: they pertain only to the saved, alongside whom remain the damned. But this is incompatible with the texts cited above.

A narrow and therefore inadequate interpretation of the doctrine of redemption allows for such a final division that lasts forever. But this is completely incompatible with the straightforward content of those texts that prophesy a universal salvation. Reconciling these latter texts with those of another and apparently opposite and contrary content, without contradiction, is possible only if we understand them in relation not only to the ontological but also to the temporal sequentiality of events in which judgment, damnation, and even the "second death" are not yet the last and final determination and condition but instead are only transitional. The incarnation is the very foundation of created being, its very goal and not merely the means for its partial healing and salvation—in which case, the victory of death and Hades over a portion of creation would remain irreversible. Granted such an irreversibility, it can clearly no longer be said that "God will be all in all"; otherwise the very same thing could be said of Hades and death as well. The redemption must be understood as the very foundation of creation, as its second act that follows the first and is connected with it. Only in such an ontological interpretation does its power entail the perfecting *divinization* of creation. If on the paths of human salvation this divinization appears only partial or, as we understand it, sequential, then this gradation pertains solely to the form of its accomplishment, to its becoming, and not to its complete fullness and power.

But to admit this fragmentation as the final outcome and thereby to accept the redemption's wholly limited reach would mean to admit the weakness and feebleness, if not the downright impotence, of the incarnation itself as the sacrifice of Christ, and so also to admit the victorious—albeit not complete but only partial—power of the devil, a power he already possessed at creation. This, however, is contradicted by the testimony of

---

6. Bulgakov here alludes to the negative adverb of the Chalcedonian definition, "indivisibly." —Trans.

Revelation (20:10): "The devil who had seduced them (the nations) was cast into the lake of fire where the beast and the false prophet are, and they will be tormented day and night for the ages of ages" (20:14). The question arises, however, to what extent exactly the fullness of these torments is compatible with "death and Hades" being cast into the lake of fire (20:14). Clearly, victory over the devil demands and presupposes the annihilation of death and Hades in creation, but it also thereby presupposes its final liberation and salvation from these as well. This passage concerns only the times and periods required for the final defeat of Hades and Satan, not merely externally—in the image of his "being restrained" ("for one thousand years" [Rev 20:2])—but also definitively. This defeat is possible as a result of Satan's becoming conscious of his impotence and as a result of his . . . conversion. Otherwise our only option is to admit the indestructability of the devil in his satanism, before which Divinity itself is impotent, to acknowledge the devil as the victor in this duel between absolute Good and created being— that is, we must acknowledge him to be mightier than God.

Here, of course, it is appropriate to ask whether the power of redemption covers the human world only or the spiritual world as well. But there are no grounds for denying the latter. At least, this is impossible to deny with respect to the holy angels, ministers to Christ himself and of his work, and witnesses too since they are partakers of the resurrection of Christ. If this is indeed the case, then what possible ontological grounds can we find for denying the redemption's power for the fallen spirits as well, who even during Christ's earthly ministry asked him "not to torment them before the time" and "not to send them into the abyss" (Matt 8:29–31; Mark 5:7–13; Luke 8:28–33)? And if the demons were already at that time susceptible to the influence of Jesus and obeyed his authority even in his earthly ministry, much more so is it necessary for them to accept these in relation to his advent in power and glory. These are the grounds for expanding the—inner and outer—power of the apocatastasis to the coming age or the ages of ages.

The disparity in destinies granted at Christ's judgment relates therefore not to the power of the ontological verdict, which would witness to its finality and immutability, but rather to the form of salvation's accomplishment in which it appears for a time incomplete, still partial and not definitive. But the power of redemption is unconquerable and irrefusable, as the gift of divinization offered through the incarnation. And in this sense we can actually *equate* the redemption with the apocatastasis in its inner essence, as not limited in any way except solely in the form of its accomplishment.

8

Augustinianism and Predestination

The Teaching of Blessed Augustine
on Freedom and Predestination

BLESSED [HENCEFORTH 'BL.'] AUGUSTINE did not directly occupy himself with problems of eschatology, and in his numerous works there cannot be found a single treatise devoted exclusively to one of these problems. Nonetheless, it belonged precisely to this father of the Church as to no other to pose, in the series of numerous works from his industrious life, a number of essential questions concerning the interrelationship between Creator and creature, freedom and grace, self-determination and predestination—questions equally decisive for eschatology. A general introduction to eschatology therefore naturally begins with this problematic of Augustinianism.

Generally speaking, this holy father did his thinking in polemics, repelling or opposing this or that current of thought hostile to him at the given moment (and in this, we might add, he resembles many other fathers). His thought was not calm and self-sufficient but rather determined by its opposite and thereby not infrequently falling into one-sidedness. Through the different stages of his life, new waves of thought replace the last in the mind of this father, who nonetheless remains the greatest thinker of the patristic era and the defining theologian of the Western world. In particular, the general problem of the relationship between God and the world, as well as its derivative problem of theodicy, appear before us in turns, first in its anti-Manichean and then with its anti-Pelagian formulations. It was necessary for Bl. Augustine in the first instance to intone more loudly human determination in freedom, but in the second, the action of God on the human being through predestination. Bl. Augustine never could provide a synthesis for this dialectical duality and opposition, although he tried to assure himself (in the *Retractiones*) that all was well and that there was no contradiction. Both problematics led him to the question of the relation between creaturely freedom and divine predestination, a relation consisting in God's creative act and in the providence that rules the world.

Toward a Characterization of Augustinianism

The uniting principle of the entire doctrine of Augustinianism proves to be *praedestinatio* [predestination], which Bl. Augustine identifies with *praescientia* [foreknowledge]. As the question is posed in Augustinianism, it is, undoubtedly, a system of double-predestination or fatalism, a fact for which Bl. Augustine was, in complete fairness, upbraided by his Pelagianizing opponents. It is simply inconsistency and evasiveness on the part of Bl. Augustine that he does not want to recognize *reprobatio* [reprobation] as one of the possibilities of shared *praedestinatio*. After original sin, the entire human race is doomed to perdition, is the *massa perditionis* [the mass of the lost]. From this mass are elected some who are predestined for salvation and who receive for this the corresponding means of grace; the rest are left to their own fate. Without any exaggeration, we may compare this position with a hospital that contains hopeless and dying sick patients: a doctor who has the means to heal them gives this healing, at his whim, only to the elect, leaving the others to die. Can it really be that this inactivity by the doctor does not also constitute *activity*, no less than his direct help for the elect does? And who can be satisfied by this verbal, terminological distinction between *praedestinatio* and *praescientia*, especially since Augustine himself asserts their identity (in contrast to the Pelagians who distinguish them)?

Naturally, it is around precisely these points that the greatest number of contradictions are concentrated, and the evasiveness of Bl. Augustine himself in the question of *reprobatio* confounds many. But how could it be otherwise if the system of Augustinianism lacks proper human self-determination arising from freedom (the latter, at least, being exhausted with the original fall into sin and afterwards ceasing to exist)? If we have two quantities that are connected, the absolute omnipotence and omniscience of God on the one hand, and impotent, sin-enslaved human nature on the other, then it is clear that the latter, *in all possible conditions*, either positively or negatively, is determined by God's decision. And this decision, in its inscrutability and concealment from man, functions as divine *despotism*. Augustinianism just is a system of divine despotism that administers love and condescension to some people but justice to others— although, in the face of such radical determinism, can we even speak of justice, since justice presupposes the ability to hold someone liable and, therefore, the capacity to be responsible for one's actions? In penal law, at least, justice puts aside the sword and refuses to judge those whom it recognizes to be, due to their own personal state, not responsible for themselves and not able to answer for themselves; but here we see handed over to merciless judgment not just adults but even newborn children. In effect, it turns out that Augustine lays all responsibility for the fates of creation on God.

If Bl. Augustine formally overcame Manicheism—he spent his youth struggling against it, both externally and internally—then in his system of predestination he nevertheless absorbs it internally and makes God responsible for good and evil. For this reason, Manicheism, with the greatest consistency, confessed two gods: the good god and the bad god. Soteriology here becomes eschatology. God in his pre-eternal plan, even before our birth, foreordains some for salvation and abandons others (that is, he negatively foreordains them to perdition). As it would later be expressed with complete consistency by Calvin: God created a part of humanity for hell, and hell itself, to the glory of his might, *sovereignty*, and yet Bl. Augustine can sarcastically name the Origenists "pitiers," *misericordes*! Here the question of eschatology can already be traced back to Bl. Augustine's general teaching on God and on the foundations of the creation of the world; here diverge the paths of Christianity and . . . Islam.[1]

It should be further noted that this feature of predestinationism is an anthropomorphism—i.e., without remainder, it inserts God into the temporal process (just as Calvinism does too, of course). Although on occasion an *aeternum propositum* [eternal purpose] is spoken of, nevertheless it is precisely here that we unexpectedly find introduced the temporal *prae*: *praescientia*, *praedestinatio*. It is as if God, before creating the world, thought things over, predested them, and then created the world according to the previously decided plan, which he then implements (here we see a resemblance to deism, the only difference being that in deism everything is already included beforehand in the mechanism of the world, such that God no longer interferes in its life, but here the interference is continuous). Such a conception (clearly inspired by the deliberately anthropomorphic language of the apostle Paul in Rom 8:28–30) is, obviously, insufficient for

---

1. It was a regular trope of Russian religious thought of nineteenth and twentieth centuries to compare Christianity and Islam (negatively) precisely on the question of God's absolutely omnipotent and determinative will. —Trans.

expressing the relationship of God to the world, but we find no other in Bl. Augustine (despite the fact that it is precisely in his works—in the *Confessions*—that we encounter the most powerful teaching in all of patristic literature on time in relation to eternity). In Bl. Augustine, the prologue in heaven contains the entire historical drama as well as its epilogue, and the actors are only marionettes set in motion from without (here again one feels in Bl. Augustine the lack of a christological anthropology, of a teaching on divine-humanity). The relationship between God and the human being is determined extrinsically, mechanistically; the human being is a thing in the hands of the Creator, for whom this thing is an object of ontological indifference. The relationship is determined by omnipotence and despotism, more broadly by divine absolutism, in which love occupies a place of only subordinate detail. But an inner co-imaging—if it may be thus expressed—a mutual connection and mutual grounding of God and the human being in anthropology, is simply lacking. The human being remainsfor God an external object for domination.

These features of Augustinianism are most pronounced in his interpretation of the foundations of predestination, when he feels himself called to perform the role of Job's friends, to act as God's lawyer. Defiance is the natural response for a human mind (if it has not been darkened) when it encounters this *apologia for despotism*, even if it be a despotism divine.[2] Such a theodicy—*sic volo sic iubeo* [as I wish, so I command]—can satisfy only those who are already satisfied and hypnotized in submissiveness. But then in others this theodicy provokes this Karmazovism: "It's not God that I do not accept, but rather God's world."[3] Bl. Augustine, as we have seen, responds to all questions concerning the foundations of the divine election of some and the non-election of others by professing his ignorance and by appealing to the inscrutability and unknowability of the ways of God. (He also employs here the text of Romans 11, not noting that the apostle in this text speaks precisely of universal compassion: "for he enclosed all in disobedience that he might have mercy on all"; but in Bl. Augustine the text has the direct opposite meaning.) The postulate of negative theology in this case is, of course, completely appropriate and cannot be disputed, but nevertheless there should be a defined place for it, so that it might not otherwise become

2. In contrast to Bl. Augustine. St. John Chrysostom says, "But when he says, '*Which He prepared for glory*,' he expresses by this that not everything happens by God alone, because if this were the case, then nothing would prevent him from saving all. And although the greater part belongs to God, nevertheless we add something small from ourselves" (*Homilies on the Epistle to the Romans*, 16).

3. A reference to Ivan Karamazov's famous "rebellion" against God. See the chapter "Rebellion" in Dostoevsky's *The Brothers Karamazov*. —Trans.

a refuge for craftiness and evasiveness of thought. Unfortunately, it is precisely the latter that we find in Bl. Augustine. He develops a neatly rational,
logically tight theory of the salvation of some and the perdition of others,
and this for him functions simultaneously as a theodicy as well, one that, by
design, ought to satisfy the questioning of human inquisitiveness. But then,
after he takes his deduction to the logical dead-end of despair, where the
human mind raises the question that it is necessarily compelled to ask, Bl.
Augustine's answer is ignorance and the inscrutability of God's ways. This
refusal to answer is experienced not as a feat of faith that has humbled itself
before the inscrutable but rather as an evasive self-deception. This completely groundless *despotism* in election or non-election that Bl. Augustine
teaches here cannot and ought not to be accepted by the undarkened human
conscience, even in the face of threatening prohibitions against thinking
(which is generally taken to be the case in questions of eschatology). His
own theory of predestinationism—which is both a theodicy and an eschatology—*commits* him to this answer: if he affirms the one, then he must also
admit the other. If he rationalizes the force and meaning of election, then he
ought to identify its foundations too. Otherwise we find a hole in the very
foundation of the doctrine. With this irrational tear in the cloth, the entirety
is undone from top to bottom. Bondage of thought is not theology. This is
neither antinomy nor legitimate ignorance but simply a dead-end.

In the constructs of Bl. Augustine there is no place at all for *mystery*:
on the contrary, here everything is rationalized, all questions can, in principle, be answered. If the great apostle speaks of the unfathomable depth
of the Wisdom of God on the paths of universal salvation, then here this
unfathomability applies to what has been made completely comprehensible,
as the despotism of election, and in this arbitrariness nothing of mystery
remains. Truly the ways of God are inscrutable, and yet just are his paths.
But here, under the pretext of inscrutability, what is abolished is justice itself. It is not possible, under the pretext of ignorance, to ascribe to God
that which our conscience and reason cannot accept as truth and justice,
thereby discovering a contradiction in God himself. This is blasphemy and
not humility—doctrinairism, but not *docta ignorantia* [learned ignorance]
or wise and pious ignorance. And one must not quiet the conscience by
quoting texts that bear no relationship to the matter at hand.

Thus Augustinian predestinationism disintegrates from within; it suffers a catastrophe, although it also remains an unforgettable monument of
human thought; to the very end it walks its notorious road. It is, so to speak,
an experiment of theological thought, destined sooner for a historical mu-
seum of theology than for life, where it remains a dead ghost.

There remains one more side of Augustinianism yet to be analyzed, namely its exegesis—its biblical foundation.

On Predestination according to the Apostle Paul: Romans 8:28–30 and Ephesians 1:3–12 in Blessed Augustine's Interpretation

When setting forth his teaching on predestination, Bl. Augustine relies, in terms of exegesis, primarily on the previously indicated texts from the apostle Paul, subjecting them to an abstract-literal interpretation, *outside* of the overall context in which the apostle Paul develops his thought. His main text is, of course, Rom 8:28–30:

> We know that for those who love God, for those called according to his choice (*toîs katà próthesin klētoîs oûsin*) all things work together for good, because those whom he foreknew (*proégnō*) he also predestined (*proŏrisen*) to be conformed (*symmórphous*) to the image of his Son, so that he might be the firstborn among many brethren. And those whom he predestined, he also called (*ekálesen*), and those whom he called, he also justified (*edikaíōsen*), and those whom he justified He also glorified (*edóxasen*).

Bl. Augustine repeatedly refers to this text, seeing in it an expression of God's total and exhaustive relation to the world, a relationship defined by a universally penetrating determinism, and—to all appearances—a relationship that also denies any significance to man's free self-determination. This interpretation is capable of acting on the soul in a confounding and scandalizing manner. Beginning already with Pelagius and Chrysostom,[4] has attempted to save itself from these horrifying assertions through distinguishing and,

---

4. Such a way out of the difficulty, following in the footsteps of Tridentine theology, is also indicated in the Epistle of the Eastern Patriarchs, chapter 3: "We believe that the all-blessed God predestined for glory those whom He elected from eternity, and that He rejected those whom He handed over to judgment, not, however, because He desired thereby to justify some but others to leave behind and to judge without cause . . . but insofar as He foresaw that some would use well their free will, and others in an evil manner, He therefore predestined some for glory and others He judged. . . . But what blasphemous heretics say, that God predestines or judges without taking any consideration of the deeds of those predestined and judged, this we consider madness and wickedness. . . ." Cf. Thomas Aquinas, *Commentary on Romans*, chapter 8, section 6: "Predestination differs from foreknowledge for the reason that foreknowledge indicates only the knowledge of what is future, whereas predestination indicates a certain causal influence on the what is future."

to a certain degree opposing, foreknowledge (which ostensibly concerns human freedom) and predestination (which becomes, as it were, the consequence or outcome of this foreknowledge). Bl. Augustine insists—implacably and not without certain formal grounds—that God's foreknowledge is also his predestination and is thus identical with it in one pre-eternal act. Here he adds Ephesians 1:3–12, where it is said that "God elected us (*exeléxato*) in Christ before the creation (*katabolês*) of the world . . . having predestined to adopt us to himself through Jesus Christ according to the good-pleasure of his will," with this "us" being interpreted, with insufficient grounds, in a restrictive manner, in opposition to those *not* elected for this. (However, this text possesses only a secondary and, so to speak, supplementary importance for him.)

Without going into detail concerning the complicated exegesis of the Epistle to the Romans (the best representatives of contemporary scholarship on the text refuse to see even a shade of deterministic-fatalistic meaning in Rom 8:28–30), we can nonetheless establish the invalidity of a literal, Augustinian exegesis. St. Paul expounds his thought in this text in a deliberately anthropomorphic manner, applying to the pre-eternal determination of God *temporal* terms—*fore*knowledge, *pre*destination—and thereby inserting the acts of God into the temporality of the world, into its past ages. It goes without saying that such a use of words demands a new, theological interpretation (see below). Bl. Augustine *exaggerates* the anthropomorphic side of the apostle Paul's exposition and in a deistic manner transforms God into a mechanic who starts the machine of the world and pre-establishes everything and everyone in it (and of course, in complete contradiction to Bl. Augustine's own doctrine of the freedom of the will).[5]

But this deistic-deterministic interpretation *does not* in the first place fit the general context of the Epistle to the Romans, just as it does not match the completely practical—or rather volitional—spirit of the apostle Paul's epistles. The main theme of the Epistle to the Romans is salvation not by works of the law and not on the grounds of election understood as a legal title and privilege, but rather by *faith* in the redeeming sacrifice of the Son of God and the corresponding life of faith. And, in fact, it is specifically in chapter 8 that the apostle exhorts us to live not according to the flesh but according to the Spirit (vv. 12–13), not in the spirit of bondage but of adoption (v. 15), being inspired and sustained by the Spirit in our infirmities, sufferings, and endurance. And as a *special consolation* the apostle testifies

---

5. Bulgakov refers here to Augustine's teaching on the freedom of the will in his early, anti-Manichean writings, such as *de libero arbitrio* (*On the Freedom of the Will*). Bulgakov had analyzed this text earlier in this excursus from which this chapter is taken. —Trans.

to the good will of God towards men, expressed in his universal determination that they be *conformed to the image of his Son*, and therefore the apostle
also testifies to the corresponding providential guidance and help given to
men, without which they would not be able to attain this lofty goal: for those
who love God, "*all things work together for good.*"

The expressions *foreknowledge* and *predestination* are simply special
verbal forms for expressing this love on God's part, but they do not in any
way contain that limiting sense that was put into them by Bl. Augustine
(and later by Calvin), namely that God elected some and rejected others,
or that the text here speaks not only of the elect but also of the *non*-elect.
On the contrary—here the apostle Paul speaks of (pre)-election and (pre)-
determination *in general*, as the common foundation for both the creation
of man and for the relationship of God to the world (the same thing, and
even more self-evidently, is true of Eph 1:4 also): this is in the fullest sense
the good news of salvation. And this is confirmed with complete clarity in
the following triumphant words from the very same text, Rom 8:31–32: "If
God is for us, who can be against us? The one who did not spare his own
Son, but rather gave him up *for us all—hypèr hēmõn*—how will he not give
us with him *tà pánta*—everything?" Precisely this juxtaposition of *pántōn*
and *pánta* bears a logical stress completely opposed to that which Bl. Augustine gives it; it speaks not of a limited, exclusive salvation, as the privilege of
some, but speaks rather of its universal scope, of the universality of the work
of Christ. (And this same thing is confirmed by 2 Tim 1:9 as well: "Having
saved us and called us—*kalésantos*—with a holy call—*klḗsei*—not according to our works, but according to his purpose (*próthesin*) and his grace
given to us in Christ Jesus before the ages of time," and especially by 1 Tim
2:4–5, "who desires that *all men—pántas anthrṓpous*—be saved and attain
the knowledge of the truth, for God is one, and one is the mediator between
God and men—*anthrṓpōn*—the man Christ Jesus." As we can see, this text,
which speaks of the universality of salvation, Bl. Augustine is forced to interpret in an obviously contorted manner against its straightforward meaning, in a limiting fashion: "*all*" = "*all the elect.*" Chapter 8 of Romans ends in
full accordance with this good news of salvation (and of course, in complete
contradiction to Bl. Augustine's limiting interpretation) with a hymn to
God's love: "Who will separate us from the love of God?" (vv. 35–39). All
trials and temptations—"we overcome them all through the one who loved
us. . . . Nothing can separate us from the love of God in Christ Jesus, our
Lord." Furthermore, if we take into consideration that, even for Bl. Augustine, election constitutes the mystery of God, unknown to mankind, then
we must necessarily refer this election not to a limited number of the elect

but to humanity as a whole, or, more accurately, to *divine-humanity*, which in fact is the pre-eternal foundation of *created* humanity.

All of the previous content, chapters 1 through 8 of the Epistle to the Romans, functions as it were as the general presupposition for the discussion of the problem—agonizing to the apostle himself and scandalizing to all others—concerning the election and rejection of Israel, the *"Jewish Question"* in its religious formulation.[6] The antinomy of this question consists in the simultaneous recognition both of the incontrovertible nature of election and of the rejection of Israel, which has not accepted Christ. In developing this antinomy, the apostle Paul, going from thesis to antithesis and back, touches on the paths by which God's providence directs *history* (for Bl. Augustine these "historiosophical" problems are imperceptibly transformed into problems of eternal salvation and perdition as well). In the development of his ideas, the apostle Paul admits—in addition to a rabbinic style of thought and exposition[7] that is felt here more strongly than in other places—certain texts that *sound* deterministic-fatalistic, which are then used by Bl. Augustine as a confirmation of his own doctrine. This includes, first and foremost, the famous text concerning Rebekah, and later on, the one concerning Pharaoh. When outlining the paths of God's guidance in the genuine election of the "children of God," which does not depend on "works," that is, merits (for no merits are sufficient to justify election, no merits are adequate to it), the apostle says:

6. The term "Jewish Question" already had a long history in European political and religious life, encompassing everything from the political status of Jews in the new nation-states to the enduring religious significance of Judaism in its relationship to Christianity. In the Russian context, the "Jewish Question" revolved largely around the issue of the Pale of Settlement and the anti-Jewish pogroms that took place therein. By Bulgakov's time this grave situation had already received serious political and theological attention from writers of the Russian Religious Renaissance, and especially from Vladimir Solovyov In this essay, Bulgakov uses the term "Jewish Question" in a more strictly theological register, applying it to the question of Israel's eschatological salvation as St. Paul pursues it in Rom 9–11. For critical commentary, see Rowan Williams's *Sergii Bulgakov: Towards a Russian Political Theology*, specifically the appendix, "Bulgakov and Anti-Semitism," and now "On the Question of Sergius Bulgakov's 'Anti-Semitism': The Report of a Devil's Advocate" in Robert F. Slesinski, *The Theology of Sergius Bulgakov.* —Trans.

7. Specifically, this relates to that sharp expression of predeterminism that we find in Rom 8:28–29. According to Flavius Josephus, "the Pharisees ascribed everything to Destiny and to God (*heimarménē kaì theôi*), while, nevertheless, the choice of good and evil remains with man." In *Pirke-Abboth* III: 24 we read: "all is foreseen, and free will is given, and the world is judged by grace, and everything corresponds to works" (Sanday and Headlam, *Romans*, 1:349).

For when they (the children of Isaac) had not yet been born and had done neither good nor evil, so that the will of God in election might come to pass not from works but from the one who calls, it was said to her, "The older will be in bondage to the younger" (Gen 25:23), as it is written, "Jacob have I loved, and Esau have I hated" (Mal 1:23). What shall we say? Can there be injustice in God? By no means. For he says to Moses, "I will have mercy on whom I will have mercy; and I will pity whom I will pity" (Exod 33:19). And so "Mercy does not depend on the one desiring or striving, but on God who has mercy." (Rom 9:11–16)

First of all, what is being spoken of in this example of Esau and Jacob? It speaks of a particular choice made for the sake of the definite goals of providence in history, but it certainly does not speak of salvation or perdition (the expression "hate" in the prophet Malachi by no means bears a literal meaning and refers only to the divergent destinies and privileges of Israel in comparison with Esau, who also receives from his father a blessing, although not the blessing of the firstborn). Here we find general evidence for the idea of God's participation in history, from which there naturally arises the related special problematic of the *interaction* of God and the human being, of its foundations, and of the relation between human self-determination and God's determination; even more precisely, there arises the problematic of the *relativity* of human freedom. But this is, of course, completely different than what Bl. Augustine sees here, for here it is not a question of predestination as it is spoken of in chapter 9, but on the contrary, here a completely different problem is taken up.

This problem is developed further in the example of Pharaoh: "For the Scripture says to Pharaoh: 'For this very reason have I established you, to show My power over you, and that My name might be proclaimed throughout the earth'" (Exod 9:16). "And so, he has mercy on whom he wishes; and he hardens whom he wishes" (Rom 9:17–18). And further on: "And what, if God, wishing to show his anger and display his might, with great long-suffering spared vessels of wrath prepared for perdition so that along with them he might display the riches of his glory on the vessels of mercy that he prepared beforehand for glory" (vv. 22–23). Related to this are the following parallel texts: "The Lord hardened the heart of Pharaoh" (Exod 9:12, cf. 4:21). Yet again, what is spoken of here is not election or rejection but rather the fact that God, for the sake of his purposes, directs human infirmities and even the hardening of hearts; in its explanation of the historical fates of Israel, the passage speaks of the *List der Vernunft* [cunning of reason] and nothing more. The text, in any case, bears no relation to the question of the paths of personal salvation or rejection.

It is this same idea of God's relationship to the world, as both its Creator and Providential Guide, that is expressed by the apostle in his paradoxical comparison of God with a potter: "And who are you O man, that you argue with God? Will that which is made say to its maker: 'Why did you make me like this?' Is not the potter master over the clay, to make from the same mixture one vessel for honorable (usage) and another for shame?" (9:20–22). The paradox of this comparison consists in the fact that it singles out, isolates, from the entire complex of relationships that the Creator and Providential Guide has to the world, only *one* side, namely the *active* relationship of the Creator to creation—so God creates Adam from the clay to afterwards breathe into him a living soul. But it in no wise follows that the comparison of the potter and the clay may be applied to the *whole*, that we may see here a characterization of *all* the interrelations between God and man, and consequently to completely preclude freedom and any self-determination on the human side. God is *not* a potter, and the human person is not clay. When elucidating any parabolic image, it is important to establish the right point of view, to find the *tertium comparationis*. In this case, the comparison refers to the omnipotence of the Creator in creating the world, who by his creative act determines the *what* of creation in all of its varieties. Here we have an expression of the character of *creaturehood*, according to which man has not created himself but is *given* to himself by God. This by no means excludes, however, his own (albeit created) freedom and self-determination. And all creatures, for all their differences, have in themselves the love of God, they bear the seal of this love, are *dignified* in having their being *conferred* on them, and in turn are worthy of it, in their own way, even if they are *differing* vessels. The comparison of vessels for honorable and shameful use in no way need be understood *in malam partem*, as an expression of the exaltation of some and the disdainful humiliation of others. Here it is most appropriate to recall another comparison from the apostle Paul concerning the different members of the body of the Church who are equally important and necessary in all their differences (1 Cor 12:14–26).

But the positive side of the apostle Paul's image of the potter and the clay consists in the fact that by God's creative act the ontological foundation and fate of every creature have been established together, creaturely freedom included. This freedom is not absolute but relative, and it operates only within the bounds of its ontological limits. In this sense is it said: "For the gifts and calling of God are immutable" (Rom 11:29). God-Creator does not *pre*-determine but rather *determines* the form of all creation, and he includes all creation's variety—as one of many pre-conditions—in the inscrutable paths of his Wisdom as it providentially orders the world. Applied to the "Jewish Question" the apostle Paul was considering at that moment, this means that according to his purpose, God created the Jewish nation as such, as well as the *non*-Jewish nations, the gentiles (just as in an egg we find both the yolk and the white). Later on the characteristics of true Israel and its mysterious fate are explained. But what is most remarkable in this entire judgment on the fate of Israel—which constitutes, indisputably, the pragmatic center of this *Epistle to the Romans concerning the Jews*—is that in this letter no verdict is given separating the elect and non-elect, those called and those rejected, but instead, *pace* Bl. Augustine, we find a verdict of universal mercy both for Israel and not-Israel. And this applies not only to the quite remarkable, mysterious, and greatly significant question of the salvation of *all* Israel (a question that at the moment lies outside of our consideration), but also to the fates of the gentile world, which are tied up with Israel. "Just as you were once disobedient to God and have now received mercy in accordance with their disobedience, so too are they now disobedient for you to be shown mercy, so that they too might themselves receive mercy. *For God has enclosed all* in disobedience in order to have mercy on all" (Rom 11:30–33). And this contemplation of divine fates makes the apostle's heart burst forth with a triumphant hymn (which Bl. Augustine abuses so violently for his own totally opposed view, applying it to our inability to give an answer for election not just to salvation but also to perdition). "O, the depth of the riches and wisdom and knowledge of God! How inscrutable his judgments and how unsearchable his paths! For who has known the mind of the Lord? Or who has been his counselor? (Ps 40:13). Or who has given to him, that he should repay? (Ps 40:13–14). For *all is from him, through him, and to him—ex autoû kaì di' autoû kaì eis autòn*. To him be praise forever. Amen" (Rom 11:33–36). These words constitute the center of the entire epistle, its main idea, which is completely opposed to the Augustinian interpretation. If we can find here a teaching on predestination (within, at least, generally acceptable limits), then we must do so not with respect to an Augustinian-Calvinistic predestination of some for salvation and the abandonment of others for rejection, but rather a predestination for universal mercy.

And so, the analysis of this complicated and difficult passage of Romans 8:28—11:36 leads to the general conclusion that it does not in any way bear the meaning that could be given to it when taken out of context. The text concerning foreknowledge and pre-election has a meaning that is not eschatological but only providential. It expresses the general idea that the salvation of the human person is not acquired by the *works* of the law, by right or on legal bases, in accord with the rabbinic doctrine, which has been partially inherited by Catholic dogmatics; instead it is granted by God through the power of the redemptive sacrifice of Christ and realized through the guidance of God's providence, which operates by paths unsearchable for man. These paths, as they appear before man, are expressed in anthropomorphic images as God's foreknowledge and predestination. The mystery of the providence of God in its wisdom and knowledge are united with the mystery of the omnipotence of the act of creation in its manifold diversity that establishes the faces and qualities of creation. All these together define the universal, divine determination of creation that does not exclude, but rather includes and presupposes the participation of human freedom, its self-determination.

It is the business of religious philosophy and theology to unite in a general conceptual framework both theses—which from the outside sound like contradictions or at least antinomies (by no means the same thing)—to unite them, therefore, as thesis and antithesis. In the theological richness of his epistles, the apostle Paul provides us with materials to thematize in theologizing—a task he himself did not undertake. With the regal majesty of a Spirit-bearing evangelist and with the inherited rabbinic technique of the epistle, he postulates a series of *yesses* and *noes*, sometimes even in the very same phrase. One of his most characteristic combinations of antinomistic affirmations of this same sort is found in Phil 2:12–13, to whose second, deterministic-sounding part Bl. Augustine so often appeals for confirmation of his own doctrine: "*With fear and trembling work out your own salvation, for God—Theòs—is the one who works—ho energôn—in you both the will and the activity according to his good-will.*" The first half of the text is addressed to human will and freedom, and the second speaks of the divine activity within us. This interrelation constitutes the main problem of historiosophy that is given to us in the apostolic epistles. In his letters, the apostle Paul with equal ease passes between thesis to antithesis. More specifically, in the Epistle to the Romans, after 8:28—11:36, the apostle moves to its *exhortatory* section, just as this section itself is preceded by the teaching on faith as a feat of human freedom (an idea developed with particular clarity in the Epistle to the Hebrews, chapter 11). And indeed, if we presuppose the Augustinian determinism that Augustine inserted into the Epistle to the Romans, the entire teaching—not only of the Old Testament (and especially of the Decalogue), but also of the Gospel and of the entire New Testament—would, as it were, lose its meaning, for all of it is addressed to man, to his activity and freedom.

9

The Sophiology of Death

All that your hand can do, do it according to your strength, because in the grave where you are headed there is neither work, nor industry, nor knowledge, nor wisdom.

—Ecclesiastes 9:10

MAN, AND IN HIM all creation, is uncreated-created Sophia, created divinity, a creaturely god by grace. God has granted him life, but he has not granted him death; "God did not create death" (Wis 1:13) but merely permitted it. Death entered the world through the path of sin, which destroyed the stability of human existence and as it were separated within man the uncreated from the created. The created, since it did not possess in itself its own power of being, became mortal, having acquired an undue independence from the uncreated. Such is the nature of death. And that very nature imposes limits on death. Death is neither absolute nor all-powerful. It can only tear at and fracture the tree of life, but it is not invincible, for it has already been conquered by the resurrection of Christ. Humanity rises in Christ and with Christ, although for this and before this it must die with Christ and in Christ. The death of humanity is precisely Christ's death, and we must take part in the fullness of this death, just as he partook in our death after becoming enfleshed and human: "he was crucified for us under Pontius Pilate, suffered and was buried" (after accepting death). What could this death of the God-man mean, this focal point of death, mortality itself? How can the

117

God-man die, in whom God himself "indivisibly and unconfusedly"[1] has become united with man? How, in Christ's very self, could the divine and created principles, God and man, not only be joined but divided, as it were? Or, insofar as his divinity is Divine Sophia, how could she be separated from created Sophia? The form of death—division itself—remains one and the same both for man and for the God-man. The God-man dies in the image of man, and man dies in the image of the God-man, in a marvelous mutuality. How to understand it?

Christ's death is included under the general power of the divine *kenosis*, as Christ's willed self-abasement and self-diminishment. God in the God-man leaves behind, as it were, his divine fullness; it is as if he stops being God, yet at the same time preserves his divinity in full force. He, while unchangeably abiding as God, nevertheless does not simply taper his divinity; no, he even casts it off, as it were. This antinomy of kenosis—God and not-God—is, generally speaking, the greatest mystery of God's self-revelation: God is Absolute Being, possessing life in himself, but at the same time he is Creator, indivisibly united with creation and with its relative and organic life. This antinomy penetrates to their depths all relations existing between God and the world. The antinomy is expressed in the incarnation and divine-humanity and finds its utmost realization in the divine death, which is united with the complete fullness of divine life: "in the grave bodily, in Hades with thy soul as God . . . and on the throne, Christ, wast thou with the Father and the Spirit."[2] Kenosis is not limited only to the second hypostasis; it covers the entire Holy Trinity, according to the character of each of the hypostases. But kenosis is directed towards the world and man through the second hypostasis, it is fully disclosed in the God-man "who humbled himself unto death on the cross" (Phil 2:8). The revelation of the God-man for us is thus also necessarily the revelation of his *death* in us, and we must comprehend the entire immeasurability of his sacrificial love towards us in his co-dying with us. But this is possible only through our co-dying with him.

Immortality stands opposed to death, it pre-exists the latter and is presupposed by it as its precondition. If God did not create death, then that means that at man's creation there existed in him at least the *possibility* of immortality, and that implies that death was not a necessity. Death as a mere possibility ceased to be a reality and became instead an inevitability on account of original sin. Nevertheless, this inevitability did not exist for

1. These adverbs are taken from the Chalcedonian definition. —Trans.

2. Paschal Hours, Troparion, Tone Eight; also recited before every Divine Liturgy during the censing after the Proskomedia rite. —Trans.

the only sinless One[3] by virtue of his freedom from sin, both original and personal. Death is sacrificially assumed by him through freedom, it is accepted by him for our salvation from death—"having trampled death by death."[4] Nevertheless this freedom cannot operate as the direct coercion of divine despotism over creation or as a new creative act, as it were. It must be *ontologically* grounded in creation. In other words, in the incarnation and in the divine-humanity there must be room . . . for death.

With the incarnation, as the acceptance by God of the entirety of human nature—soul and body, in their indivisible and unconfused union with Divinity—it is as if human nature is already deified[5] through the God-man's communication of his immortality to his human nature. In any case, it is clear how this deification would have occurred if the incarnation had been accomplished in the absence of original sin, and, accordingly, if God in his divine-humanity had assimilated an unfallen human nature. *Posse non mori* [possibility of not dying] here would have crossed into *non posse mori* [impossibility of dying], and the immortality that was merely a possibility would have become an overwhelming reality. Human nature would not have suffered the dissolution of death, and the beginning of life [in humanity] would have multiplied and been fortified through the action of Divinity. That state of risen and glorified humanity, which corresponds to the God-man sitting at the right hand of the Father, would have been proper to the humanity united with him. The transitional state that corresponded to the earthly ministry of the Lord up until his crucifixion, death, and resurrection and that includes the *posse mori*, the possibility of death, would have been excluded.

But such a supposition is only an abstract possibility; we can introduce it only as an auxiliary hypothesis, but it has no place in reality. The incarnation was accomplished in the first place not only as the divinization of man, his ultimate *telos* from the beginning, but also as redemption—liberation from original sin through Christ's acceptance of death and the victory over death in the resurrection. In the incarnation, the Lord brought not human nature *simpliciter*, created Sophia, into relation with his own divinity—this relation being the very foundation of the created world—but rather a human nature that was fallen, diminished, weakened, and mortal. Fallen human nature, even in the incarnation, was no longer—or not yet—capable of receiving the divine nature in all its fullness. It too, in fact, had to travel the

3. The term "only sinless one" alludes here to the communion hymn spoken by the deacon in the Liturgy of St. John Chrysostom. —Trans.

4. Paschal Troparion. —Trans.

5. Reading *obozhestvliaet* for *obozhaet*. —Trans.

kenotic path of divinization, of glorification: "Now the Son of Man is glorified, and God is glorified in him" (John 17:1). And on this kenotic path the
humanity of Christ assumed mortality: "Having diminished himself, having
accepted the form of a slave, having become obedient even unto *death*" [Phil
2:8]. It is this mortality, originally only the possibility of death, that Christ
incessantly encounters on the entire path of the earthly ministry, beginning
with his birth. King Herod endeavors to murder the God-child, and there is
no indication that Herod's intention was, in principle, unrealizable; on the
contrary, the flight to Egypt proved to be necessary for Christ's salvation.
Throughout the course of the Gospel narratives the Jews repeatedly wish to
kill Jesus, who, evading this, "passed through them" [Luke 4:30]; even if we
understand this "passing through" as something miraculous, it was no more
than a form of evasion and in any case does imply the impossibility of that
very murder that, in the end, became a reality on the cross.

The susceptibility to death that the nature of Christ possessed is accompanied by the complete fullness of the sufferings of the cross. This
susceptibility does not signify, of course, sinfulness, which would have
been proper to the human nature found in Christ and by itself would have
grounded the mortality of that nature in the only sinless One. The Son of
Man remains free from sin, both personal and universal or "original"; then
again, we have here the complete coincidence of the personal and the universal, insofar as the New Adam is the pan-human. But although free from
sin, he is not free from its power in humanity, insofar as Christ's humanity
is not a new creation. The God-man is the Son of Man, and the New Adam
assumed humanity from the old Adam. "Jesus was the son of *Adam*, the son
of God" (Luke 3:23–38). But to be the son of Adam, and in him and through
him the son of all humanity, means to assume Adamic humanity, i.e., no
longer primordial but rather fallen nature infected by sin, although it does
remain free from *personal* sin in the God-man himself. As a consequence
of sin, this humanity is reduced to that mortality which is for man now an
inevitability but for the God-man only a possibility; although it is *posse non
mori*, it is also *posse mori*. The Son of Man entered into the world unpro-
tected against death. The Adamic humanity in Christ could, of course, by
virtue of its union with Divinity, manifest as free from the internal necessity
of death and thereby remain immortal, but it also remained free to yield to
a violent death, from crucifixion, as the Lord's death on the cross attests.
In the resurrection and glorification, his humanity still had to receive the
power of immorality through the feat of the redemption. "After suffering
death he was crowned with glory and honor, Jesus, who was made a little
lower than the angels (since they do not know death), so that he, *by God's
grace, might taste death for all*" (Heb 2:9).

And so, anthropologically, the incarnation in and of itself is not already the overcoming of death, which still remained to be conquered. Death was included in the divine kenosis: "*having become similar to men*" . . . he humbled himself, "having become obedient even unto death, even death on a cross" (Phil 2:7–8). Liberation from death by an omnipotent act of God, as a *deus ex machina*, would have meant the abasement of humanity, the diminishment of its freedom, its reduction to the state of an object passively receiving salvation, i.e., the abolishing of human nature itself. But humanity deserves nothing less than a victory over death through the overcoming of mortality itself, the transition from *posse mori* to *non posse mori*. But this was unattainable through human power alone. The fall of man means his debilitation as well: "if a tree falls to the south or to the north, then there it will remain, where it fell" (Eccl 11:3). Mortality in man can be overcome only by divine power, through the God-man. And yet to overcome death, it had to be assumed by the God-man in the hypostatic union of two natures. This assumption cannot be restricted only to the human nature but instead must also reach even the divine hypostasis of the Logos who hypostatizes the humanity in Christ, and in him and through him it must also reach his very divinity, i.e., the Divine Sophia. In other words, there arises the most complicated question of Christology and sophiology, the question concerning mortality in the God-man. How can we understand and accept this idea, this dogmatic truth that from the outside appears to be the most, as it were, *blasphemous* contradiction—the death of the God-man, of man in God and of God in man?

It is necessary to recall *by what means* the incarnation occurred. On the one hand, it is the union of two "natures," divine and human. Divine "nature" is Divine Sophia, the unity of life and self-revelation of the three hypostases. In the Divine Sophia, there is no division of God's triunity in the Holy Trinity. Divine "nature" even in the incarnation belongs to the entire Holy Trinity in its heavenly, pre-cosmic being and in its hypostatic unity, unity in trinity and trinity in unity. The divine second hypostasis is incarnated, but he is not thereby isolated or removed from the entire unity of the Divine Sophia. Here is the mystery of the incarnation together with its antinomy: the identity of trinitarian and Filial Sophia. The very same Divine Sophia belongs to the Holy Trinity in "the heavens," and she is the same divinity of the Son as God-man on "earth." Yet there is more to this antinomy: in "the heavens," Divine Sophia is the very glory of God by which the Holy Trinity is illuminated, as well as the Trinity's Wisdom. She is the *fullness* of divine life, which inheres both in the divine triunity in the Holy Trinity and in each of the hypostases, and in particular in the hypostasis of the Logos, the Son of God. She is, in this sense, "true God from true God."[6] In the heavens, this fullness suffers no diminishment of glory, no divine abasement. And yet—antinomically—she is abased in the kenosis of the Son of God, "having come down from heaven"[7] in the self-diminishment of Christ. Christ's nature (*estestvo*) in the union of the two natures (*prirod*), in the descent from heaven and in the hominization, suffers the diminishment of divinity—all this just *is* the very union itself.

Human nature does not reach its definitive divinization already in the very beginning of the incarnation insofar as it is only the beginning and not the end of the path, that as yet unreached goal that is the fullness of glorification: "I have glorified, and I will glorify again" (John 12:38), "glorify your Son" (John 17:1), "Glorify me, Father, with the glory which I had with you before the existence of the world" [John 17:5]. This glory is received by the Son from the Father in the resurrection and ascension, but only after he has traveled the path of earthly suffering. This kenosis of Divine Sophia in Christ, the self-diminishment of divine nature, constitutes the very foundation of the incarnation as the union of two natures: it is not the human nature that is made equal to the divine—whose level the former from its very origins is always striving to attain—but rather it is the divine nature that diminishes itself to the human level, all while remaining itself. Only under such a kenotic self-diminishment of divinity could human freedom be preserved in the redemptive feat of Christ, which would otherwise become an act of God's omnipotence exercised on the human nature of Christ. In other words, the very possibility of the sacrificial redemption would be lost.

The kenosis of the divine nature in Christ is manifested not only in the assumption of human nature, in becoming equal with the latter, but also in the assumption of *Adamic* nature weakened by original sin. Insofar as this weakening is manifested in the mortality of man, it is necessary to conclude that the kenosis of divinity too must to be manifested in the acceptance of precisely *mortal* human nature. This expresses the whole depth of the human kenosis. In a manner inscrutable for man, the divine nature diminishes itself up *to the point of accepting* the death of the human nature united with it, albeit in an unconfused yet also indivisible manner. The divine nature is not separated from the human nature even in death, and to that extent and in this sense it *co-dies* with it. Clearly, we can speak here of "dying" only in a completely unique sense, different from human death; specifically, it is a some kind of passivity, an inactivity, which permits the death of the human nature on account of a certain incompleteness in the latter's divinization.

6. From the Nicene Creed. —Trans.
7. From the Nicene Creed. —Trans.

Divinization comes into its fullness only in the resurrection and is accomplished only by the Father's power through the action of the Holy Spirit.

The kenosis of Christ is expressed in the acceptance not only of death but also of mortality. The latter also include the acceptance of suffering, as came to pass in the passion of the cross (not to mention the possibility of experiencing hunger, thirst, fatigue— the frailty of the human body in general). All these together are proper to the possibility of the human nature assumed by the Lord in his humanity, and his divine nature permitted their realization; all these were included in the life of the God-man as a son of Adam. The difference between the death of the God-man and the death of the sons of Adam lies in the unavoidable nature of the latter and the violent imposition involved in the former. But even this violence already presupposes for its possibility the Lord's assumption of the mortality of human nature together with the capacity to assume bodily sufferings. Christ's corporeality, and more generally his humanity—although distinct from typical humanity and surpassing it by virtue of his incipient divinization—is still weakened from the start by virtue of the original sin living in man. The humanity of Christ is created Sophia, permeated by Divine Sophia and in this union with it already pre-deified. Nevertheless, this creaturehood remains damaged in comparison with its primordial condition, which was free from mortality (though not incapable of it), as the very possibility of the original sin demonstrated. Created Sophia, as the human nature of Christ, admitted of further sophianization or divinization, which is exactly what was progressively accomplished in the resurrection of Christ and in his glorification. The latter is the fullness of divinization, the sophianization of created Sophia in Christ, its full penetration by Divine Sophia, perfected divine-humanity. Over this divine-humanity in its glory, death and suffering no longer have any authority; rather, divine-humanity itself already wields authority over them with respect to all humanity, for it bears within itself the power of universal resurrection. That is, the very possibility of resurrection, as a perfected divine-humanity, presupposes the sophianicity of Christ's nature in the union of the two natures of Sophia, the divine and the created. And in this lies the order of the universe, as the union of eternity and time, of fullness and becoming.

But here we must focus our attention on another side of the incarnation, this time not just the sophiological side but also the trinitarian, specifically in relation to the incarnation in the life of the second hypostasis and with it in the life of the entire Holy Trinity. The incarnation in its hypostatic aspect must to be understood, first of all, as the hypostatic kenosis of the Son, which expresses itself in his acceptance of the limits of human nature: "Having humbled himself, having accepted the form of a slave." The antinomy of kenosis consists in the fact that the Son, while preserving his abiding "in the heavens," "on the throne with the Father and the Spirit," also during his incarnation lives in the world as man in the process of divinization and only at the end of the journey as the fully deified man, or more precisely, the God-man. And on the paths of this life there is accomplished that acceptance of the entirety of human existence—of course, without sin—the acceptance of suffering and death. This acceptance must be understood in the most realistic sense, i.e., not only as the permitting of it and agreement to it but also as the very exhaustion and eradication[8] of death— as dying. It is a fearsome thing even to utter a thought such as "the dying of God," but it is precisely this that the Gospel tells us, that revelation attests. And there is no place here for any sort of docetism, the acceptance of which would turn our entire hope into a myth. The matter at hand concerns exactly dying and death . . . of God in man, of the God-man.

But to what extent can we speak of the *God-man's* death in particular? Here in the first place let us draw upon the analogy of human death. Even in this latter case we distinguish death from annihilation. The death of the human person is not a complete annihilation but only the dissolution of the complexity of human nature, that tearing away of the spirit from its (soul-animated) body that occurs in dying. Furthermore, death, as a division, presupposes as well the possibility of a new reunification of spirit and body in the resurrection. Their division in death thus presupposes a two-fold process—a spiritual and a bodily one. The spirit, after that most agonizing separation from the body, is handed over to the post-mortem state in all its inferiority; the body gives itself over to decay while nonetheless preserving in itself the vital power for resurrection together with the immortality attendant on the latter. And so, of course, *a fortiori* in the case of the death of the God-man.

The inscrutable mystery of the divine-human death unites in itself not only human death but also the dying of God. Yet in this inscrutability there are revealed to us certain features connected especially to hypostatic triunity. The guiding principle in comprehending the inscrutable mystery of the incarnation still remains the fact that it must be comprehended in light of trinitarity. Although it is the specifically the Son, the second hypostasis, who is incarnated, still in his taking on flesh he is not separated from the Holy Trinity but instead abides in divine union with the Father and the Holy Spirit. This union, indestructible in eternity, "in the heavens,"

---

8. The verb Bulgakov uses, *iszhit'*, finds no economic translation into English. Here it expresses an eradication that follows upon a full experiencing or living out of some trial, such that in our case Christ eliminates death precisely by exhausting it in fully living through of the process of dying. —Trans.

is also indestructible, in its own way, in the incarnation as well, "on earth." And in the incarnation we find the co-participation of all three hypostases, each in its own manner: the Father sends the Son, and this sending is an act of fatherly sacrificial love, the kenosis of the Father, who condemns to the cross the beloved Son, who takes on himself this feat on the cross. The feat of the Son is also the self-denying love of the Father who, in "sending" the Son, condemns his very Self to co-suffering and co-crucifixion, though in a manner different than the Son. Because there is the God-man's passion on the cross, there is also the fatherly passion on the cross, the passion of co-suffering love, of fatherly self-crucifixion. We must understand the "sending" of the Son by the Father not as an act of authority, as a command, but rather as an act of agreement, initiative, origination, all of which are hypostatically proper to the Father. This sending includes the complete fullness of accepting the God-man's passion through the divine fatherhood. Even human fatherhood gives us an image of the oneness of the life of a father and son in their destinies, despite the wholly limited nature of fatherly and filial love in humanity. Still, the Father and the Son possess one life, one joy and suffering, although in a different manner. We cannot even say that the Son suffers but the Father does not suffer, or that the first suffers more and the second less—rather, both co-suffer together. The salvation of the world and the redemption, the divinization of man, is one act of the Father and the Son. The Son accomplishes the will of the Father, and this unity of will and of mutual knowledge ("no one knoweth the Son, but the Father, neither doth anyone know the Father, but the Son" [Matt 11:27]) testifies to the unity of life and the unity of suffering in their common—although distinct for each—kenosis of love.

But the same co-participation in the redemptive sacrifice of the Son is proper to the Holy Spirit as well, who *is sent* into the world by the Father, both onto the Most Pure Mother of God, in order to accomplish the divine-maternal conception, and onto the Divine Son in his ministry. The Holy Spirit rests on the Son as the abiding principle of the incarnation. But to that extent the kenosis also includes him. "The Spirit of the Lord is on me, for he has anointed me . . ." (Luke 4:18). The ministry of the Son is the ministry of the Holy Spirit as well, or more precisely, his co-ministry. This co-ministry is the love of the Father for the Son uniting them in bi-unity, just as this very union is hypostatic Love itself, the Holy Spirit. But we must understand even this hypostatic love of the Holy Spirit as a participation in self-diminishment, dying, and death, although not the death on the cross. It is impossible that when the Son dies the Holy Spirit resting on him should not also co-die with him and in him, if only because the Spirit "abandons" the Son in this dying. The dying of the God-man is therefore not only the co-dying of the Father but also of the Spirit, of the Holy Trinity one in essence and undivided.[9] But how is this Trinitarian co-dying expressed?

Let us pause at the Son of God's vexation at death, about which he himself says, "My soul is sorrowful unto death" (Matt 26:38). What can this mean, this abjection of the Son of God on whom rests the Holy Spirit, Love and Joy itself, Glory itself, by which he is glorified by the Father? Does this grief not signify a certain activity of the Father towards the Son and the Spirit? This activity is expressed in the first place with the prayer of the suffering Son: "My Father! If it is possible, let this cup pass from me; however not as I will, but as you will" (Matt 26:39). And "again, having withdrawn another time, he was praying, saying, 'My Father! If it is not possible that this cup pass from me, that I not drink it, let your will be done'" (Matt 26:42), but the Father sent him to suffer, he commanded the Son to drink the cup that, to that extent, the Father himself drank with him, in his fatherly love. But this same activity of the Father is expressed not only in the command to drink the cup and in the sending of the Son to the passion, but also in the *abandonment* of the Son: "around the ninth hour Jesus cried with a loud voice: 'Eli, Eli, lama sabacthani?' i.e., 'My God! My God, why have you forsaken me?'" (Matt 27:46). What could this abandonment mean—for the Father, for the Son, for the Holy Spirit, for the Holy Trinity one in essence and undivided, for its one substance in Divine Sophia? We must, of course, immediately reject any understanding of this abandonment that would suggest the separation of the second hypostasis from the divine triunity, and, consequently, that would entail the division of the Holy Trinity; such an idea would be blasphemous. The eternal (ontological) triunity of the Holy Trinity is susceptible neither to diminishment nor to division.

Yet the "economic" triunity in relation to the creation of the world and the redemption—although expressed in the distinct activity of the individual hypostases—also remains unshakable, and only in its accomplishment is it accompanied by a changing interrelation of the hypostases. One such change is the descent from heaven and incarnation of the Son who was sent from the Father, together with the sending down of the Holy Spirit into the world and onto the Son who was taking flesh; but a similar change also occurs in the abandonment of the Son by the Father. Such a change, of course, must be understood economically and not ontologically as it applies to each of the hypostases, and most of all with respect to the Father. What does the "abandonment" of the Son by the Father mean? Is it the cessation of the Father's love for the Son? But this is impossible and

9. "The Holy Trinity, one in essence and undivided" is a quotation from the Liturgy of St. John Chrysostom, spoken by the people before the recitation of the Nicene Creed. —Trans.

completely out of the question. Nevertheless what is not impossible, and, on the contrary, what does in fact take place is the cessation of the palpability, of the manifestation of this love. The fatherly love as it were withdraws into itself, it does not reach the Son. The Son as it were feels a separation or distance from the Father, a kenotic-sacrificial solitude on the cross. The cup did not pass, it had to be drunk by the Son—such was the will of the Father. But this will was not merely some imperious and powerful, authoritatively commanding will. It is a rending action within the Holy Trinity: for the Son, the fatherly love withdraws in the Son's utmost suffering, and this is the greatest sacrificial aspect of the Father's love. The Father "abandons" the Son not in that he stops loving him but rather in that he ceases to manifest to him this love, he makes it impalpable, it is hidden in the heavens whose veil becomes impenetrable: a darkness covers the earth in which the Son of God, alone, tastes death on the cross. "From the sixth hour a darkness was over the earth until the ninth hour; and around the ninth hour (when the darkness of divine abandonment was completely exhausted) Jesus cried with a loud voice (as if in the person of this entire God-forsaken world)[10] 'Eli, Eli, lama sabacthani?'" (Matt 27:45–46). And this was already death: "Jesus, *having cried out again* with a loud voice, gave up the spirit" (Matt 27:50). The command of the Father to drink the cup of death was fulfilled. But the verdict extended as well to the Father who commanded: of course, in this case *not* in the divine-human but in the divine acceptance of co-tasting the Son's death through fatherly love. On Church murals we often see the Father depicted grieving over the Son's death on the cross, but the Son was alone in his abandonment, from him was concealed both the love of the Father and his grief. The Son remains alone in his dying, just as Father is, as it were, deprived of the Son in his sacrificial "It is finished" [John 19:30]. "For God so loved the world that he gave his only-begotten . . . so that the world might be saved through him" (John 3:16–17). Not long before had he taught his disciples: "I have come from God. I have come from the Father and I have come into the world; and again I am leaving the world and am going to the Father" (John 16:27–28). But this coming from the Father and into the world was not yet an abandonment. On the contrary: although "you all will abandon me, still I am not alone, for my Father is with me" [John 16:32]. But the hour came when the Father hid himself and God abandoned him. "Eli, Eli, lama sabacthani?"

But how can we understand this abandonment of the Son by the Father in the former's dying? The answer to this can be given only in light of our

10. "Divine abandonment" and "godforsakenness" both translate the same word (*bogoostavlennost'*), although now in a noun form and then in an adjectival form. I alternate between these two terms as context necessitates. —Trans.

understanding of the very *bond* of the Father and Son in their co-abiding, their union *before* the onset of the Son's division from and abandonment by the Father. This bond of love is their hypostatic union in the Holy Spirit. He is the hypostasis of love and hypostatic love itself. And by the Holy Spirit who proceeds from the Father onto the Son, the Father loves the Son, just as the Son, receiving onto himself the reposing of the Holy Spirit, in him loves the Father. The abandonment of the Son by the Father means the removal of the Holy Spirit who reposes on the Son. The Father as it were ceases to send his Spirit onto the Son. Once again, we must remember that, ontologically, in "the heavens," in the life of the Holy Trinity, the mutual bond of the hypostases is unbroken and there can be no room for any sort of mutual abandonment. But "economically," in the relationship of God to the world, as Creator to creation, there occurs, as it were, a division of the hypostases because the very hypostasis of union, the Holy Spirit, in "abandoning" the Son ceases, as it were, to unite the Son with the Father and instead remains with the Father.

This can be explained in the following manner: The Holy Spirit, as the incarnating hypostasis, by whose activity the incarnation is accomplished, abides on the Son, yet no longer by the deliberate sending from the Father, as it was at the baptism [of Christ], but rather by his own activity. The world in the God-man is as it were separated from the Father, although the Holy Spirit, by his own power, maintains the world in being, even if the world is shaken to its foundations. "And behold, the curtain in the temple was torn in two from top to bottom" (Matt 27:51)—this is a symbol of the separation of heaven from earth during which the divine hypostatic presence is as it were interrupted as a result of the cessation of the power of the Old Testament temple as the place of divine presence, namely the presence of both God and his Glory.[11] And this mystical shock is accompanied—and could not but be accompanied—by a convulsion in the elements of the world (although this was limited in its outward visibility): "and the earth shook, and the rocks split" [Matt 27:51]. What was accomplished then prefigured the final hour of the world at the second coming of the Son of God.

But it is appropriate to pause here at the thought of what exactly this abandonment of the Son by the Father in the Holy Spirit meant for hypostatic love itself. Although the Word of God does not directly speak of it, we nonetheless have all the data necessary to draw a conclusion on this matter. If the Holy Spirit is the hypostasis of the Father and Son's love in the Holy Trinity, then what could it mean for the Trinity, the cessation, as it were, of

---

11. For Bulgakov's understanding of God's Glory, see the excursus, "On the Glory of God in the Old Testament" in Bulgakov, *The Burning Bush*, 117–30. —Trans.

this love in the "abandonment of the Son by the Father"? We can comprehend this only by analogy with the mutual separation of the Father and the Son. The abandonment of the Son by the Father can be understood only as the Father's participation in the dying of the Son, in the suffering of a love that is self-denying, sacrificial. But what then can we understand concerning the hypostasis of love, for whom it becomes impossible to love, since the work of this love has become "abandonment," an involuntary inactivity, as it were? Love not loving, as it were, for the sake of love, perfect efficacy abiding in inactivity—this inscrutably contradicts the hypostatic quality of the Holy Spirit. Human language does not even possess the words to express this impossibility of Love itself becoming unable to love, and there is no idea by which we can comprehend it. "The Spirit blows where it wills" (John 3:2), but now the Spirit stops blowing on the Son, he ceases, as it were, his respiration. Perhaps it would be most natural to express this impossibility—which makes love impalpable, non-existent, as it were, for the beloved—as "death," or more accurately, as that same dying in common with the Son. Together with the dying Son the Father co-dies, the Holy Spirit co-dies, each in his corresponding hypostatic character, and only in this trifold co-dying is the dying of the Son accomplished. Precisely this is the death of the Son, its precondition.

The co-dying of the hypostasis of love relates not only to this one hypostasis in its separation from the others; the Father and the Holy Spirit co-die in their mutual union, alongside the dying of the Son, one together with the other—the Father with the Holy Spirit. For the union of love unites them in the deathly grief of co-dying as well. Even in humanity, in the dying of a son and in the grief of a father who loses his son, is there not at the same time also the grief of a brother or daughter, and not just grief over the deceased but also grief for the one who is losing him? The grief is mutual, two-fold. Therefore the image of the Holy Trinity, although preserving its trifold character, nevertheless in this grief appears as if in an eclipsed light. This is not a division but rather a union in dying for each of the hypostases in its own way, true both individually and for all of them in conjunction. There can be no ontological disunion of the Father and the Holy Spirit from the Son, even though he be abandoned by God; instead, this "economic" abandonment is accomplished in full measure as the Son cries no longer to the *Father* (as was still the case in Gethsemane, Matt 27:39, 42) but instead to *God* in the words of the Psalm: "My God, my God, why have you forsaken me?" (Ps 21:2). And the psalm continues further: "Far from salvation is the word of my crying; my God; I cry throughout the day—and you do not hearken to me—by night, and there is no comfort for me" (Ps 21:3; Matt 27:46; Mark 15:34). It is through this abandonment that the dying of the

Son occurs, a dying that concludes with the "*It is finished*" addressed to the Father in the Holy Spirit: "Father, into your hands I commend my spirit" (Luke 32:45), the death on the cross. But here we read specifically of *dying*, in which the power of death, mortality, becomes manifest. And the dying of the God-man is for the God-man himself a divine abandonment. If the grief of [the Father and Holy Spirit's] co-dying consists in the abandonment of the Son, in separation from the filial hypostasis, then [the Son's] dying itself consists not only in grief but also in the *power* of this abandonment: "Being one of the Holy Trinity,"[12] he remains alone and solitary in this abandonment. This terrible loneliness—for him who speaks of himself in the following manner: "The one who sent me is with me: The Father has not left me alone" (John 8:29) and "The Father is in me, and I in him," (John 10:38)—now attests that he is abandoned by the Father, and this constitutes the onset of death, dying itself.

What then does it mean, the abandonment by God of the God-man who is God according to his divinity—how can this occur? Or did the union of the natures cease, and the one abandoned was no longer the God-man but merely a man, such that the incarnation did not, as it were, succeed, having ended with a division of the natures? But this idea—by itself blasphemously ridiculous—is subverted by the testimony of revelation concerning the resurrected and glorified God. What then does this deadly abandonment mean for the God-man himself? Or does it signify, if not a division, then such an extreme measure of kenosis of the divinity in Christ, such a diminishment of it, that we have practically already arrived at that same division of the natures? And yet such a division does not, in any measure, occur; furthermore, it is not even approached. Instead, divinity kenotically reduces itself to potency, abolishing itself, as it were. How can this be? Through the salvific love of the Father and the Spirit, a love that fully divides itself from the Son, in accordance with the decree of trinitarian love. The Son himself kenotically empties himself, "diminishes himself" [Phil 2:7]. Although he is the God-man, he reveals himself only as a man. And he thereby exposes himself to death, becomes susceptible to it, assumes mortality.

But one may ask, is such a measure of kenosis possible without already being a "division of the natures"? Is such a victory of death possible, which is followed not by resurrecting life but by the onset of decay? No, it is impossible, for it has been said, "You will not abandon my soul in Hades and you will not let your holy one to see corruption" (Acts 2:27; Ps 15:10). Kenosis is nothing more than a *state* that may be adopted by divine being—temporary

---

12. A quotation from the hymn "Only-Begotten Son" from the Liturgy of St. John Chrysostom. —Trans.

and transitory, as the *path* to resurrection. But kenosis is not mortal existence itself, which is what divine existence would be transformed into in such a case. In the depths of kenosis there is a weakening, as it were, of divinity, but only until the end of kenosis, when this weakness is overcome. Such is the immanent dialectic of kenosis in divine-humanity. In its kenosis it is capable of dying, but the death of the God-man can only be a victory over death: "having trampled death by death." And yet, if death is impossible for the God-man, then through kenosis he is made susceptible to dying. Nevertheless, this dying, while not representing the genuine death of decay, is still that *condition* of death in which the Lord rests in the grave. The God-man fully experiences death, he partakes of it, although he is not handed over to its power in his divinity and in his divinized humanity. His divine-humanity enters into the fullness of power and glory precisely through dying.

The kenotic character of the humbling of Christ is expressed in the fact that while it represents the fulfillment of the Father's will through the removal of the Holy Spirit, it remains at the same time something he *voluntary* accepts. When Judas arrives with the multitude of people carrying swords and spears who were sent by the high priests and the elders of the people, the Lord says to the one who cut off the ear of the high priest's slave: "Or do you think that I am not able to pray to my Father now and he will not offer me more than twenty legions of angels? But how then will the Scriptures be fulfilled, that it must be so?" (Matt 26:53–54). This is a mysterious admission of the possibility, as it were, that the suffering of Christ could have *not* been accomplished on account of his prayer to the Father concerning the matter, and that the command of the Father for him to take the cup was after all not a coercion of the Son but instead represents the Son's voluntary acceptance of it: "Not as I will, but as you will . . . let your will be done" (Matt 26:39, 42). And only after this acceptance do the sufferings of Christ begin: the insulting, the spitting, the striking, the exhaustion (right up to the "I thirst" from the cross [John 19:28]). The will of the Father and the Son meet and become identical in the Holy Spirit: "It is finished" (John 19:30). Divine abandonment is overcome. This kenosis unto death must be understood not only with regard to the hypostasis but also to the nature of Christ in the unconfused and undivided union of divine and human nature, of Divine Sophia and created Sophia. In the divine abandonment of Christ, the Divine Sophia becomes, as it were, inactive in him; what remains in full force is only the human nature, created Sophia, although in a state of suffering and mortal frailty. This sophianic kenosis—which *prima facie* appears to be a division of the natures, as it were, in the humanity's loss of divinity—is the *path* to their fullest union in the resurrection. Humanity, created Sophia, needed to be revealed in the depths not just of the positive power belonging to it as the image of Divine Sophia, but also in its Adamic nature, weakened by the fall and communing with death. But in this union with Divine Sophia, created Sophia communes in this divine nature, and in this union she reaches the greatest depth of kenosis: the depth of human frailty is disclosed to the utmost through Christ's voluntary acceptance of humanity's fall for the sake of humanity's restoration and salvation.

Butthis kenotic character of the death of Christ does not make that death easier or, so to speak, illusory. There is no room here for docetism. It is precisely its kenotic unnaturalness that makes it the death of all deaths, mortality itself (see *The Lamb of God*),[13] the universal death of all humanity. The difference that remains consists in the fact that what takes place for man in dying is the fullness and victory of death; this, of course, is not the case in Christ's death. Christ through his death conquered human death on the path to resurrection. Christ is the one who resurrects, freeing his humanity from death, but for the full completion of this liberation he must drink the entire cup of death, which the Father gave to him for the salvation of humanity, with all that cup's bitterness. We can say that in this fullness of death, or more accurately, in the fullness of Christ's dying, the death of every human and of all humanity is included. If Christ redeems and raises every person, then it is only because he co-dies in every person and with every person. It therefore follows that Christ, glorified and sitting at the right hand of the Father, even now suffers and dies with the humanity whose collective suffering and death he once took upon himself and exhausted on Golgotha. We pause here at the idea of the identity of the one, unique, personal, and universal death of Christ and the multiplicity of all personal human deaths included in this "pan-death." This paradox of death leads inevitably to the conclusion that Christ continues to partake of the cup of death together with every dying person, continues to suffer with him the pain of death and to co-die with him in deathly exhaustion. We have already had occasion to express this idea in connection with the interpretation of the Gospel narrative (John 19:34) concerning the outpouring of blood and water from the side of Jesus, the story concerning the Holy Grail.[14] This story encompasses the more general idea of the co-presence, co-living, and co-suffering of Christ on the earth together with his humanity. The Holy Grail, the blood and water from the body of Christ which remain on earth, is the most general symbol of the continuing feat of Christ in which temporal extension is identified with accomplished and abiding eternity.

---

13. Specifically, chapter 5, II. C: "The Death of Christ and His Descent into Hell," in Bulgakov, *Lamb of God.* —Trans.

14. Bulgakov, *The Holy Grail and the Eucharist*, 1997. —Trans.

How can we approach this holy mystery, to what degree is it accessible to us? It is dreadful thing, but it must be said: it becomes accessible to us, in full measure for every person, in his own particular dying—which just *is* the death of Christ, as a dying with him, the revelation of death concerning death. For, as an act of dying, the death of Christ is precisely a human death. In the maximum degree of kenosis, the one abandoned by God is humanized; in dying, Christ has cast off divinization. The God-man in dying is a man whose divinity is concealed from his very self; it is concealed for us too who are divinized through him. In death Christ abides with us on the same level, as it were—the level of human helplessness, suffering, and the horror of those sitting in darkness [Ps 107:10]: "Thou hast laid me in the pit of the netherworld, in the darkness of the vestibule of death" [Ps 88:6]. If Christ honored human nature by assuming it, then he also honored it by the assumption of human mortality, because without the latter the assumption of human nature would have been incomplete, docetic, and therefore powerless as well. And to the extent that we know, or rather, *will* know our own particular death, in it and through it shall we know the death of Christ too. But until we have reached the very threshold of death and have drunk the cup of death, we can only foreknow our death, and in it and through it Christ's death. Such *fore*knowledge is accessible to us and possible, for it reveals to us our own—as well as Christ's—humanity, in its depths and in its terrible abyss; in the light of death it manifests to us our very selves. And to whom it is granted by the will of God to approach this edge of the abyss, let him from *thence* become a herald, that *thence* which for each person will at some point become a *thither* and a *there*.

It was granted to me to become such a herald, and I sense a call and duty to relate what I learned there. But how deeply I feel my own impotence—a dumbness that grows as I am further removed from that place. The frailty of forgetfulness and the force of profanation, of immersion in the elements of the world, blunt this revelation of death, or more accurately, of dying. The expanses of forgetfulness gape wide, swallowing up more and more of what I lived through, and I feel that a sinful muteness prevents me from speaking what God commands me to say. It is a fearful and joyful thing to fall into the hands of the living God [Heb 10:31] . . . .

***

In March of this year (1939) my disease was diagnosed: a throat cancer that demanded a quick operation, two in fact. The most probable outcome was death, and the best case scenario—the loss of my voice forever. I poorly understood the medical side of things. But I can say that the way I met and experienced this enormous news was truly a miracle of God. I experienced neither fear nor grief; rather, I experienced a joyful rousing in response to the call of God. What saved me from anxiety (I knew already that both operations would take place without general anesthesia and therefore portended great suffering) was a certain feeling of curiosity related to the danger—a characteristic quality of mine. Here is how Pushkin describes it:

> There is a thrill in battle,
> at the edge of the dark abyss;
> All that threatens with death's rattle
> conceals for mortal hearts
> inexplicable bliss.[15]

At the time of the first operation I observed the procedure by a mirror placed above me on the ceiling, which reflected all the details of the incision on my throat (tracheotomy), and it was somehow still interesting to me, even if also agonizing. In the second operation certain measures were taken to prevent such observation, and my consciousness was dulled anyway by narcotics. Nonetheless, here too I heard the doctors' evaluations and remarks, and as much as I was able I observed the procedure with full consciousness, taking in,[16] of course, all the pain, but no fear. From grief and fear was I liberated by the power of God, and I recall this with a joyful feeling of deep tenderness. Yes, this state was some kind of delight, which I was able to share even with others. On the final Saturday and Sunday before the operation, I heard the confessions of and gave communion to my friends and bade them farewell, and, insofar as I can judge, there was no grief found in them either, just as there was none in me. There was only the delight of love. Now, I considered myself then and consider myself now a man of cowardly spirit, and I receive this joy as a miracle of God, as an act of the Holy Spirit. Of course, it was a difficult and terrible thing on account of those near to me, my family, but this too was somehow miraculously tempered.

In such a state did I arrive at the clinic the day before the operation,[17] just as cheerful and calm. The second operation followed two weeks after

15. These verses are culled from different sections of Alexander Sergeyevich Pushkin's *A Feast in Time of Plague*. —Trans.

16. Here Bulgakov uses a key verb, *vosprinimat'*, which we have translated as "assumed" in the directly christological portion of the text. It is a recurrent feature of this portion of "The Sophiology of Death" that Bulgakov will apply to his experience the christological language and scriptural citations that he explored at length earlier in the piece. —Trans.

17. This is the note that I composed (unexpectedly even for me, since I had long ago already stopped writing anything down) not long before the operation. 6 March 1939.

the first—the second fell on Holy Tuesday, during Holy Week. I had already lost my speech after the first operation and had unreflectively transitioned over to the pen. This was somehow taken for granted and not even burdensome. My sufferings began on Holy Week, when my throat had been cut open and breathing became especially agonizing and difficult on account of the suffocating, mucusy, revolting bandaging, which turned me into some sort of immobile bundle deprived of movement and sleep. It goes without saying that I was deprived of food as well, for I was not able to open my mouth for any swallowing movements, and much less was I able to swallow through my bisected throat. There was placed on my nose a revolting pipe through which some sort of liquid was poured. "I thirst." And "I tasted vinegar" (John 19:28, 30).[18] But it was not this that was most agonizing; it was not the pain but rather the suffocation, the shortage of breath joined with the deathly, unendurable weakness. There were a few occasions, primarily at night, of terrible, murderous suffocation when I was objectively on the edge of death. During the entirety of my illness I had never lived through anything as agonizing as this. Sometimes this was relatively short, though violent, and at times it was prolonged, accompanied by a state of darkened half-delirium, and on top of that, I did not escape the state of humiliating dependence on the machine that freed (or more often did *not* free) my breathing from the mucus.

This was dying—with reprieves, but without any ray of hope. I was immersed in some kind of darkness, with a loss of consciousness of space and time and with only a confused memory that it was Holy Week, that Good Friday fell on the same day as the Annunciation.[19] I was chronologically conscious of the beginning of Easter: I received Easter greetings, but the darkness of Golgotha did not dissipate and remained unbearable; Paschal joy was lacking for the one who was dying and yet to whom it had not been

"Thy will be done. Today death looked me in the face—either death from a cancerous tumor of my vocal cords, or from the operation with equally deathly dangers, or from unavoidable muteness. I humbly and submissively, even calmly, accept God's will. I am not so bold as to say: 'My wish is to die and to be with Christ,' but I warmly greet life beyond the grave. The only thing that makes my heart ache is parting from my loved ones and their future, but I trust the Lord, the Master of life and death, that he will not abandon them. I am trying to ponder how and with whom I must be reconciled, whom I ought to console and to show affection, what to do. . . . I am trying to recall all people and not to forget anyone. May the Lord send his angel of light. Once already I died spiritually at my ordination, and now, dying in the flesh, I would like to make my peace with it and to come to love all . . . Glory to God for everything."

18. Bulgakov here is quoting the Scriptures, but the Russian past tense for "he tasted" is equivalent to the Russian "I tasted." The verbal ambiguity heightens Bulgakov's assimilation of his sufferings to Christ's. —Trans.

19. 1939 in the Julian calendar. —Trans.

granted to partake of death. Yes, death did not approach—it was only dying. In days past it had been granted to me to experience death with its joy and its liberation, but here only its fetters and gloom were felt. What became of that joy and what remained of that delight I was granted to know before the operation? It was as nothing, or rather, worse than nothing, only a deathly shadow in the pit of the grave [Ps 88:6]. The light of life was extinguished; what set in was that ungraced insensibility of which it is written: "why have you forsaken me?" True, there remained a dull awareness that I abided in the will of the Almighty, and more specifically that this will had determined for me to suffer or that it had somehow permitted this for me as something inevitable. As far as I can recall, there was no thought of death, it seems, not even for a moment. There was no expectation of it, no horror in the face of it—my consciousness was severely suppressed and my thinking was blunted. I was too far from the light of death in my dying, too immersed in my suffocation, my soul was too cast down by my bodily suffering. Nor was prayer any longer a way of ascending to God, just as there had been no ascent for the Abandoned One. It was all a joyless night without dawn, without morning. There remained the feeling of physical sufferings, but even this paled in comparison to the general feeling of losing strength of spirit, it paled in comparison to the abandonment . . . perhaps it was precisely this that was most terrible . . .

So what did remain in me that was still human? Did anything remain at all? Yes, something remained, and this was some sort of final miracle in my suffering soul: love remained. I loved my brothers, and I loved all people. Moved by love, I ran in my mind through all whom I knew from the past, both those I loved and those I did not, as well as those whom it was an easy and joyful thing to love and those whom I found it difficult to love. But I could only love, and I loved all whom I could remember. I do not know whether this was love in God. It seems that it was, and probably it was so—how else could I have loved? Of course, from among those at my bedside, some brought me more joy than others, some comforted me and others tired me, but no one was able to destroy the harmony of love that somehow broke through the dissonance of my day of death.

But where was my thinking? Was it ever extinguished in me? Where were the "problematics" that were always drilling their way into my head? Where was that complex of ideas, both inspiring and gladdening, with which I crossed the threshold of this very hospital? It was as if all of it was extinguished, as if it had stopped existing. I was empty; thinking was, apparently, no longer endurable for me. My existence was impoverished, simplified to the point of just bodily existence, having become only the possibility of suffering. Did I feel the nearness of God? Yes, it was palpable insofar as nothing distanced me from God except bodily suffering, since everything else had fallen away. This nearness of God, this standing before him face to face, was a tremulous thing. In my illness I neither earlier nor later, never and in no way opposed God's will, nor did I grumble or ask him for mercy or for freedom from suffering; I received it as God's unchangeable and undoubtable decree. And in this respect it was a terrible and holy nearness, as it was for Job. But . . . it was not joyful, for . . . it had been thoroughly permeated by one thought: why have you abandoned me?

But along with this there was another thought that up to that point I had not known and that constituted for me a genuine spiritual event, which will forever remain for me a revelation—not of death, but of dying, with God and in God. It was my dying—with Christ and in Christ. I was dying in Christ, and Christ was dying with me and in me. Such was the terrible and shocking revelation that at that point I, most likely, could not have been able to express in words and concepts and that I came to recognize only later. Only one temporally incalculable moment passed between "why have you abandoned me" [Matt 27:46] and "he gave up the spirit" [Matt 27:50], between the dying of Christ in his divine abandonment and his death. But this moment contains the non-temporal extension and fullness of dying for each person insofar as he dies by it and in it, for no man can die except through divine abandonment, and the same was true for the All-Man, the New Adam, in the God-man.

I knew Christ in my dying, his nearness was palpable for me, almost bodily, but . . . it was the bodily nearness of a "corpse injured and bruised" lying beside me [Isa 53:5]. He was able to help me in my suffering and in my dying only by co-suffering and dying with me. I saw this image with my inner vision, I felt him as Holbein had felt him and Dostoevsky after him in his terrible image of the death of Christ,[20] which communicates to us not death, however, but rather dying; not the power of a posthumous transfiguration concomitant with resurrection and on the path towards it, but instead a death that is frozen and halted in the process of dying. This perfectly corresponded with the deathly days of Holy Week, which had entered and penetrated my being. Previously, in days of health, I had opposed Holbein's image of the corpse as an unbelieving and blasphemous depiction. Today it has come to life for me in this image of death as dying, as the revelation of death in human dying in the God-man. There is another, equally soul-rending image of the suffering of Christ: the Christ of Matthias

20. The painting in reference is The Body of the Dead Christ in the Tomb, by Hans Holbein the Younger (1497–1543). It is famously described in Dostoevsky's novel, The Idiot, as a painting that could provoke the loss of faith. —Trans.

Grünewald.[21] But this was something different, and for that reason it did not come to mind. Grünewald's crucifixion is only a moment in the dialectic of death, a moment inseparably connected with the resurrection in glory, which a number of other depictions in the polyptych portray. Grünewald presents a terrible image of death in its cadaverous state, after dying is finished and is therefore exhausted. But in Holbein—though also through an image of a corpse—we can get a sense not of accomplished death but of a dying that is still in progress, a sense of dying's very power.

That is how I felt it, not in ideas but with an inner knowledge, at that time when I myself was lying together with him, not dead but only dying, not yet a corpse but in a cadaverous state that was not living and yet not dead either. To this Christ I was not able (or I still at that time did not know how) to pray; I only could love him and co-suffer with him insofar as he was co-suffering with me. Through my—human—dying was revealed to me his—human in the God-man—dying. Divinity was, as it were, extinguished in divine abandonment, and it was the humanity that was dying. The dying that took place in the death of the God-man could only be accomplished in a human manner, i.e., in the divine abandonment of the man. That dying was identified with all human dying and in this sense it was universal, encompassing all forms of human dying, all deathly illnesses; it was their synthesis. And the common content of all these myriad dyings was death. The God-man in his divine abandonment revealed himself, made himself susceptible to dying. Death came to him in his humanity. And this dying was the torment of all human torments. In his humanity the dying that took place was natural, i.e., it was not made easier by some dissolution in divine power. It was accomplished in extreme kenosis, as if in a division of the natures, which, of course, could not occur *as such* in the ontological sense, by virtue of the undividedness of both natures in Christ; rather, in the inactivity of one of the natures the other remained in its own proper power. In this self-abasement of the God-man lies the salvific power of his death, with its humanity serving as the path to its divine-humanity. Christ was dying our *human* death in order to make it the death of the God-man. For this very reason, our dying, as a co-dying with him, becomes a revelation of the death of Christ, though not yet a revelation of his glory. Here I came to know the meaning of these words of the apostle: "We always bear in our body the death of the Lord Jesus so that the life of Jesus might be revealed in our body. For we, though living, are unceasingly handed over to death

21. The painting in reference is Crucifixion, the center panel in the Isenheim altarpiece commissioned for the Monastery of St. Anthony. The painting was meant to bring solace to the disfigured to whom the monks tended. It is considered Matthias Grünewald's (1470–1528) masterpiece. —Trans.

for the sake of Jesus so that the life of Jesus might be revealed in our mortal flesh, so that death is at work in us, but life in you" (2 Cor 4:10–12). And furthermore: "All creation together groans and suffers until now; and not only creation, but we ourselves also, having the first-fruits of the Spirit, and we in ourselves groan, awaiting the adoption and redemption of our body" (Rom 8:22–23).

In dying I did not die and I did not come to know the light of death (as it had been given to me earlier), but thus I remained in dying, if not forever, then for a certain and prolonged period of time. And when the doctor, after one of his regular visits, unexpectedly said to me: *"Vous êtes guéris"* [You are healed], and he proposed to send me home from the hospital, I had not sensed any improvement, except perhaps that at this point there were fewer bandages. And the agonizing weakness, the absence of the feeling of life, as is the case in dying, accompanied me all the more now that there occasionally arose the need to move, and more generally to *live*. I began to force myself to engage in any kind of activity, like reading, while as if in a fog, and half-consciously did I again pick up my usual religio-philosophical subjects. This was still bearable and somehow natural. But the feeling of divine abandonment, which had not left me, remained a continuous dying. In this gloomy silence my soul languished, prayer became mute, and life was unjoyful and ungraced.

Oh, at that time too there was no room anywhere in my being for grumbling. On the contrary, "Thy will be done," and "Glory to God for everything," unyieldingly resounded in me—so unyieldingly that they admitted of neither verification nor doubt. If it is possible to call this un-yieldingness joy, some sort of grace of faith, then this was granted to me, this joyful fortitude in bearing what had been sent to me. But the joy of encountering God did not accompany this nearness of God, a nearness that I had nonetheless come to know even in my dying. My life was left joyless. And what is most important, joy in the Church was lost, in Church prayer and Church feasts. The weeks of Pentecost came and went, and I recognized this with my mind but not with my heart. My life was shrouded in gloom, and the cross of my muteness lay heavy upon me. I was forced to use hand-written notes to speak with my family, with my wife,[22] my son,[23] with those close to me, and this created a unique suffering of degradation and shame, as it were. But the main suffering came from the recognition that I would never again be able to stand at the Holy Altar and celebrate the liturgy. It is impossible to communicate this in words. True, even this failed to wrest

22. Elena Ivanovna Bulgakova (*née* Tokmakova), 1868–1945. —Trans.
23. Sergius Sergeevich Bulgakov, 1911–2016. —Trans.

from me any hint of grumbling, for my heart was resolved in resignation:
"God has given, and God has taken away, blessed be the name of the Lord"
[Job 1:21], but its gloom remained undissipated. This gloom deepened especially after I was told by an allegedly competent source that I could count on
regaining my speech. Although I had been told the opposite as well, still this
did not penetrate my consciousness. This continual dying lay on my life in
the Church like a dark cloud. I was still in no state to go to the liturgy. But I
felt no need for this. I was still not able to begin receiving holy communion.
The day of the Holy Trinity approached, as well as the day of Holy Spirit, the
21st of May, the anniversary of my ordination—and these days, which had
always been so solemn and holy for me, I now contemplated with anxiety
and abjection, like a dead man. . . . It was in this feeling, it seemed, that my
suffering was concentrated, this dying without death . . . .

And suddenly it was interrupted by God's mercy. This miracle occurred
by means of a faithful, loving friend who brought me joyous news from the
doctor, whom he said had vowed that my voice would return. Of course,
now I know what a complete exaggeration this vow was. But how shocked I
was then and how delighted by this news, which nonetheless promised me
the overcoming of my silence! It was as if heavenly light had broken through
the darkness of my being. God showed me his kindness. With tears of joy I
sobbed like I had never before in my life. Blessed be the Name of the Lord!
On the eve and day of the Holy Trinity I was at church, and on the day of the
Holy Spirit I participated in the Holy Mysteries (after confession) in my own
home. The day of my ordination was more joyful for me, it seems, than ever
before. My friends made my home overflow with their presence and with
flowers as they greeted my resurrection to life.

Dying came to an end. Life began, with its new tasks and difficulties.
Dying did not eventuate in death, but it remained only the revelation of the
path of death that, in the footsteps of Christ, lies before every person, like
it or not. Death lies in man's fallen nature itself, which Christ assumed in
his mortal human nature. Every illness is already knowledge of mortality,
a revelation concerning it, which no one can escape, and the extent of that
revelation is determined by the strength of the illness, by its nearness to
death. Objectively, I was a hair's breadth away from death in the first half
of my illness, but subjectively I was almost completely engulfed by death
and therefore came to know it. I came to know it as the dying of the Lord
on the cross in his divine abandonment even unto death, from the "why
have you abandoned me" to the "into your hands I commend my spirit."
Dying does not contain a revelation of death itself; it provides only a taste
of it, and precisely to those who have left this world irretrievably behind.
Beyond the gates of death follows the revelation of life beyond the grave as

the beginning of a new existence, concerning which this-worldly human existence can tell us nothing. Dying in and of itself knows the revelation neither of post-mortem life nor of resurrection. It is the night of day, original sin itself. We may forget about death, turn away from it, and, of course, the sole content of life should not consist in the premonition of death. But by forgetting it one cannot escape from it—it comes sooner or later to every person, and this is only a matter of time.

Nevertheless, if in dying itself the experience of death in its reality and fullness remains inaccessible to us, at least some anticipation of this experience remains possible. This anticipation is even independent from that sequence of time between dying and death. In a strange manner it was granted to me to experience just this anticipation of death, approximately fifteen years before this latest illness. After the deadly torments of dying, it seemed to me then that I had once already crossed the threshold of death with its light, joy, finality, as well as with its escape and liberation from dying. At that time everything became other than it was: instead of darkness—light, instead of divine abandonment—theophany. I cannot recount this except by reproducing the record that I made then immediately after the illness, when strength permitted.

***

My Illness (January 1926)

I have not suffered any serious illness in life. And often, especially lately, I had become perplexed (particularly when this is occasionally pointed out to me by others) that all those around me were ill while I had always been healthy. And this became especially difficult because the multitude of my sins pressed upon me more and more heavily. I could sense both God's anger and his saving love, and I was inadvertently expecting something to happen, knowing that God is not mocked [Gal 6:7]. I was living with the feeling that God's hand was upon me.

I fell ill on the day of St. Seraphim, and for the first two days I remained on my feet, though feeling feeble. But on the third day my temperature rose and I felt that I had entered into a grave and dangerous illness. Day to day my temperature was rising. My suffering was great, especially in light of the fact that I was not sleeping at night, and my consciousness—as it seemed to me, at least—would not fade for even for a minute. Time stood still. I don't know if my fever continued for a month or for a year. In any case, whatever was happening then is impossible to measure with time, much less with such a short duration. I was living with such intensity and tension, with all the strength of my sinful and repentant soul, that the minutes opened out to eternity; there was God and I before him with my sin. Overall I lost consciousness of any definite place in space and time; only temporality and extension remained. I completely lost awareness of the fact that my body, my sensorium, was located on a bed, since for me it bled into the other rooms and into space in general, and only with difficulty could I find a small part of myself in my immediate possession. A similar blurring occurred also with respect to the unity of my "I" because I felt myself as some sort of "*we*," a plurality, and only with difficulty could my proper "I," as a certain confused point, enter into this plurality. Broadly speaking, time came to me only in flashes, whenever something was done to me, particularly the operations for my flow of urine, which had stopped; these were very agonizing for me.

In a word, my "I" melted in the heat and became fluid and flowing. But my spiritual "I" reached an increasing acuity and consciousness. It was the unvarnished judgment of my life. I was in fear and trembling [Phil 2:12]. It was like walking from ordeal to ordeal, during which the searing wounds of my soul were being uncovered. But the Lord had mercy on me then and protected me from demonic visions. Yet the feverish state together with the spiritual agonies created a fiery furnace. Only now do I understand why the Church so loves the image of the fiery furnace and its burning, only now do I understand what the Church says about this image. For I was burning in it, but I was saved as if through fire [1 Cor 3:15]. Suddenly, in this burning furnace, I felt a certain coolness. That guardian-angel who descended to the youths in the furnace, he approached me as well and cooled my blazing body and saved me. It is impossible to express this in words, but as of that day, I now know how one can burn without burning in the fiery furnace.

It was in the first period of my illness—whether long or short, I do not know—that I experienced this fiery furnace.

***

And suddenly—after this burning—a cooling and comfort penetrated into this fiery furnace of my heart. How to communicate this miracle of God's mercy, this miracle of forgiveness? But I felt it with all my being, I felt its limitless joy and ease. The guardian angel who was constantly with me put this into my heart.[24] I suddenly felt that nothing separated me from the Lord, for I was redeemed by the Lord. . . . Even in the act of confessing my sins I felt that I already possessed forgiveness. The feeling was this: my sins have burned up, they are gone.

But this mystery of forgiveness was revealed to me only in connection with the mystery of death, for simultaneously I felt that my life was coming to an end and that I would die. But where, then, was that fear of death? It did not exist; there was only the joy of death, joy in the Lord. Joy—heavenly, ineffable for the human tongue—filled my entire being.

This is how it happened. On Saturday the 10th (this entire turning point took place on Saturday the 10th through Sunday the 11th, when the Church was praying for my recovery), I felt I was at the end with this debilitating illness—and I was horrified at the thought of death. This horror was predominantly connected with an agonizing concern for my family that would be left behind, a concern for their life after me and without me. My heart was filled with cowardice and lack of faith. But at this time support was sent to me, just one word from a friend, telling me that everything was kept in the will of God and that it was not necessary for me to worry about my family. This word entered directly into my heart, and I felt with joy that God, who was granting me mercy and salvation, would save and have mercy on them also, that I must entrust them to God. And when I, in my heart, thus entrusted them to God, I felt the unknowable joy, peace, and freedom of the "now let your servant depart" [Luke 2:29]. And that very second I felt like my family, which this whole time had been inextricably connected to my heart by love and concern, as had all my other loved ones, became *separated* from me, had withdrawn somewhere, that I had died and was beyond the border of this world.

In me everything shone with a special joy. An awareness arose in me that everyone was alive and near, both the living as much as the dead. I spiritually sensed that *everyone* was with me, and at the same time I somehow realized that my physical sufferings would still not allow me to bodily communicate with those at my bedside. By turns I summoned to myself and spiritually kissed those who were long, long dead, and I did the same for the living too. I was equally free with respect to my sense of place: I was now in my beloved, dear Crimea, and it was the summer of my son's death in 1909, with its rays of sunshine.[25] But even to this place I was not bound: the pres-

24. For Bulgakov on guardian angels, see chapter 2, "The Guardian Angel" in Sergius Bulgakov, *Jacob's Ladder*. —Trans.

25. Bulgakov's third child, Ivan (Ivashechka) Sergeevich Bulgakov, died before reaching four years of age (1905–9), as a result of complications from dysentery. Bulgakov writes of his son's death in *Unfading Light*, 14–16. —Trans.

ence of God reigned over *everything*. I had always understood that there is only God and his kindness, that we must live only for God, must love only God, must seek only the kingdom God, and that anything that overshadows this is self-deception. I was calling for and could sense the nearness of the More Pure Mother of God, but I lacked the strength to ascend. Later I moved—as if by some sort of inner command—forward, out of this world and to that place: to God. I was racing with swiftness and freedom, with nothing holding me down. I knew by some sort of trustworthy inner feeling that I had already passed our time and current generation, that I had passed the next generation too and that after them the end had begun to shine. Brilliant were the ineffable lights accompanying the approach and presence of God; the light became brighter and brighter, the joy more inexpressible: "which no man can utter" [1 Cor 12:4]. And at that moment a certain interior voice from a fellow-traveler—I was alone, but together with a certain *we*, which was my guardian angel—said to me that we had gone too far ahead and that we must return to life. And I understood and heard with my inner ear that the Lord would return me to life, that I would recover. Today I can no longer comprehend what this was, but the *very same* voice and command that had liberated me from the life of this world had at the same time and by the same word also decreed my return to life.

Within myself I already knew that I would recover. I was still not better, yet I was completely at peace, because I had heard God's command. But from death I returned to life, my entire sinful being having been completely consumed in the fiery furnace. I felt I was liberated from the heaviness of sin and tried not to hold on to it even in memory. I felt like a newborn, because in my life there had occurred an *intermission* through which the liberating hand of death had passed by. I cannot fathom and do not want to sinfully pry into what the Lord was pleased to do with me, but I testify with my mute tongue to the deeds and wonders of God. Lord, accomplish your will! Every day of my existence and every beloved human face I now meet with a new joy. Only may the Lord grant to me and to them to live in the light that God has revealed. Who is so great a God like our God? Thou art the God that doest wonders [Ps 77:13–14].

***

At that time, I experienced a pre-revelation of life after death and the joy of the age to come, as well as of the continuation and end of history. This was completely different from dying. In dying I did not yet feel myself to be totally isolated, insofar as solitude still contains within itself the sense of a lost connection; but here even that was lacking—I was just left alone. At that time I was disconnected from people and events, from ideas and hopes, from history; it was empty, dark, dark and terrible. By contrast, in death—to the degree to which it drew near to me—I experienced myself as included in the fullness, in the apocalypse, in the revelation of the age to come. Death was pulled away like a veil concealing the life of the age to come. Naturally, only its beginning was partially revealed to me who was dying but not yet dead. Yet even this beginning was already qualitatively different from the darkness of dying. In it I was granted the experience of knowledge of the spiritual world in connection with the human world (inaccessible within the limits of our life here). Of course, each person dies in his own manner, just as destinies and states beyond the grave are different for each. But alongside the horror of dying there was experientially revealed here as well the joy of death as the continuation of life, its triumph, the victory of death with Christ, "having trampled death by death."

Of course, these images of revelations are fragmentary and incomplete, and it is precisely their disintegrated and unfinished character that leaves us in ignorance and later plunges us again into the waves of forgetfulness. But a certain knowledge and comprehension remain all the same. And this is necessarily sophiological. How can we understand dying and death in light of sophiology?

The dying of the human nature in Christ correlates to his abandonment by divinity. This abandonment, as we have already grasped, is expressed not only in the suffering of the Son, become human and sent by the Father into the world through the Holy Spirit, but also in the co-suffering together with the Son of both these hypostases, in accord with the hypostatic character of each. This shared suffering of all the hypostases in the abandonment of the Son is a triune act of divinity that expresses itself in its sophianic self-determination. Although Divine Sophia in her mutual relationship with created Sophia is not separated from the latter—which would be impossible, for that would abolish creation's very being—she becomes as it were inactive, and it is this that constitutes Christ's dying. Although human nature or created Sophia bears the image of Divine Sophia, thereby manifesting within her the features of divine triunity, she nonetheless abides in this her *human* unity, albeit in a weakened and as if devastated state. For fallen man, this weakness and devastation is the natural condition. His connection with Divine Sophia does not yet contain in itself the immutable durability that would ensure immortality. But human nature in the God-man, sharing the possibility of death with man despite also bearing within itself the image of divine triunity, nonetheless also suffers as a result of the divine abandonment of man. The connection of Divine Sophia with created Sophia is, of

course, preserved, for otherwise a division of the natures would take place—
something excluded by virtue of their indivisibility and lack of confusion.
But the connection's *effectiveness* is suspended. Such a suspension is possible precisely on the grounds of the lack of confusion between the natures,
thanks to which each of them preserves itself and in no case dissolves in
the other. It is for this reason that this relation between them is possible, in
which each of the natures, while remaining in union with the other, abides
in a mutual inactivity, and the created Sophia in Christ becomes receptive
to dying, although not to death. She, so to speak, allows herself to undergo
this dying, yet with a view towards forfeiting this possibility in the resurrection, in which the actuality of divinity is restored through its activity in the
God-man. God, through the Holy Spirit, raises the God-man, who himself
is raised by virtue of his salvific feat. This raising-resurrection signifies precisely the overcoming of death through the restoration of the fullness of the
union of Sophia, both Divine and created, in the Holy Trinity: the Father
raises the Son by the Holy Spirit and the Son is raised in him for the Father.
His divine-humanity is restored in its fullness.

***

There arises a final, most dreadful and difficult question of Christosophiol-
ogy: *why* was death permitted in Christ, with all the torment of his dying
and divine abandonment? Surely it could have been removed by the power
of divinity in the union of divine and human nature? Surely it would have
seemed more natural not to conquer death by death, as the Church testifies:
"having trampled death by death," but instead to have destroyed it through
immortality?

In becoming human, Christ accepted Adamic, mortal nature: fallen
Sophia. This fall and mortality of human nature was weakened in him personally through his holiness as the only sinless One. The qualities of human
nature were raised to the level of *posse non mori*, to the possibility of *personally* not tasting death. Nonetheless, this possibility was, so to speak, only a
de facto state of the still-mortal Adamic nature, but it was not yet a victory
over death. The overcoming of death by divine power was merely its *de facto*
suspension, but by no means was it an inner victory over it. Such violence
against human nature would have been nothing other than the abolishing of
the incarnation itself, which presupposed the assumption of a human nature
both genuine and unalterable by divine violence. This would not have been
the genuine divine-humanity that was called to the salvation and redemption of human nature. The Lord had to assume humanity as it had become

in reality after its fall, weakened to the point of the condition of mortality. Only by having made mortal humanity immortal, "having trampled death by death," could the Lord restore fallen human nature and, having accepted death, raise it to immortality. It was not a new, re-created Sophia, or one forcibly freed from mortality, that the Lord had to accept for the restoration and renewal of her fallen image in man, but precisely the genuine, fallen created Sophia. Christ's acceptance of fallen humanity had as its goal the raising of that humanity to the capacity of receiving complete healing, no longer locked behind the inner gates of sin. This was possible not on the basis of divine violence or some sort of new creation but rather on the basis of a free feat of love, obedience, and sacrifice. The sacrifice on the cross was manifested in the "It is finished," which opened the gates of immortality and healed created Sophia of Adam's fall. Nevertheless, the object of this restoration had to be accepted in its fallen form, to the point of the cry, "I thirst," and only through the divine quenching of this "I thirst" did the "It is finished" occur—the sacrifice of love was finished, manifested by created human nature in its relation to God and to man. The divine nature in the God-man, Divine Sophia, in its kenotic self-diminishment, awaits this salvific, human "I thirst" of the dying God-man so that through the "finished" union of the natures it might trample down death by death, might bestow immortality to human nature. Not through the omnipotence of a new creation by God but through the sacrifice of love was the victory over death accomplished, the overcoming of kenosis with the fullness of both natures in the life of the God-man. This is how the victory was accomplished—a victory not only over death but also over mortality itself.

Thus the sophiological meaning of the concept of mortality in the God-man becomes apparent. Created Sophia, the fallen nature of Adam, was assumed into Divine Sophia through the union of the natures; it had to be elevated precisely from the depths of its ontological fall, the latter itself being the mortality of the God-man. This depth needed to be exhausted to the utmost by Christ's tasting of pan-human death together with his personal death. The entire fullness of human nature in its perfection was revealed in the created Sophia, in the human nature of the God-man, albeit with a weakened vital force, with mortality, which is precisely what had to be overcome in the God-man. It is in this that the sophiological meaning of the death of Christ becomes apparent, its necessity as the path to glory. "Now is the Son of Man glorified" [John 13:31], for "a grain of wheat does not come to life unless it dies" [John 12:24].

But another, further question arises. Human dying, which the Lord accepted for the salvation of men, concludes with death. "He was rejected from the land of the living, for the crimes of my people he endured the punishment, . . . the Lord was pleased to strike him, and he handed him over to torment" (Isa 53:8, 10). This is clear, but when and how did this begin? There stand before us here two facts in all their expressiveness. The first fact consists in the Lord's natural freedom from illness, connected to his holiness and his imperviousness to death: *posse non mori*. In the Gospel there is no direct indication of the fact that the Lord, though he experienced the power of bodily weakness (hunger, weariness, thirst), was subject to personal illnesses inherent to his own life. On the contrary, we can say that the personal path of his life could have proceeded as free from illness as it was from death. And yet he turned out to be susceptible to death and to dying. How then could this prove possible? Still, we know that the Lord's death was not a natural but rather a violent death. In this sense it was also a death free from illness, i.e., it did not occur as a consequence of any illness of the body or soul. True, it is said of him: "A man of sorrows, acquainted with illness" (Isa 53:3), "He took on himself our weaknesses and he bore our illnesses" (Isa 53:4), "His countenance was more disfigured than any other man, and his appearance—more than the sons of men! (Isa 52:14). And the prophecy of Isaiah is confirmed by St. Matthew: "He healed many with demons, and he cast out the spirits with a word and he healed all the sick, that what was spoken through the prophet Isaiah might be fulfilled, who said . . ." (see above, Isa 53:4).

What could this mean, this acceptance by the Lord of our weaknesses and his bearing of our illnesses? He "gave his spirit over to death" (Isa 53:12). There was not and could not be another path to death besides this handing over of himself to torment, the bearing of our weaknesses and illnesses. But these were not illnesses in the strict sense, like the inevitable bodily diseases that are proper to man in all their diversity. On the contrary, this was a voluntary acceptance of them—"He was oppressed, but he suffered willingly" (Isa 53:7), for "the Lord was pleased to strike him, and he handed him over to torment" (Isa 53:10). For this to occur it was necessary that the human nature in the God-man become susceptible to mortal suffering, and this was his will, in agreement with the will of the Father: "The Lord was pleased to strike him, and he handed him over to torment; when his soul offers the sacrifice of propitiation; . . . the will of the Lord will prosper by his hand. He will look with satisfaction on the feat of his soul: through his knowledge he, the Just One, my Servant, will justify many, and he will bear their sins on himself" (Isa 53:10–11). This means that the Lord became susceptible to mortal suffering not, however, because this was unavoidable for him, but rather because it was accepted by him willingly. Therefore, this mortal suffering needed to have a beginning, and this corresponds with the doom of the cross, with the acceptance of the cup. This spiritual event is indicated with perfect clarity in the Gospel, first as an inner event, after the confession of Peter on the mount of transfiguration (the conversation with Elias and Moses concerning the "exodus" to come) (Luke 9:31) and later in Gethsemane: "He began to be sorrowful and abject. . . . My soul is sorrowful unto death. . . . My Father, if it is possible, let this cup pass from me; nonetheless not as I will, but as you will" (Matt 26:37–39). "My Father! If it is not possible that this cup pass from me, that I should not drink it, let your will be done" (Matt 26:42). "See, the hour has come, and the Son of Man is handed over to the hands of sinners; . . . see, my betrayer is at hand" (Matt 26:45–46).

If the impassibility of Jesus, just like his immortality, was supernatural, having its foundation in the union of the two natures, then in the kenosis of Christ, which was realized in the sufferings of the cross, this supernaturality leaves room for the weakness of the human nature, which here comes into its own. The passion of Christ occurs already on the foundation and within the limits of the human nature. Of the Christ who stands wearing the crown of thorns and the scarlet robe after his beating, Pilate says the following: "Behold the Man!" (John 19:5), and as the Man he humanly exhausts human sufferings and death.

Yet this relates to the kenosis of the passion by which Jesus Christ "was made like man," having become obedient unto death on the cross" (Phil 2:7–8), "in all things having become like his brothers" (Heb 2:17). There was a time, before the acceptance of the cup, when Jesus was *not* like his brothers, but instead only concealed within himself the possibility to be such, when he *differed* from all humanity by the illness-free perfection of his human nature, when he appeared as the *Healer* of humanity. The greater part of the Gospel narratives concerns these healings: the casting out of demons, the freeing of the sick from various illnesses and even the raising of the dead (although this was not a total victory over illness and much less over death). The quantitative measure of these healings are described in the Gospels in the strongest of terms, such that we would imagine a *universal* healing, if this were compatible with the other testimonies of the Gospels and with the general flow of human life. It is said that, "He went around all Galilee . . . healing every disease and illness among the people" (Matt 4:23), and in all of Syria and the like. This same power was given also to the apostles, "to cure every disease and illness" (Matt 10:1 and parallels).

But what exactly does this healing mean, what relationship does it establish between those cured and the Healer himself, who is free of disease? On the one hand, there is clearly established here a border between him and those healed, but at the same time it also unites them, and not only by the very fact of the healing, but also by his "taking upon himself our

illnesses and by the bearing of our diseases." The Lord accepted the humanity of Adam, weakened by mortality and burdened by sin, but at the same
time he remained free from it personally. In the presence of this freedom,
the Adamic nature in Christ preserved its power and its connection to his
divinity. Precisely through this connection was healing possible in Christ,
the same healing that he communicated to the apostles as well, just as this
healing activity was also proper to holy men in the Old and New Testament.
The Lord was carrying out his healings by his human, albeit divinized,
power—by his divine-human sanctity, but not by the divine omnipotence of
the Creator, which can initiate a completely new life. The decisive witness in
favor of this fact—that here we have only healing and not a new creation—is
the presence of illnesses and diseases in man. In the Gospel story we see
Christ who is invariably surrounded by the sick and who grants them healing. Their quantity is defined with the strongest of expressions: "He healed
all the sick" ("every disease and illness"). Nevertheless, this statement cannot be taken literally, because the sick are mentioned again and again. It
follows that the sick received healing but illness was not rooted out in humanity, this illness that up to now remains in humanity with all its strength;
Christ came to diseased humanity and was surrounded by it. Diseases in all
their diversity are tied to man's very nature. Sometimes these were simply
bodily diseases that arose due to unknown causes, just as they do now; at
other times, their cause is known, as in the activity of an evil power that
cripples and disfigures human life. But, in the final analysis, there is not and
there cannot be any man who is free from disease, and this basic fact is not
abolished even by the appearance of Christ in the world. The Lord does not
obviate this fact itself but instead only offers individual healings, just as the
discrete instances of raising the dead do not annihilate the general mortality
reigning everywhere as it had before. The cemetery and the hospital are the
abiding companions of human existence, neither one abolishing the other.

Although the Lord made use of various forms of healing the sick (and
raising the dead), all these were accomplished not through omnipotence
but rather through the God-man's *prayer*,[26] just as other Old and New Testament healings were accomplished. Although disease and death are for each
individual the consequence of causes unknown to him, as if from some
personal *fatum*, like the fate of Job, nonetheless they remain susceptible—
once again to a degree unknown to us—to the power of *prayer*. Prayer ac-
companies man in his illness and dying. Christ abides with him at his sick
bed and on his deathbed: this is a necessary postulate of faith. We pray to

26. See my essay "On the Gospel Miracles" [translated into English by Boris Jakim
and published as *Relics and Miracles: Two Theological Essays* —Trans.].

Christ, to the God-man, to the Healer and Resurrector, to God who has
returned to heaven and sits at the right hand of the Father, to God who is the
Holy Trinity (and also to the Most Holy Mother of God, in addition to the
saints). We pray to him with our *human* prayer. But if all that has been said
above concerning our dying in the Lord is correct, then we must necessarily
conclude that in our dying we are accompanied also by his divine-human
prayer in human divine-abandonment. "Why have you forsaken me"—he
uttered this not only about himself and from himself but also in the person
of all humanity. There are no grounds for exceptions here, unless someone,
through his personal resistance, should prove capable of making himself
an exception. Nonetheless, this is one of death's mysteries: to what extent
such resistance is possible once a person finds himself before the face of
God. I think the possibilities of unbelief and rebellion in the afterlife are not
as unlimited as they are often considered to be. But I repeat: the personal
lot of a man, his form of participation in disease, is a mystery that remains
hidden. This is especially apparent with respect to hereditary diseases. There
are no words to express the human grief over these diseases and their rending inscrutability. In the Gospel many diseases, especially spiritual ones, are
explained by the direct action of evil spirits. Yet even the very allowance
of their influence is a mystery (as was shown in the story of Job). Not only
psychic illnesses, however, but also all other inherited diseases bear in large
part the character of a heavy, evil doom weighing on humanity due to the
power of original sin ("in diseases you will bear children" [Gen 3:16] can
refer not only to physical childbirth but also to the diseased nature of the
child born).[27]

The Lord dwelt in the world, "healing and doing good"—for this the
Spirit of the Lord had sent him (Luke 4:18; Isa 61:1–2). Nevertheless this
pertains only to those who met him on his path, but the diseased condition
of humanity remains in full power even after these healings, which had the
significance only of a personal, individual act of charity. And this power is
preserved undiminished even to this day. It pertains to the very condition of
humanity that was assumed by the Lord. Therefore, although the Lord himself was personally free from disease, he did not reject even for himself the
possibility of illness inherent in the weakness of human nature. Therefore, it
was he alone who could assume it, who could "bear our diseases." He made
himself susceptible to them, so to speak, in the incarnation. Infirmities and
diseases were the path to death, with death being, as it were, their integral.

27. The Russian word *bolezn'* ("disease" or "illness") comes from the same root as the
related *bol'* ("pain" or "ache"), thereby enabling Bulgakov's interpretation here. —Trans.

The Lord accepted infirmities in order to conquer them in himself: having trampled infirmity by infirmity and death by death.

Hence, we must conclude that the sufferings of Christ, bodily and psychic, were included in their entirety in his dying and in the passion of the cross. They contained in themselves the entire fullness of human diseases—not quantitatively, of course, like their collective sum (that, of course, would be ridiculous), but qualitatively, as the torment of all torments. This means that the dying and death of each person, just like the sufferings from every disease, are included in the sufferings and death of Christ. And this allows us to understand that every person dies with Christ, and that Christ co-dies with each person in his disease, in his suffering. This is the cost of redemption, as it were.

And when I return again to my personal, miserable, and unhappy condition in disease and dying, they become comprehensible, those troubled thoughts and anxieties to which I was subject on the bed of my unfinished dying, and afterwards also, even up to the present day. These tell me that my illness (operation included) was illness in Christ, an illness of his divine abandonment, and that I could lean my unhappy, wounded body against his suffering human nature. That was not and is not blasphemy but rather revelation. And how could it be otherwise? How could Christ, who has become human, separate himself from any of us after he has united himself with us? If he healed the sick in his earthly ministry by his touch, gaze, and word, then here, in deadly illness, will he not touch our mortal, dying body? And therefore again we say: in the diseased, dying human body it is Christ who co-suffers and co-dies.

This idea, insufficiently recognized in theology, is sometimes revealed to the intuition of the artist. In iconography, the Lord in the tomb is often depicted with certain conventional, dignified features, even in his beatings, torture, and most extreme torments, or he is depicted in a state of post-mortem calm, in the quiet victory of the spirit over death. The requirements of pious contemplation conceal from the eye the rending and humanly unbearable depiction of Christ's passion, although for fostering a prayerful disposition, such stylization may in fact be fitting. But besides the demands of iconographic depiction, there remains another possibility for artistic theological meditation that finds its expression in the religious art wherein such contemplation is inscribed. While not pretending to exhaust this immense theme, we cannot help touching on this once more in connection with the depictions of Christ by Holbein and Grünewald. With both depictions, and differently in each case, one is shocked by the lacerated and disfigured human image of Christ, "the naked and lacerated corpse" (*The*

Lamentation of the Mother of God),[28] "marred beyond human semblance" (Isa 52:14): "There was in him no beauty or majesty . . . there was in him no beauty that would attract us . . . to him" (Isa 53:2). Here we find depicted the dead human body in its painstaking natural anatomical features, to the point of wounds and pains.[29] What is this? Merely the efforts of impressionism achieving the greatest impact, more strongly striking the nerves? That is, is this all just something contrived? Or is this the salvific, albeit also dreadful, thought that he truly "took upon himself our infirmities and bore our pains," in all their cruel, ruthless reality, from which we cannot turn our face and divert our thought, even if not all can bear it, or rather since only a few can? In any case, depicted here is a contemplation of paramount importance, one that is also expressed in its own way in our divine service books (especially in the divine services of Holy Week). Here this takes on artistic form, through which the dreadful, ruthless thought becomes as it were weakened. In both these artists, beauty is sacrificed to ruthless truth, and it is precisely the hideousness that shocks us. This is precisely that horrible truth of human dying . . . and to him to whom it was once granted to come to know co-dying with Christ, it is no longer possible to bypass this truth to which art testifies and instead to prefer sentimentally embellished depictions, just as it is also impossible to prefer iconographic patterns with their abstract conventions of theologoumena, which lack any anthropological data. Icons exist for theologically meditative prayer, and religious art for human comprehension. . . .

There is a profound reason why the depiction of the human sufferings of Christ and his dying became the lot primarily of religious art as opposed to iconography. This is because iconographic depictions of Christ have as their subject his divine-humanity: here through the human face his divinity shines through, and all that is human becomes a symbol of divine-humanity. In this sense the icon is symbolic. It has as its subject unrepresentable, transcendent-immanent being, which strives to transcend the image. Included here is everything related to Christ's glory, to his glorified state, to the resurrection and to all that follows after the resurrection and is connected with it: the appearance of Christ on earth, the ascension and the sitting at the right hand of the Father. Here a painting would be inappropriate and even impossible; only a symbol is fitting, albeit a symbol of divine-humanity, meaning

28. A devotional prayer focused on Christ's crucifixion from the perspective of Mary, known as the *Lamentation of the Most Holy Theotokos* and composed by Symeon Metaphrastes (ca. tenth century). —Trans.

29. Art history testifies that Holbein used as his model the corpse of a drowned Jew. Grünewald too depicts him not merely in dreadful pain but also by endowing him with a body that is similarly dreadfully distorted and lacerated.

that the features the symbol portrays as illuminated by divine radiance are still *human* features.

But something similar occurs in the iconographic depictions of the entire earthly life of the Savior, from the birth of Christ up to the death on the cross. On the one hand, paintings of events from the Gospel are possible here, but only if they have no symbolic intentions of depicting Christ's divine-humanity. Deliberately limiting themselves to the human image of a certain historical figure, they can be free of any relation to religious truth and can even be foreign to it. On the other hand, in these too there can be a religio-symbolic intent—to reveal the face of the God-man, the incarnation of God on earth. Here naturalism encounters a limit, insofar as its very purpose is removed, with all historical events being depicted as metahistorical or metaphysical. The kenosis of the incarnation does not conceal in these depictions the radiance of divinity. The same applies as well to the depictions of Christ's passion, not in its human divine-abandonment, in the depths of kenosis, but in its divine-humanity, in which the radiance of divinity shines. Included here are the various kinds of images of Christ's passion, of his burial, of the "shroud."[30] In all these there is not and cannot be any depiction of suffering and death, which would be proper to religious art in the aforementioned sense or, in fact, proper even to a simply historical painting. We can say that in both instances the very theme or intent will be different: in one the human kenosis predominates, though not without the vision of and awareness of divinity; in the second, the veil covering the kenosis is completely transparent, it abolishes those dreadful features of human suffering that are proper to human dying. Therefore, it becomes completely clear that the first depictions either cannot in any way possess the significance of an icon (Holbein) or they receive this meaning only in connection with another icono-symbolic depiction (like in Grünewald's triptych, in which the crucifixion is only *one* of various paintings, with the others relating to the resurrection and glorification).

The question can be posed, finally, yet another way, specifically concerning the character of the pains and infirmities borne by the Lord. The book of the prophet Isaiah speaks in a universal fashion concerning the Lord's acceptance of our infirmities and pains, indicating no exceptions (chapter 53); it speaks of his face as "disfigured more than any other man, and his appearance more than the sons of men" (52:14). Perhaps it is precisely this that gave biblical grounding to the depictions of Christ by Grünewald and Holbein, both of whom went further on this point than

---

30. The "Shroud of Turin," a linen cloth believed by some to be the burial cloth of Jesus of Nazareth. —Trans.

other artists. They in fact gave expression to the most horrific and repulsive pains that disfigure man beyond all measure. But are there grounds to include in the number of these pains even those that have their origin in sin and vice? "No place in my flesh is whole because of your fire; there is no peace in my bones because of my sins. For my lawlessness hangs over my head, like a heavy load it drags me down. My wounds stink and fester because of my folly . . . for my loins are inflamed, and no place in my flesh is whole" (Ps 38:4–6, 8). What is the psalmist describing here that bears the marks of Job's pain and that is connected at the same time with our sins and with the wrath of God upon them? And yet the psalmist prays to the Lord for help and salvation (vv. 23–34). But how then can this help be given other than through his being accepted into the Lord's bosom? It may seem audacious and blasphemous if from this we draw the straightforward conclusions about the Lord's body that Grünewald and Holbein did in their artistic work. Here artistic "silence is simpler."[31] But is it possible simply to avoid an answer here, even if only through silence, and thus to *limit* Christ's acceptance of human pains, excluding certain sorts of pains? And does this mean that these pains remain unhealed even beyond the resurrection, such that those suffering from them will be doomed eternally to "diseased loins" [Ps 37:7], that all those Jobs will remain on the bed of suffering? But then there arises a further, even more unanswerable question: if it is still somehow possible to understand, even if not to accept, the eternal decay of those who have sinned, what then can we say of their children or their children's children who languish under an unbearable responsibility and who also decay from illness? Such an idea is unacceptable. And if at first it was said, "the fathers have eaten sour grapes, and the children's teeth are set on edge," i.e., that the power of a bad, grievous inheritance is justified, then later (Jer 31:29 and the following) this blind destiny is expressly rejected and personal responsibility affirmed.[32] But because of this, the inherited transmission of illnesses and the fateful power of heredity become still more tragic and incomprehensible.

It remains for us to recognize that there is not and there cannot be any limit to Christ's assumption of human illnesses and sufferings. Yet at the same time we must completely leave behind the idea of ever enumerating how many illnesses he accepted, of cataloguing these illnesses. We

31. Cf. the *zadostoinik* from the Feast of the Liturgy of Nativity of the Lord. —Trans.

32. In those days they will no longer say, "the fathers have eaten sour grapes, and the children's teeth have been set on edge" (Jer 31:29). "Why do you employ . . . this proverb, saying, 'the fathers have eaten sour grapes, and the children's teeth have been set on edge.' As I live, says the Lord God—henceforth they will not say this proverb in Israel" (Ezek 18:2–3). Cf. Deut 24:16; 2 Kgs 14–16; 2 Chr 25; Ezek 18:19–20.

must simply believe that the Lord accepted *all* illnesses, as the "illness" or infirmity of the entire fallen human nature, with no exceptions, and that by himself or in himself he healed this nature and redeemed it.

But this by no means implies that the Lord, so to speak, underwent all these illnesses in their empirical discreteness, which, clearly, was not and could not have been possible within the given time, and which in any case would have been completely unnecessary. But the Lord did assume and did live through the entire *power* of all illnesses and sufferings in the *form* of his passion on the cross, which contained this power as a certain integral of human infirmity and mortality. In him every human illness and suffering found a place for itself, and that was sufficient. It was not necessary that the Lord personally experience every individual ailment, but it was necessary that he himself not remain a stranger to any human suffering—not externally, but internally, assuming it and sharing it. *All* illnesses are the *one* illness of fallen Adam whom the Son of Man came to heal and to save by his cross.

***

And so, what then is death in the light of sophiology? Is it a certain ontological mistake, one that could have not been and even should have not been? In that case, it can simply be removed by an act of divine omnipotence, through an amendment of creation. But on this view, would not the sacrificial death of Christ itself be nothing more than such an amendment? Clearly, such an idea is both confused and blasphemous. It must be rejected without discussion, as diminishing divine creation and its Creator along with it. Death must be understood not negatively, as a certain "minus" in creation, but positively, as flowing from the latter's very foundation. Its true source is original sin, which weakened and injured humanity; the source of sin, on the other hand, and that which determines its very possibility, is created *freedom* as the highest good and most valuable possession of man. Man could not handle the possession of freedom with which his Creator honored him, and in his fall he lost his spiritual equilibrium, he became a *slave* to his nature, and this slavery is both death and mortality. To save man from sin and to restore his human nature by a victory over death, two paths were possible: the first path available to the Creator—if one could even consider it a path—is the destruction of the Old Adam, the overcoming of fallen man through the creation of a new, recreated man. This idea implies, essentially, a certain acknowledgement on God's part of his, as it were, failure in creation and of the necessity of correcting it. But if this is so, how then could a new creation be made? If it were repeated, then where is the guarantee that the new man would prove worthy of this freedom and would not sin again —a repetition recurring without end? In such a case the only conclusion turns out to be that man is completely unworthy of freedom and is incapable of using it other than on the paths of sin and satanization, instead of divinization.

The removal of sin from the world (in the form of an imaginary victory over it) can be understood in yet another way besides as an act of divine omnipotence manifesting in a new creation or the recreation of man. It can be understood instead as an act of human might, a "common task"[33] that physically overcomes death. It is impossible not to bow before the enthusiasm of that great thinker who felt death to be the main, central, and unchanging task for all humanity and who never on this point allowed any deviation of thought. At the center of human creative work he placed precisely this victory over death as the universal resurrection. To be precise, it is a matter of resurrecting dead bodies through collecting and vivifying (through spermatozoa?) their decomposed parts. The idea here represents, in a certain sense, the technological victory of human compassion, of the familial love of sons for their fathers. But this view lacks the victory over mortality in freedom, the trampling down of death by death. What remained to the end unrecognized by Fedorov was the problem of victory over death; the problem was always conceived within the limits of a mechanico-naturalistic achievement, as a "regulation of nature." Fedorov was indignant that there was ascribed to him (by Vladimir Solovyov) the idea of resurrecting our ancestors back to that condition in which they had lived on earth. He understood that such a resurrection could not be resurrection as new eternal life. Nevertheless, he did not have at his disposal the means for overcoming death other than through mechanical "regulation," and this was not the resurrection, which must be accomplished not from without but from within: not a bodily victory but a spiritual overcoming.

The power of death is the power of original sin, which made itself known through freedom in the acceptance of the world's captivity and, in the end, in slavery to mortality and to death. The overcoming of death can take place only through a restoration of freedom, through combat between slavery to death and freedom from it. This freedom is the return to the sinless and pre-sin state of man, which, however, had already become the state of sinfulness after man's sin. Christ, although having accepted a body weighed down and bound by sin, was not subject to this slavery but instead fulfilled

33. Nikolai Fedorovich Fedorov (1829–1903), Russian philosopher and futurist who greatly influenced the Russian Religious Renaissance. See also n29. —Trans.

the will of the Father through his feat of freedom of spirit in the flesh. This freedom was realized by an acceptance of death, which was, nonetheless, a work of freedom and not of the slavery of the flesh: "trampling down death by death." According to the comparison used by the fathers, the devil wished to rapaciously devour the living corpse, but it was he himself who was caught by the bait. From the grave there shone the light of immortality, the new power of life, which was given to all humanity. For this reason a "regulation of nature" has become completely unnecessary, because there is no longer anything or any reason to regulate. The heavy shroud of mortality that was hanging over the world has already been taken away, though for a time it still displays its former, lost strength.

But for victory over death it is necessary that death be revealed completely and in all its depth, that is, not only as the common death that no one can avoid, but also as Christ's death—which had no basis in his human freedom—as the fulfillment of the Father's will. And only this freedom proved to be the path back to the realization of the image of the first Adam: "in order to renew in us his image which had fallen, decayed by passions."[34] Concerning this, the Golden Mouth says in his *Paschal Homily*: "Let no one fear death, for the Savior's death has set us free. He that was held prisoner of it has annihilated it. Christ is risen, and life finds a dwelling place."[35]

But this reveals to us the foundational truth of the sophiology of death: death is the gate of immortality. Death—precisely the death of Christ, and with it and in it all human death—is disclosed in this light as a necessary and thus a grace-bestowing and joyous event in the sophianization of the world: "Where, O death, is your sting? Where, O Hades, is your victory?" [1 Cor 15:55]. Why was it necessary and why was it possible for Christ to die, and why is death necessary for all of humanity? Does not this universal death represent a diminishment of the sophianicity of the world as well as evidence, as it were, of God's inability to create a perfect, sophianic, immortal world that would be "very good" [Gen 1:31]? In the face of death, would it not be possible to doubt the sophianicity of the world as well as the very possibility of this sophianicity?

To answer this question it is necessary, of course, to distinguish two aspects of sophianicity: the divine foundation of the world and its creaturely face. The first cannot be diminished, for it is divinity itself: divine essence, nature, glory—divine Wisdom—*this* is the indestructible and eternal foundation of every created being. The second aspect—the created or becoming

34. From the Ochtoechos, Tone 4. —Trans.

35. St. John Chrysostom's *Paschal Homily*. English translation found here: <<https://oca.org/fs/sermons/the-paschal-sermon>>. I have slightly adapted the translation to fit Bulgakov's Slavonic text. —Trans.

Sophia—is realized in time. She, of course, is "very good," but as one still being perfected, of whom it can still be said: "God *will* be in all" [1 Cor 15:28].
And this "Let it be" of the coming divinization must be accomplished *in
a divine-human manner*, with the participation of God's power acting in
creation, in created Sophia. And if God honored created freedom to the
point of permitting even the fall, original sin, and if this state determined
the being of created Sophia, then it is precisely this state that was assumed in
a divine-human manner in the incarnation. And in this *divine-human* path
the willing acceptance of death, and not its violent removal through divine
omnipotence, is the genuine, profound fusion of divinity with creation, the
sophianization of the latter. If death had not been assumed, then there could
have been no resurrection either, for only by "death has he tramped down
death." And furthermore: for each person this partaking of death is not only
inevitable but also salvific, for only in this manner is it possible to come into
communion with the death of Christ, and thus also with his resurrection.
The grain of wheat cannot live unless it dies: "The Lord who raised Jesus
from the dead will raise us also through Jesus" (2 Cor 4:14). "We are heirs
of God, co-heirs with Christ, provided that we suffer with him so that we
may also be glorified with him" (Rom 8:17). Victory over death can occur
and inwardly already has occurred through Christ's resurrection, but not
through a human resurrection brought about by a mechanical regulation
of nature. In and through such regulation there cannot occur the necessary
step for the sophianization of the world. The regulation of nature, just like
the entire development of human life, remains immanent to the world. Such
regulation discloses the world's possibilities (which in its own way is also
necessary for the world's total unfolding on the way to its end), but it is powerless to arrive at and to realize the world's transfiguration, the transcensus
to a *new* existence, a new heaven and new earth—"Behold, I make all things
new" [Rev 21:5], and the image of this new creation is resurrection.

Of course, it is impossible to say of death that it is sophianic—this
would be a ridiculous and strange paradox, like saying that original sin
was also sophianic since it too was included in the paths of created being.
Nevertheless, death can and must be included—in the fallen condition of
the world—in the necessary path of the life of the world in its sophianization, on the way to the world's liberation from slavery. Death grants freedom
from the burden of the world, and without it this freedom is unattainable
and unrealizable. Death is the exit from the fallen world for the sake of a
return to a renewed world. Death has two faces: the first—dark and horrible, turned towards non-being; this is dying or death properly speaking.
For the sake of sacrificially accepting this face of death, Christ came into the
world. Its other face is bright, peaceful, joyful, leading to freedom, to divine

revelation and the coming resurrection. Naturally, in this transition there is no room for automatism. In the disclosure of his freedom, man even in death finds a path to the light only to the degree to which he himself realized such a possibility in his life, and only in this context is the sophianicity of death disclosed. Dying is the only path to the final overcoming of original sin and death. Death is the "final enemy" (1 Cor 15:26). But death has been overcome by Christ. "For, as death through one man, so also through a man the resurrection of the dead. As in Adam all die, so in Christ all are made alive" (1 Cor 15:21–22). . . . In our dying, death becomes for us the most horrifying reality, but beyond its threshold it loses its power. "Let no one fear death, for the Savior's death has set us free. He that was held prisoner of it has annihilated it" (see: John Chrysostom, *Paschal Homily*)

Nevertheless, does it not follow from this that death is a good that one can prefer even to life itself, and that therefore the voluntarily termination of life through suicide is the only logical conclusion? Without mentioning the fact that a most powerful life-instinct speaks in defense of life, the main thing is that we must mature into death as into a state of life—which is what death is—and the violent and willful attempt to prematurely breach death, as the violation of the organic order of life, carries within it its own inner judgment and punishment (for life is *given* to us by God). There is a natural norm of life for different people that is variously justified in accord with their ages and destinies. Here we again stand before the mystery of individuality and personal destiny. We can comprehend this only by analogy, on the basis of the image of dying that reveals this mystery to us to the degree we can bear it.

"Fear not: I am the First and the Last, and I live; I was dead, and behold, I live unto the ages of ages, amen" (Rev 1:17–18).

10

"Even so, Come"

THE QUESTION NATURALLY ARISES: what is the meaning of the promise "the time is at hand" [Rev 20:10], "Surely I come quickly," in connection with its response "even so, come, Lord Jesus"? [Rev 20:20]. It has been pointed out more than once by interpreters that "soon" is rich in its signification. It can refer not only to the second coming of the Lord, to the parousia, but it also *embrasse toutes les manifestations de la puissance du Christ, sans être bornée à la Parousie* [encompasses all the manifestations of the power of Christ without being limited to the parousia].[1] Nonetheless, this multivalence in the context of the Apocalypse and in its concluding chapter has a particular, concrete meaning. First of all, we must ask ourselves: how does it sound in the hearts of the faithful, this promise based on the Synoptic texts containing the words of the Lord about the second coming? It sounds like a threatening and dreadful anticipation of the dread judgment at which it will be required of everyone according to his deeds, to the uttermost farthing [Matt 5:26]. The human soul trembles "before the day of judgment" and the Church in its liturgical texts (on the week of the dread judgment) discloses precisely this side of the promise (it is similarly expressed in the apostolic epistles of the apostle Paul, the apostle Peter, the apostle Jude). To summon this day of judgment, to hope for it joyfully, clearly surpasses human weakness, which can only bear, at the very most, the *memory* of judgment day and the tremulous fear it provokes. But—and such is the antinomic nature of this dogma too—in the promise of the Lord's new coming into the world there is contained the greatest joy of joys, which can be revealed only to the believing

1. Ernest Bernard Allo, *Saint Jean. L'Apocalypse*, 331.

heart: to see the Lord coming again with glory; even if it be "to judge the
living and the dead," still "his kingdom shall have no end." And we find the
very same testimony concerning this in the Gospel of the same John, in the
words of the Lord himself in his farewell conversation with his disciples
whom he comforts and encourages with this promise: "I will not leave you
orphans, I will come to you. A little while, and the world will no longer see
me, but you will see me, for I live and you will live" (John 14:18–19). "And
I will come and will prepare a place for you, I will come again and call you
unto myself that where I am, you may be also" (14:3). This promise, with
all its breadth, is never qualified and so is all-encompassing. It contains in
itself diverse aspects, both eschatological and apocalyptic. As addressed to
the disciples, whose fidelity and courage would undergo a dreadful trial that
night, the promise, at least at that point, did not yet cause dread. On the contrary, like the entirety of the farewell discourse, it has the sound of a blessing
and of a loving act of affection, despite the fact that it contains a sorrowful
warning: "see the hour is coming, and is now come, that you all will scatter,
each to his own, and will leave me alone" (16:32). Nonetheless this does not
preclude what is said later, in the high priestly prayer: "These things I speak
in the world, that they might have complete joy" (17:13). Thus, in light of
the Fourth Gospel, the tragic horrors of Revelation are, in a certain sense,
undone and overcome, since—and this we must remember—both books
belong, according to the Church's witness, to one and the same holy writer,
the beloved apostle, and what is more, the Gospel was written not before
but after Revelation. Therefore, we can say that already within the limits of
the Fourth Gospel there is a twofold or, in any case, a complex reception of
the parousia not only as the dread judgment but also as the joyful encounter
between the orphaned apostles (who represent us and all of humanity) and
the Christ who returns to the world, "coming again with glory."

But what then does it mean and what is its resonance, this "Even so,
come, Lord Jesus" in Revelation and, alongside it, in all of apostolic Christianity (in the apostle Paul, 1 Cor 16:22; *Didache* 10.6: "Maranatha," the
Aramaic "Lord, come!")? In the first place, a complete difference in nuance
is evident concerning how the Lord is to be expected in this passage when
compared with the Gospels, or with the Synoptic Gospels at least. Can
he, ought he, dare he—the creature who trembles before the "dread judgment"—at the same time summon it? This is not the case and cannot be the
case with respect to the *dies irae, dies illa* [that great day of wrath]; on that
day, *quid sum miser[2] tunc dicturus*? [what shall I, wretch that I am, say?] In
the liturgy of Meatfare Sunday of the Lenten Triodion we also find nothing

2. Bulgakov's text reads *ego* for the original *miser*. —Trans.

but varied and repeated expressions of fear and trembling before Christ the Judge and (as is true in other liturgies, incidentally) there is absolutely no place for the bright images of Revelation but instead only room for images of the utmost horror. Only occasionally, and as it were in spite of the more general tonality, do we meet, as the rarest of exceptions, some individual expressions of a different character, from the prophets and Revelation,[3] and predominantly in Paschal liturgies (such, for example, is the "Shine, shine, O New Jerusalem, for the glory of the Lord hath risen upon thee; dance now and be glad, O Sion").[4] It is perfectly evident that there is a complete incompatibility between penitent horror, with its prayers for personal salvation and forgiveness, and the final summoning prayer of Revelation, "Even so, come": our only option here is an *either-or*. It is perfectly clear that the prayer "Even so, come" does not at all fit the context of the "Meatfare" trembling before the coming Christ; it is not boldness but audacity, not inspiration but spiritual deception. Therefore, we are left here only with that same attitude towards apostolic Christianity that we have towards apocalyptic Christianity, and in this we see yet another common feature of that attitude the historical Churches, including the Eastern Church, take toward to the Apocalypse; it remains, if not under direct prohibition, then under a suspicion bound up with a sort of apprehensiveness—a fact reflected in the absence of the Apocalypse from the liturgy.[5]

And so, the general and foundational question arises: what is the concrete meaning of this prayer: "Even so, come Lord Jesus," which is the final word of the final book of the entire Bible, and to that degree also the final word of all of Christianity? Does it refer to the Judge coming to judge the living and the dead as he is depicted in the Synoptics and in all New Testament literature, and even in Revelation itself too (22:11–15)? Or is it not even a direct reference insofar as it is cordoned off in the context of chapters

3. A survey of Orthodox liturgical texts connected with Revelation would be its own interesting subject of investigation.

4. The Paschal Canon, Ode 9. Translation accessed: <<http://ww1.antiochian.org/pascha-ninth-ode-canon>>. —Trans.

5. In discrete instances this absence is striking. Here is one such instance. The Paremia readings of the liturgy of the Archangel Michael and other fleshless powers are neither the eleventh chapter of Revelation (vv. 7–11)—where the foundational and exhaustive work of the Archangel Michael and his angels is described, namely the war in heaven with the dragon and his angels, which concludes with the latter defeated and cast down from heaven—nor even the apocalyptic chapters of Daniel (10:13; 12:1). Instead, we have the narration of Old Testament appearances of angels that are of relatively secondary dogmatic importance: the appearances to Joshua son of Nain (Josh 5:13–15) and to Gideon (Judg 6:27, 11–24), as well as Isa 14:7–20 (the latter concerns the casting down of the King of Babylon, analogously to Rev 11, although it depicts this only with the images of historical allegory).

21–22, which are dedicated to the heavenly Jerusalem and the city of God? The very same question can be expressed otherwise: with what content is the prayer "even so, come" invested, what is its "intent"—eschatological or chiliastic, or both at the same time? It cannot be straightforwardly or only simply eschatological insofar as the trepidation at the dread day of judgment stops mouths and strikes one with horror at such a prayer. And it is not just this, but it is also the fact that the very subject of the prayer is too transcendent to be the concrete content of a prayer. The parousia lies beyond the borders of the life of this age and it is not accomplished within its borders, and in this sense it is generally *outside* of our time.[6] It is, therefore, shrouded in darkness, that is, it is practically non-existent for our time. It refers to the new creation of God in the world by an act of divine omnipotence.[7] It is in this sense that it is said: "of that day and hour no one knows, neither the angels in heaven, nor the Son, but only the Father" (Mark 13:32; Matt 24:36: "of that day and hour no one knows, not the angels in heaven, but only my Father alone").

For this reason, in regard to the second coming all we can do is watch, which is what the Lord summons everyone to do, that is, to relate to the second coming as a guiding idea, the general orientation of life, but not as an event or goal that could become the object of prayerful hope (in contrast to our prayerful hope for a positive outcome to the entirety of our life, namely "a Christian end to our life and a good defense before the awesome judgment seat of Christ").[8] Otherwise, if it is taken in the other, literal sense, our prayer for Christ's second coming for judgment becomes an ontological misconception containing an inner contradiction, a certain religious presumption that is simply inappropriate because inapposite.

6. On this, see the section on eschatology in Bulgakov, *The Bride of the Lamb* —Trans.

7. To that extent, the "ignorance of the Son of Man" (Mark 13:32), referring to the kenosis of his earthly ministry, is included in the universal ignorance of all creation, both of angels and of humans ("Watch therefore," it is said to the apostles, "because you know neither the day nor the hour in which the Son of Man comes," Matt 25:13). The expression "neither the day nor the hour" does not mean, of course, that the second coming will take place on one of the days and hours of earthly time (instead of exceeding it, in the *transcensus* of time). Here we obviously have an anthropomorphism of expression that is equivalent to a simple "never" in our time. To that degree we have an analogy here with personal death, which occurs in time, on a definite calendric day and hour for all who remain alive, but not for the very one who is dying; for him time is exhausted along with days and hours, yesterdays and tomorrows, time as a whole ceases (although there begins a new, post-mortem, transcendent time).

8. This prayer is said during the Divine Liturgy of St. John Chrysostom. Translation of the liturgy accessed here: <<https://www.goarch.org/-/the-divine-liturgy-of-saint-john-chrysostom.>> —Trans.

All these arguments tends towards the conclusion that, in one sense, namely the eschatological, the prayer "even so, come" is, with respect to the parousia, inappropriate and impracticable, which is why in *this* sense it is absent from God's Word and from the Church's liturgy. From this we must conclude that its appearance in apostolic Christianity and the fiery appeal to it which we find in Revelation, in its very possibility and actuality, must have another meaning beyond the eschatological: the concrete-historical. In this sense, it can receive an answer connected to time, namely: "even so, I come quickly, amen," as in the penultimate word of Revelation, in response to which this final word resounds: "even so, come, Lord Jesus" (22:20). "I come *quickly*" can also have and in fact does have, in another context in Revelation, a distinct shade of meaning. We distinguish it as either *ontological*, related to an organic fulfillment, to the onset of maturity, or as *chronological*, related to a time or season. (And so, the first verse of the first chapter of Revelation: "which must come to pass *shortly*" has an ontological meaning; on the other hand, the final verse of the final chapter: "even so, I come quickly" has instead a chronological meaning with respect to our times and seasons.) But in distinguishing these nuances there remains for us one common and foundational meaning that alone makes both the prayer, "even so, come," and the promise, "even so, I come soon," possible and intelligible. This meaning is not the eschatological but the chiliastic. We must strictly distinguish these two meanings, although often they are confused in the general concept of "eschatology." The latter relates not to the fulfillment of the historical time of this era but instead lies beyond its limits, in the life of the age to come, a metaphysical or even meta-chronological life. But the chiliastic understanding of the last days and fulfillments relates them to the life of this age, to history, although this too, in fact, is meta-history, albeit not in the transcendental sense of the life of the future age, but only in relation to its final part, the thousand-year reign of Christ on earth.

In the light of this distinction of the two meanings, chiliastic and eschatological, historical and transcendental, it becomes absolutely clear which of these meanings relates to the prayer of apostolic Christianity, "even so, come," in which meaning the prayer becomes natural, possible, permissible. For the entirety of the Apocalypse is in a sense an introduction to its final chapters, a preparation for it. The promises of chapters 20–22 are not merely incidental to the book, chapters that must therefore be bleached or weakened through allegorical or spiritualizing interpretations; no, precisely this is the very theme of Revelation and its express prophecy, through which it contains *in itself* something new that is lacking in the entirety of the New Testament (although it is not lacking in the Old, as we shall see below). Revelation of the actual distinction of these two planes, the historical-chiliastic and the transcendent-eschatological, does not allow us to mix in one common concept of the "eschatological" both that which does not apply to it and that to which it actually refers. It places between them a certain intermediate state, which in relation to our still-continuing history is in a certain sense eschatological, although it does not belong to the fullness of eschatology in the strict sense but is rather only the conclusion, the epilogue of history, as it were. The eschatology of Revelation is therefore two-fold: on the one hand, it is directed towards history, it belongs to it, even if by way of a meta-historical epilogue, but at the same time it is also *beyond* history in its relation to the life of the age to come.

In the earliest moment of early Christian consciousness, the parousia was understood in this two-fold manner: immanent-transcendent and historical-eschatological. Among the first Christians one could find this living remembrance of the abiding of Christ in the world, this intense memory of him which had yet to be eclipsed or darkened by the eschatological terror that arose later. They expected him and summoned him, spoke and thought of him as an event that could happen tomorrow and, in any case, as an event located within the limits of human life, even their own. Because of this there arose certain gross exaggerations or corruptions of this feeling, which had to be combatted through correction. We see this in the apostle Paul's exhortation to the Thessalonians, which warns them of the spiritual fussiness developing among them on this account [2 Thess 3:11]. Besides this warning from the Lord himself, which the Apostle repeats (1 Thess 5:1–2; 2 Pet 2:10), concerning the suddenness of the coming of the day of the Lord as a thief in the night and the consequent call to unceasingly remember this, we find the opposite too—a call to a certain eschatological sobriety: "we beseech you, brethren, concerning the coming of our Lord Jesus Christ and our being gathered together with him that you not soon be shaken in mind, nor be troubled either by spirit or by word or by letter as if it had been sent by us, as if the day of the Lord had already arrived. Let no man by any means deceive you" [2 Thess 2:1–3]. In effect, the apostle is warning here against any confusion of the two planes we have indicated, the apocalyptic and the eschatological, and instead he proposes his own apocalypse, as it were, in relation to the historical warning concerning the day of the Lord, thereby transferring the discussion of the question to another plane, namely the historical plane.

Yet his own proper apocalypse remains limited and bare in relation with John's, for it contains only the coming of the Antichrist, the "man of lawlessness": "[the day of the Lord] will not come before the falling away and until the man of sin is revealed, the son of perdition" (2 Thess 2:3). Thus, besides this feature proper to the book of Revelation, the apostle

Paul's writings have no trace of apocalypse as the path to the millennium, which constitutes the subject of Revelation. Naturally, Paul's apocalyptic is not the sort to arouse any feelings today besides terror or, in the best-case scenario, courageous preparedness to meet the final trials and temptations (which the Lord himself also warns of; see Matt 24 with parallels). In any case, it is clear that in this kind of apocalyptic there is no place either for the prayer "even so, come" or for its answering promise: "I come quickly," both of which constitute the exclusive property of the seer of mysteries. Thus the prediction of the apostle Paul casts a heavy shadow over the bright hope of apostolic Christianity concerning the soon coming of the Lord. If we were so inclined, we could even discern a certain conscious and deliberate contradiction in the two apocalypses, the Pauline (along with the Petrine) and the Johannine. The latter's goal was reestablishing, in a certain sense, an apocalyptic, prayerful, and contemplative inspiration. This juxtaposition of the two apocalypses underlines for us even more the special character of Revelation in relation to its conclusion. If the apostle Paul had to reckon with an unhealthy mystical fussiness, then the apostle John by contrast wished to reestablish a healthy and necessary Christian sense of the Apocalypse (something we wish to avoid in our modern times) as well as, more specifically, to reestablish the prayer for the coming of Christ taken in its proper context and with all its apocalyptic fullness.

And this holistic context necessarily also includes all the revelations and promises of the Apocalypse, which refer not only to the second coming of Christ but also to its anticipatory events in earthly history. To this category belongs first of all the mystical prophecy about the coming of Christ to earth for the final battle with the armies of the Beast and the False Prophet; and later the equally mystical promise of his reign on earth with the saints in the first resurrection; and finally the promise of his abiding in the heavenly Jerusalem as the center of his kingdom on earth. All this, if we may express ourselves this way (despite our consciousness of the complete imprecision of such a definition), *precedes* the second coming of Christ, his parousia; it belongs to history, albeit on its supernatural and supra-historical plane. All this must be accomplished on earth and in history, it belongs to our earthly life and to our time, we can hope for it and summon it in prayer, and all this is covered in that exact prayer, "even so, come." We repeat once more: it is chiliastic and not eschatological, and for just that reason, it can be required of us. It is impossible to overstate the entire historiosophical significance of the orientation that such an understanding of this prayer grants us. If in an eschatological understanding of the prayer—in the impracticability and contradictoriness of such an interpretation—the prayer would lead to a hopeless fussiness, then in the chiliastic understanding there is enkindled a new sense of life and history, especially in proximity to Christ, in the fullness of his power and presence, through his abiding in the world and on the earth, which is marvelously conjoined to his ascension and session at the right hand of the Father. The promise "Lo, I am with you , even unto the end of the age" [Matt 28:20] is fulfilled in a new, specifically apocalyptic sense; it gives a different feeling to life, a feeling that is lost and even denied by ascetically interpreted Christianity with its transcendentalism. Earthly life and history are not just a *path to death*, to the afterlife and to resurrection, to the life of the age to come, but they also contain their own proper meaning: they indicate a christological interpretation of the progressing reign of Christ, and therefore of his royal ministry too.

The dogma of the ascension, which has two antinomically joined sides—separation from the world and a continuing abiding in it—receives its own apocalyptic disclosure and confirmation. Not shying away from paradox, we can say that the Apocalypse was written as if it did not include in its context the event of the ascension. True, it presupposes this event as already accomplished to the extent that the Lamb that was slain already abides in the heavens. But the main subject of Revelation relates to the Lamb's ministry on earth, which still continues and is still being accomplished. In the new song directed to the Lamb in the heavens, it is said that he redeemed us by his blood "and made us kings and priests to our God, and we will rule the earth" (Rev 5:9–10), reigning with him. And other voices in heaven said: "worthy is the Lamb that was slain to receive power and riches and wisdom and strength and praise and blessing" (Rev 5:12–13). Thus, concerning the *reception* of all these sevenfold adulations, the text may be applied both to what has already been accomplished (in the ascension) and to what still remains to be accomplished in his reign. The high priestly ministry is here disclosed through the royal ministry. The coming of Christ into the world and his abiding in it—despite, together with, and alongside the ascension into the heavens—continues "until the end of the age." And more than once in this marvelous book we find testimony that this reign is still being accomplished and remains to be completed. Thus, once again in a context corresponding to a definite place in history, after the trumpet of the seventh angel, "there were heard in the heavens loud voices saying: the kingdom of the world has been made (the kingdom) of our Lord and his Christ, and he will reign for the ages of ages" (Rev 9:16), and the twenty-four elders say: "We give thee thanks, O Lord God Almighty, which art, and wast, and art to come; because thou hast taken to thee thy great power, and hast reigned" (Rev 11:17). Connected with this is the figurative testimony of the reign of the "Word of God, the King of kings and Lord of lords," which is accomplished by his victory over his enemies (according to chapter 19:11–21).

Further on we also have, of course, the related passage of chapter 22:1–16, with its prophecy of the thousand-year kingdom, alongside the final concluding chapters as well.

Like all other Christian dogmas, the reign of God over the earth that is accomplished in the "royal ministry" of Christ possesses, of course, a *trinitarian* aspect. "The kingdom of the world has become (the kingdom) of our Lord and his Christ," and in response the elders thank "theLord God Almighty" for the fact that he reigns. God, the Almighty Creator, is the Father who reigns in the Son and through the Son, the God-man, "the King of the Jews." This reign, the divinization of creation, is accomplished through the activity of the Holy Spirit. It is not accidental that the second request of the Lord's Prayer, "Thy kingdom come" has this variant reading: "Thy Holy Spirit come." The Lord's Prayer for God's kingdom through the Father is directed to the entire Holy Trinity, in a manner corresponding to each of the hypostases. But even though this reign was accomplished and is being accomplished in the heavens, it nevertheless takes place on earth as well, in the human world. This meaning is also implied in the prayer for the coming of God's kingdom, concerning which the Lord says: "until now the kingdom of God is taken by force" (Matt 11:12). The universal meaning of the teaching on God's kingdom in all of its facets and fullness presupposes synergism, human action and effort, for its coming. Thereby does human history become comprehensible, as does the entire history of the Church as well; it is disclosed in the light of the teaching of Revelation, and in particular in the light of its final prayer: "even so, come." In a certain sense it is identical or consonant in content with the prayer "Thy kingdom come," whose entire power is disclosed in the following request: "Thy will be done *on earth* as it is in heaven." And to that extent this prayer refers not just primarily to our personal will, to the self-determination of individuals, but also to all of life. The prayer, we can say, is as chiliastic as it is eschatological. But in its address to the Father it refers to God's will, which providentially acts in the world *on* man, such that outside this will and apart from it a hair does not fall from our head [Matt 10:30]; but the prayer "even so, come" in its address to the God-man has in view the synergistic participation of human creative struggle: it is directed towards history, not just meta-history.

Understood in a trinitarian fashion, the prayer "even so, come, Lord Jesus," despite being directly addressed to the God-man, silently includes as well an address to the Father who sends the Holy Spirit, through whom the Holy Spirit is sent. The teaching on the Holy Spirit (pneumatology) is on the whole less clear in the Apocalypse, but in this place of decisive significance it is as it were completely missing. How can we unite the chiliastic, the first return of Christ to the world, as well as the second, the parousia, with

Pentecost, the Son's ascension from the world accompanied by the descent
into the world of the Holy Spirit? Clearly there is no direct relationship here
such as there was in the divine incarnation. Specifically, the annunciation
as the personal Pentecost of the God-Bearer, the descent of the Holy Spirit
onto the Mother of God, is united here with the descent from heaven of the
incarnate Son of God. In this present context, such a union cannot exist. On
account of his ascension, the Son abides in the heavens, but after Pentecost,
the Holy Spirit is already in the world. (This does not prevent the Spirit
even after Pentecost from abiding in the heavens, just as the Son after the
ascension does not abandon the world and his disciples but instead remains
with them until the end of the age; neither contradicts either the ascension
or Pentecost.)

Nonetheless, in a certain sense, Christ's parousia as chiliastic and as
eschatological remains for the world still something yet to come, for which
it is both possible and necessary to pray, "even so, come." On the other hand,
the new descent of the Holy Spirit, or his parousia, is something already
accomplished—to pray for it is no longer possible. There obtains a relationship here that is the opposite of that which existed in the incarnation: the
Holy Spirit accomplished the incarnation, while the Son through the Spirit
became incarnate according to the Father's sending him from above; but
in the parousia, the Son descending from heaven is met by the Holy Spirit
already hypostatically living in the world, and the Spirit prays for the coming of the Son into the world. In a veiled manner, this truth is contained
precisely in the book of Revelation, where, as a whole, comparatively little
is said concerning the Holy Spirit taken separately. But this truth concerning the Spirit is here expressed in precisely this final portion of the final
chapter. It reads: "The Spirit and the Bride say 'come.' And let him who hears
say 'come.'" And it is to *this* summoning that the following answer is given:
"The one witnessing these things says, 'even so, I come quickly.' Amen." And
in reply to this answer there resounds the final, concluding prayer, which,
clearly, again comes from the Spirit and the Bride, as well as from everyone
else who "hears": "even so, come, Lord Jesus."

Thus, in this context of Revelation, it is not simply that we do not find
the supposed hypostatic absence of the Holy Spirit, but, on the contrary,
his presence is solemnly proclaimed: he, from within the world in which
he abides through the power of his descent into it in Pentecost, summons
Christ who is coming into the world in both the chiliastic and eschatological parousia; the Spirit says, "come," the Spirit prays for this and summons
it. But the Spirit does not do this of himself in his divine essence and hypostasis, so to speak—not alone, but together with the Bride, which is the
Church, the Body of Christ. He descends into the world and abides in it in

a divine-human fashion, although in a manner corresponding to his particular hypostatic character: not through incarnation, but through descent and grace-bestowing overshadowing. The Bride—the Church, which is humanity overshadowed by the Holy Spirit and divinized by him—cries out, all together, with one voice, to the God-man in whom the one hypostasis of the Son unites two natures, the divine and human. In the person of the Bride, of divinized humanity, the Spirit intercedes for the saints according to (the will of) God: "the Spirit himself intercedes for us with groanings which cannot be uttered" (Rom 8:26–27). The Spirit and the Bride, that is, all graced humanity, and together with it the world, all of creation, with one voice say, "come." This is the entire magnitude, solemnity, and power of this summons.

But that is still not all that can be said about this. There still remains in all its import the image of the Church as Bride, which suddenly appears with such definition and significance in the context of these final chapters of Revelation, where it is said that "the marriage of the Lamb has begun" (19:7) and the New Jerusalem is shown, "like the bride of the Lamb adorned for her husband" (21:2): "come, I will show you the woman, the bride of the Lamb" (21:9). And only in the consonance and fullness of this context does the final image of "the Spirit and the Bride" appear.

If the Spirit and the Bride as the Church are indeed understood here in the entire plurality of their different aspects, then we must also necessarily include here the Church's personal head, the Unwedded Bride, the Most Holy Mother of God, the Virgin Mary, the "Woman clothed with the sun [Rev 12:1]. In other words, we need not only an ecclesiological but also a mariological understanding of this text. There is a certain ecclesiological self-evidence for such an interpretation. Namely, if it is the Church that is here crying out—the Spirit and the Bride—then the Church in the Holy Spirit does this in the person of all her living members. Each of these, crying out in the person of and on behalf of the Church, also in his own right becomes the bride in relation to the Heavenly Bridegroom, to the God-man in his divine-humanity. If such a conclusion is applied to every member of the Church, then it refers pre-eminently and in an exceptional measure to the Ever Virgin Mary as the personal head of the Church, which is and can never, in any way, be separated from her. Thus we conclude that here the one crying out as the head of the Church and on behalf of her is precisely the Most Holy God-bearer herself. This is the hidden mariological meaning of this final revelation in Revelation. Like everything else relating to the Virgin Mary, this is revealed in holy silence (the same is true for the other mariological dogmas, excepting the annunciation, which relates not just to Mary herself or, in any case, not to her alone, but also to the Holy

Spirit who descends upon the Pneumatophora). Revelation about her is communicated in Holy Scripture not through words but through silence. Similarly, there is a general silence concerning the activity of the Most Holy God-bearer in the age to come. Here too, the activity of the Most Holy God-bearer and her participation in the pan-ecclesial prayer, which can never take place without her participation, is concealed, or, rather, is shrouded in silence. And especially applicable to this revelation is her own word about herself: "For he hath regarded the low estate of his handmaiden: for, behold, from henceforth all generations shall call me blessed" [Luke 1:48]. They do indeed call her blessed with a conclusive fullness and power through this final prayer, "even so, come."

The image of the Church, which refers to "Jerusalem" as the society of saints, to the entire sobornost'[9] of the Church in its catholic unity, in its oneness of mind and feeling, finds a *personal* expression in the Unwedded Bride who is the personal representative of the Church, Mary, the Mother of God. It is she, the Pneumatophora, who by the Holy Spirit cries out on behalf of the Church and of all creation: "even so, come." It would be completely incomprehensible if in this final call, if in this final word of the final book of the entire Word of God, if in this voice of all creation, she were missing, if her voice did not resound, if there was silence concerning her and if she proved—dreadful and blasphemous to say—forgotten. But no, triumphantly Christian consciousness speaks: she is here, with the world and in the world, she summons and meets the second coming of the Son.

And so, the Most Holy One herself together with the Church, as the Pneumatophora, and in this exceptional sense as both the Spirit and the Bride, cries out: "even so, come." But if this is so, then there necessarily follows a further conclusion, namely that she summons him *together with* the world, on behalf of it. But does this not bring in its wake new dogmatic difficulties? How can we introduce such an idea in light of the dogma of the dormition of the Most Holy God-Bearer, the dogma of her resurrection, ascension and, in sum, of her accomplished glorification, which, as it were, puts her above the world and outside the world, separating her from it? How then is it that she herself, who remains departed from the world, can cry out for the coming of her Son into the world, how can she pray together with the world for this? Do we not have here a fundamental contradiction?

9. This word contains a rich storehouse of meaning comprised of such distinct concepts as "communal," "conciliar," "catholic." The word is used in the Russian translation of the Nicene Creed ("one holy, *sobornal*, apostolic Church") but it became a mainstay of Russian religious thought with Alexei Stepanovich Khomyakov (1804–60), who used it to distinguish Orthodox ecclesiology from Protestantism and Roman Catholicism. —Trans.

But this contradiction is only apparent and can be resolved by attending to the following dogmatic considerations and clarifications. In the first place, the dormition of the God-Bearer does not signify the break with the world that Christ's ascension does. As the Church directly testifies (in the troparion of the dormition), the Most Holy God-Bearer "did not abandon the world in the dormition," even if in her glory she abides above the current state of the world, which is not yet glorified and transfigured. (This general idea is confirmed and disclosed in the Church tradition witnessing to the special, maternal closeness of the Mother of God to the Church on earth, to her heavenly mantle covering this world, which she even on occasion visits, *as if* leaving heaven for the sake of this earthly contact.) Her ascension signifies only her personal resurrection and glorification before the universal resurrection and glorification. Similarly, there is no impediment to understanding the prayer of the Mother of God, "even so, come," in two senses: the eschatological and the chiliastic. In the first sense, the eschatological, the parousia of Christ accompanied by the holy angels and all the saints clearly includes in this accompaniment and return to the world the Mother of God who is not left behind. For her this will not be the parousia in the proper sense, as a return to the world, but rather only a new appearance *in* the world. This appearance can be understood both as necessarily simultaneous with the coming of Christ with his saints as well as an anticipation, in a sense, of the latter. In that case, the prayerful cry of the Most Holy God-Bearer for the coming into the world of her Son, for the parousia, merges with the cry of summons stemming from all of creation too. The Mother of God summons her Son on behalf of the Church.

But even this does not yet exhaust the dogmatic power of this marvelous prayer of prayers, "even so, come." It has not only an eschatological and mariological but also a sophiological meaning, which is disclosed, of course, only in the light of sophiology. "The Spirit and the Bride," the Logos, the Church, and the Mother of God, are Sophia, the Wisdom of God, in a dual aspect, as Divine Sophia and created Sophia, distinct between themselves but also merging in the divinization of creation that takes place in the Church and most expressly in the Most Holy God-Bearer, the Mother of God. The Church as divinized creation is divine-humanity that unites two natures, not in the unity of the hypostasis of the Logos but through the activity of the Holy Spirit, through pneumatophoricity. It is this that joins the Church to the divine-humanity of Christ as his Body. The Church-Mother of God therefore is neither Divine nor created Sophia alone: she is divine-creaturely in the union of these two, in the accomplished transparency of creation to its divine foundation. We can say that this is the sophiological disclosure of the Chalcedonian dogma on the two sophianicities, the bi-unity of the divine and created principles brought about in Christ by the Holy Spirit. The Chalcedonian dogma of the two natures of Christ, the divine and human, when applied to the Church can be expressed as the teaching of two forms of sophianicity, the divine and the created, united in the Spirit-bearing character of the Church.

The union of divine and human nature, understood sophiologically, signifies the mutual penetration and transparency of eternal Wisdom, divine Wisdom, and of creation as bearing Wisdom's image, constituting created revelation in Christ himself, in the incarnation, in the kenosis, and in all his divine-human "ministry" accomplished through the Holy Spirit. The "Christ," the Son of God, the Logos, on whom the love of the Father eternally reposes, is revealed in hypostatic Love through the Holy Spirit, just as the hypostatic God-man is also the perfect Spirit-bearer. The life of Christ, which is accomplished through the Holy Spirit, Christ's humanity, is the bi-unity of two natures, divine and created. This *bi-unity* does not turn into either a duality or a unity, but preserves exactly that doubleness of form of the one principle, Sophia, in her divine and created existence. In the God-man these two natures have a hypostatic unity in the second hypostasis of the Holy Trinity. Here divinity descends into creation, kenotically unites with it, deifies it. But the Church with the Most Holy God-Bearer at her head is created Sophia, creation, which through the Holy Spirit—not through hypostatic union in him, but rather in the fullness of its Spirit-bearing—thereby receives into itself life in Christ, that is, life in complete union with God. The Church, and the Mother of God in her as the Pneumatophora, make creaturely life equally divine-human by joining it and raising it to divine-humanity. This happens first in the Most Holy God-Bearer *qua* Spirit-Bearer, who consequently becomes the Mother of God who lives one life with her Son, the God-man; and afterwards it occurs in all human hypostases, who are called to say of themselves, in the words of the apostle Paul: "it is not I who live but Christ who lives in me" (Gal 2:20) and "do you not know that the Spirit of God lives in you?" (1 Cor 3:16; cf. Rom 8:9–11, 2 Tim 1:14). The ultimate fulfillment of this is expressed in the promise that "God will be all in all" [1 Cor 15:28]. This promise relates precisely to the fullness of the sophianization of creation, which unites the interpenetrating divine and human principles; it refers to the divinization of creation or, what is the same thing, to creation's sophianization, its transparency to its prototype in the manner of bringing to fruition the latter's power in creation. This sophiological understanding of the Chalcedonian dogma of the two natures indicates not just the fundamental fact of the union of the natures in Christ, the one anointed with the Holy Spirit, but it also represents the dynamically continuous act of divinization that is the life and power of the Church. The Church in this sense is the ongoing revelation of Divine Sophia in created Sophia, the sophianization of creation. Only in a sophiological manner can it be understood.

For this reason, we must add to this whole series of ecclesiological equivalences, corresponding with the entire Chalcedonian import of the phrase "Spirit and the Bride," this next equivalence too: "The Spirit and the Bride" are Sophia, Divine and created, in the unity of divinization or the sophianization of creation, the life of the Church in Christ as the Body of Christ animated by the Holy Spirit. But viewed in this aspect, what is the significance of the prayer "come," what is the sophiological meaning of this prayerful summons together with its reciprocal promise: "even so, I come quickly"?

Christologically, the Chalcedonian dogma indicates Christ's already completed coming into the world through the incarnation. This is the first parousia of Bethlehem, which of necessity was preceded by the coming of the Holy Spirit into the world, namely through his descent onto the Virgin Mary, the Pneumatophora. In this primordial sense, the coming of Christ into the world—which furthermore was dyadic, referring to its inseparability from the Holy Spirit as the one who anoints Christ—was accomplished for ever, and it is neither abolished nor interrupted by Christ's ascension, which is not a disincarnation or a dehominization or an abolishing of the divine-humanity in him. In Christ was accomplished the complete sophianization of creation through Christ's humanity, which was united with divinity in the hypostatic union and brought into being by the Holy Spirit through the will of the Father who sent them both.

This sophianization in incarnation and in divine-humanity, accomplished in creation according to the pre-eternal plan of God, nevertheless does not represent something new or unexpected, although it certainly appears as such for creation itself in its limitation and self-enclosure. The latter is broken open by sophianization as in a catastrophe, for into the world comes a new divine power and life—divine-humanity. This pre-eternal divine plan found expression in the sophianic prototype and in the sophianic creation of the entire world and of man within it, created in God's image. The six days are in this sense the sophiology of creation, in which the threefold Sophia as the self-revelation of the Holy Trinity is revealed. God the Father, the Almighty Creator, who creates the world by his Word, on whom reposes the Father's "let there be," is revealed in the dyad of the Son and Spirit, just as Divine Sophia is revealed in created Sophia and the Prototype of man is revealed in created man. The fullness of this Prototype includes "heaven and earth," that is, the "spiritual world" comprising both angels and humans, who are distinguished by their respective creaturely natures: embodied and disembodied, yet united in the unity of the image of God. Thus already in its creation the world is stamped by its Prototype, the Divine Sophia; in this sense it is created Sophia. But at the same time, the creation of the world is also already the beginning of its sophianization. Sophianization cannot remain at its inception but presupposes further disclosure; creation is the first but by no means the last deed of the Creator in creation. In this sense we can and must say that the world is divine-human in its creation by virtue of its sophianicity. The entire world in this respect is a natural Old Testament in relation to the New, which is its fulfillment. Hence, the incarnation and Pentecost are both natural and comprehensible as the revelation of the Wisdom of God, of divine Wisdom in created Wisdom. No break or ontological catastrophe can be admitted in relation to the sophianicity of the world; it is primordially foreordained in its sophianic fullness.

The sophianicity of the world in its depths, through man and in humanity, was already manifested in the anticipations the Old Testament (or, even before then, in the paradisical state of man), but it was realized through the union of God and man in the divine-humanity, that is, in the the Son of God's becoming human and in the Pentecost of the Holy Spirit. Through this divine condescension, the uniting of Divine Sophia and created Sophia was accomplished in the depths of the world's being, which had already *become* Sophia in its God-world (theocosmic) or divine-human bi-unity, in the divinization of creation. But even though it is already Sophia in its divine-humanity, the world in man has yet to complete the *path* towards the actualization of its sophianicity, to the fullness of its sophianization in the life of this age, in the New Testament Church. The sophianicity of the world, although already something *given* in the most profound depths of its being, remains nonetheless also a *commission*, for the world still retains its created inertia, which must be overcome in the universal resurrection and in its transfiguration in the life of the age to come, or more precisely, in the ages of ages, on the paths towards universal apocatastasis, when "God will be all in all" [1 Cor 15:28]. Only then will the sophianization of the world be complete.

With respect to the divine fullness revealed in God's condescension towards creation, sophianization can never reach completion; with respect to creation, sophianization knows no exhaustive end but is instead a life of infinite ascent from strength to strength [Ps 84:7]. It knows both ages and stages. Despite the infinity of creaturely ascent, it does possess a decisive border that in the current aeon has yet to be reached but that will be crossed in Christ's parousia and in the transfiguration of the world in glory by the Holy Spirit. It is for this that the "Spirit and the Bride" cry out, it is to this that their prayer, "come," refers, and the divine answer "even so, I come quickly" is for the crossing of this border, for the second coming of Christ, in the manifestation of Glory in the Holy Spirit. Exactly this is that ontological border, the *before* and *after*. It separates the world still in the state *before* the progressive sophianization begins from the state in which the latter is already accomplished, although this same fulfillment unfolds and in this sense continues for the ages of ages. Therefore, this very prayer for the onset of the eschatological period is bound up with this onset, it is a prayer within time and as such must cease upon its fulfillment, having been replaced, clearly, by new and more suitable prayers that will be put in our hearts by the Holy Spirit, by the one praying "with groanings which cannot be uttered" [Rom 8:26].

And so, the prayer *"come"* also refers to the sophianization of the world, but this prayer is at the same time also a prayer for the world's enchurchment, for the entire world to become the Church, which is just what "God will be all in all" means. No longer will anything remain outside the Church, nothing will be worldly, unecclesial or anti-ecclesial. This also corresponds with the universal apocatastasis, which is not only the renovation but also the enchurchment of all creation. Opponents of apocatastasis and defenders of the eternity of hell unwittingly put a limit on the sophianization or enchurchment of creation and thereby also put a limit on the effectiveness of Christ's coming. For them this coming is not universal insofar as there remains forever the unenlightened region of hell, the kingdom of Satan. It may be a conquered, fettered kingdom writhing in eternal torments, but nonetheless it ontologically abides and even asserts its satanic selfhood for all eternity. This idea represents, of course, a radical Manicheism, the admission of the inconquerability of Satan after his expulsion as the "prince of this world" [Rev 19; John 14:30]. Those advocates of eternal satanism and of Satan's inherent unconquerability do not reflect on what kind of place will be allotted for him in God's creation, for outside of this creation there is absolutely no place, that is, there is simply nothing. Neither do these advocates of eternal torments for Satan affirm the eventual annihilation of Satan and his angels in their very being (only a few uninfluential supporters of "conditional immortality" claim this), for they exceedingly desire to guarantee the existence of "eternal torments," of the eternity of hell.

But in reality, the admission of the annihilation of Satan and his hosts (that is, an ontological death penalty) would be tantamount to blasphemy against the Creator, as if he were admitting to his mistake in creating Satan and would fix this by virtue of his omnipotence. But then there arises this quandary: why did this annihilation not occur at the very beginning? Meanwhile, the very opposite took place: Satan's activity was permitted in the world, beginning with the temptation of our ancestors in paradise, something that could have simply been prevented by divine foreknowledge and omnipotence. And the same can be said of all subsequent manifestations of the power of evil in human history. In order to destroy this power, the Lord himself is crucified in the world, but even after his resurrection and ascension in glory, he comes again into the world for the continuation of his battle with Satan; this constitutes the main content of the Apocalypse. It is precisely this latter point that must be understood, however unexpected and paradoxical it may seem, as teaching apocatastasis—both its development and its completion.

This is the trifold completion that concludes Christ's victory: "and the beast was taken and with him the false prophet, both alive (that is, not killed, not executed, not destroyed in their being) . . . were thrown into the lake of fire burning with brimstone" (19:20), and "the devil too was cast into the lake of fire and brimstone, where the beast and the false prophet are, and they will suffer for the ages of ages" (20:10). Further along we find this: "and death and hell were cast into the lake of fire. This is the second death. And whoever was not written in the book of life was thrown into the lake of fire" (vv. 14–15) (cf. also 22:15: "and outside [the city] were dogs and sorcerers"). And yet, one wonders, where exactly is this place located, this "lake of fire"—in this world or outside of it; that is, is it completely outside of any creaturely reality made by God? Is this the ontological death penalty along with annihilation of being, or does this signify only a *particular state* within being that therefore cannot be viewed as permanent, as eternally abiding, but instead only as temporary, capable of being overcome, even if only from the perspective of the "ages of ages" (on which point we must remember that for God "a thousand years is like one day" [2 Pet 3:8], and that the "ontological time" of these ages of ages is different from our earthly time with its chronology). To admit the eternity of the lake of fire in creation is tantamount to confessing the unconquerability of Satan in his unchangeability, thereby putting a limit on God, who can therefore no longer become "all in all." But this would signify (something the fanatics of eternal hell cannot and do not want to understand) the final victory of Satan, at least in his own place, in hell, along with the unconquerability of satanism. There results a religio-ontological absurdity from which there are only two exits: either the annihilation of the satanic principle in the world by means of divine omnipotence, since it cannot overcome this principle from within, or the latter option, that is, apocatastasis, which means the complete sophianization of *all* creation, in which "nothing cursed will any longer remain" (22:3). Admitting the eternality of hell would signify the immortalization of the division of Divine Sophia from created Sophia, the self-affirmation of the being of the latter, which is once again an ontological absurdity.

We must not forget that "hell and the lake of fire," and within them the second death as well, find their ground, as does all of being, in divine creation, in created Sophia. For it is not only life and being that are sophianic but death too, as a state of being, as a moment in the dialectic of life. The Lord himself tasted death and descended into hell. Do we need a more indisputable and self-evident proof of the sophianicity of even death and hell insofar as they belong to *being* and not to *non-being*, to the extent that they are particular states of being? The destruction of satanism, of hell, of the lake of fire, of the second death, signifies their overcoming from within, their dissolution in the common sophianicity of being in the fulfillment of the promise: "God will be all in all." But this in fact constitutes the fulfillment of the prayer, "*Come.*" This is a new and final descent into hell by the Lord Jesus through the Holy Spirit: "When You descended into death, O life immortal, then You illuminated Hades with the splendor of Your divinity."[10] This text of the paschal chant must be understood in an ontological sense, as applied to the dogma of the descent into hell and the universal resurrection.

And so, insofar as the power of universal sophianization extends to *all* of creation, then so too does the prayer "come." It can and it must, in the end, begin to sound in "death and in hell," even in the depths of the lake of fire, by virtue of the sophianicity of creation. This sophianic prayer has power only as far as the domain of the "Spirit and the Bride" extends, that is, *everywhere.* For the Spirit, every created gate has been penetrated, and the Bride abhors not the stench and obduracy of creation. The Most Holy One prays to the Son to have mercy on sinners, and her love warms and opens hearts and souls and spirits, even in the depths of their fall. The apocatastasis of the spirits (in the vernacular, "the salvation of Satan") is accomplished through the facilitation of this love, by the power of the blood of the Lamb. If Satan was cast down from heaven along with his angels, having been conquered by the blood of the Lamb (22:11), then this same victory leads him even further in this casting down, namely through the return journey of . . . de-satanization.

The more fully is disclosed the entire universal meaning of the prayer "come," which must also be the *personal* prayer of every Christian, the more acutely the question arises: from *whom* exactly does this prayer ascend, this pan-ecclesial, universal prayer by which the "Spirit and the Bride" pray? This prayer is accepted and answered "even so, I come quickly" as if from a person to a person, from Christ to the "Spirit and the Bride" personally. How then ought we to understand this personal address, which also receives

10. Troparion sung on the night of Pascha. Bulgakov's text reads "illuminated" instead of the original Slavonic "destroyed" (*umertvil*). English translation accessed here: <<https://www.goarch.org/-/sunday-orthros#Apolytikia>>.

a personal answer? We must understand this address in all its polysemeity and therefore in its fullness and complexity. "The Spirit and the Bride" are the entire Church, the Bride praying in the Holy Spirit who "lives in us" and intercedes for us "with groanings that cannot be uttered" (Rom 8:9; 26). Though the Spirit prays in us, "intercedes for the saints according to (the will of) God" (Rom 8:27), still this inspiration by the Spirit cannot, however, signify his *hypostatic* prayer in us. The Church is Spirit-bearing in the sense that she accepts the grace of the Holy Spirit, his gifts and inspiration, but his hypostasis is not incarnated and is not made human like the hypostasis of the Son. The "Spirit and the Bride" signifies the "Bride," that is, the Church in the Holy Spirit, the Church inspired by him. But beyond that, is the Bride also a hypostasis that can *personally* address an other in prayer? To the degree that the Church, as was said above, has a personal head and focal point in the Most Holy God-Bearer, to that degree also does the "even so, come," take on a hypostatic character as *her* prayer on behalf of the Church. She prays for the coming of Christ; the one who summons him into the world is the Mother of God, and it is in response to this personal summons that he answers her. Such an interpretation is not ruled out but rather necessarily included in the prayer "of the Spirit and the Bride": this is the prayer of the Mother of God on behalf of all humanity.

But can we go so far as to finally identify the Virgin Mary with the Church in order to say that her hypostasis, as the human daughter born of Joachim and Anna, is precisely that proper hypostasis of the Church, even if she speaks only *on behalf* of the latter? Such an identification does not ultimately prove possible. As a human being, the Mother of God herself is only *one* of the hypostases belonging to multi-hypostatic humanity, and therefore she does not function as humanity's one, pan-human hypostasis. She is not the head of the Church like Christ is; rather, she only stands at its head, as its representative, who encompasses all through her personal love. We can say that she is in this sense its *sobornal*[11] hypostasis: her voice can speak *on behalf* of all humanity, its multiple hypostases sound *in unison* with it, but for all that, the entirety of humanity in its multi-unity is *not* hypostasized in her but instead abides in its sobornal multiplicity. Humanity in its Spirit-bearing capacity as the Church accordingly recognizes in her its unity through the Holy Spirit.

Thus we conclude that the Bride as the Church is not a uni-hypostatic personality; as a multi-hypostatic being, the Church remains personally *un*-hypostatized. This corresponds with Church's sophianic character, insofar as Sophia, which possesses in God her divine foundation, is not a "fourth

11. See p. 58n53 above. —Trans.

hypostasis" in God. In order to comprehend this question we must here ascend to the very essentials of sophiology. Sophia is not the tri-hypostatic God but rather his divinity, united with him and inseparable, as his self-revelation in nature, essence, and life. But this tri-fold self-revelation of the Father in the Son and the Holy Spirit, in Wisdom and Glory, in its indivisibility, also possesses its own being in itself, non-personal and non-hypostatic; it is divinity in God. And the relationship between the divine hypostases and nature or Wisdom, Sophia, is defined not only as God's possession of his own essence but also as the life and being of this essence in itself. This self-existence of Sophia in God grounds her revelation in the world as well, both as its very creation and as its progressive sophianization.

It is according to the image of divine trihypostaticity that creaturely hypostases, angelic and human, are created with their capacity of personal love and mutuality. But personal mutuality does not exhaust the forms and possibilities of love. There still remains the possibility of the non-hypostatic, non-personal love, which exists between divinity and the tri-hypostatic God. This is the nature of the non-hypostatic love of the Church for Christ. The Church loves him as Sophia loves God. Between God and divinity, between Christ and the Church, there exists a relationship of mutuality in love that is personal and impersonal, tri-hypostatic and non-hypostatic, and yet at the same time multi-hypostatic. The Church as a multi-unity of hypostases is not a "collective" but rather a real being that reveals itself in the life of the multiplicity of created hypostases created in the image of God. This multi-unity is not personal but *supra*-personal; in it exists the divine fullness, the revelation of divine life, and it *loves* God, even if impersonally, like the world with its nature loves and praises God with its very being.

Hence we conclude that the Church as a supra-creaturely, impersonal-multi-personal unity can also express herself: she *speaks*, in the full multivalence of this definition. She speaks *personally* in the person of its highest representative in the Mother of God; she speaks in the person of each of her members, in their prayer; and she speaks, finally, impersonally, as the Church, through the groanings of the Holy Spirit. This is her voice and it merges with all voices, remaining higher than them yet without swallowing them. And this meaning—of the non-hypostatic love of Sophia for the Church—"speaks" here as the "Spirit and the Bride": "come." And in response to this summons—multi-personal and non-personal, and that should resound in the soul of each in his individuality and in the souls of all in their sobornost'—the Lord responds: "even so, I come quickly."

And so, the Church as the Body of Christ animated by the Holy Spirit calls out to Christ: come! At the same time, it is evident that we have juxtaposed here various forms of the Lord's abiding in the Church, both as the already accomplished and the still remaining to be accomplished coming. Of the first the Lord says: "Lo, I am with you always, even unto the end of the age"; of the second: "even so, I come quickly." The first coming remains hidden in the sacraments, but the second will be manifest. Both the first and the second are revealed in different images of the union of Christ with humanity in his divine-humanity, in its different stages. This union is already accomplished in the depths of being, but it is still being accomplished and must be accomplished in its manifestation. Something similar to this is taking place in the relationship of the Holy Spirit to creation. The Holy Spirit descended into the world at Pentecost and remains in it. And yet we still pray to him: "come and abide in us."[12] Clearly, here too we must distinguish two different forms of coming that nonetheless remain identical precisely as the common activity of the Holy Spirit in the world: the immanent-historical and the transcendental-eschatological bestowal of grace on the world and its glorification. Similarly, the abiding of Christ in the world and his coming were and are immanent-historical, but in the future we expect also a transcendent-eschatological coming.

This parallelism between the coming of Christ and the Holy Spirit into the world, between the incarnation and Pentecost, can be further filled out by the following idea. We can distinguish, strictly speaking, not just a two-fold but even a three-fold coming into the world by the Lord. Specifically, besides his first coming we know not just one but two forms of his second coming: the chiliastic and the eschatological, and while our prayer "come" refers to both these forms, it refers to the chiliastic no less, and even more so (in accord with our explanation above), than it does to the eschatological. This very same distinction can be applied to the prayer to the Holy Spirit to "come and abide in us." The bestowal of grace and sanctification provided through the Holy Spirit, "from strength to strength" [Ps 84:7] and "not by measure" [John 3:34] knows an equal multiplicity of chiliastic levels and stages, as does the chiliastic meaning of the "coming" of Christ into the world, insofar as it is dyadically indivisible from the activity of the Holy Spirit. Christ as the one anointed by the Holy Spirit always brings the Spirit into the world and thereby sends him too, with all the diverse forms of this "sending down." Therefore, chiliasm is not merely the anticipation of the parousia as the preparation for the coming of Christ into the world but also

---

12. From the Orthodox prayer known alternatively as the "O Heavenly King" or "Prayer to the Holy Spirit": "O Heavenly King, the Comforter, the Spirit of Truth, Who art everywhere and fillest all things; Treasury of Blessings, and Giver of Life—come and abide in us, and cleanse us from every impurity, and save our souls, O Good One." Translation accessed: <<https://www.oca.org/orthodoxy/prayers/trisagion>> —Trans.

represents, as it were, a new coming into the world by the Holy Spirit who has already descended into it at Pentecost.

And here we need not be brought up short by this phrase from the book of Revelation: "and the Spirit and the Bride say, 'come.'" We ask ourselves: how and in what sense can the co-coming of the Holy Spirit with Christ be united with the prayer addressed to Christ by the same Spirit: "come"? This two-fold possibility is inherent in the dyadic union of the Son and the Holy Spirit, as is revealed in their being sent down into the world from the Father: according to the first possibility, the activity of the Spirit precedes the revelation of the Son; according to the second, it follows it. Thus, in the incarnation, the Spirit incarnates the Son through his descent onto the Ever-Virgin God-Bearer, the Pneumatophora, and at the same time the Spirit reposes on him and is given by him. And the same relation, a unique dyadic synergism, continues throughout the entirety of the Lord's ministry, both on earth and above it: the Holy Spirit, who descends on Christ at the baptism, baptizes, although the Lord, since he came to John for baptism, is to that extent himself the one who is baptized. The Holy Spirit leads Christ to be tempted by the devil, although Christ himself is the one who goes. "The Spirit of the Lord is upon me, he has anointed me," [Luke 4:18] Christ himself proclaims in the words of the prophet Isaiah when beginning his prophetic ministry. The Holy Spirit is the Glory that overshadowed the Lord with his light on Mount Tabor, although it was the Lord himself who recovered and received this manifestation of the Glory that belonged to him "before the foundation of the world" [John 17:5]. By the Spirit he is resurrected by the Father, although it is Christ himself who rises from the dead. The same thing is also true with respect to his ascension, which is as much something that happens to him as it is something that happens by him, by the Holy Spirit and in accord with the will of the Father.

In a word, over the course of the entire ministry of Christ, the dyadic relation of the hypostases is "economically" the opposite of its order in the "immanent" Trinity. Here the work of perfection belongs to the third hypostasis, and to the second its fulfillment, not the other way around. The only exception is Pentecost, in which the Holy Spirit is sent by the Son from the Father, but such a relationship proceeds from the very essence of the act, in which it is precisely the very "sending" of the Holy Spirit that is done to him by the Son: in this there is certain parallel, but at the same time it is the opposite of the incarnation. In the latter, the Son himself comes down into the world, but here it is the Holy Spirit, and naturally so because one and the same hypostasis of the Holy Spirit cannot itself be both the one sent and the sender. Nonetheless, in what concerns the Holy Spirit being sent into the world and his activity, the dyadic relationship between the second and third

hypostases is not changed by this sending into the world of the third hypostasis through the second. The Holy Spirit once again takes its proper place
of primacy as the perfecting hypostasis. It is precisely a new descent into the
world by Christ— both in its anticipatory, chiliastic sense and its conclusive,
eschatological senses— that is also accomplished by the Holy Spirit.

This common theme of triadology is not clearly expressed in Church
tradition, just as it is not in theology, as a result of the generally undisclosed
nature of eschatology. But it is precisely to such a triadological understanding of the eschatological dogma that we are compelled, first and foremost by
the entire general context of the revelation concerning the Holy Trinity and
the incarnation. If Christ's first coming into the world was accomplished
in accord with the will of the Father by the activity of the Holy Spirit, as
was everything else connected with his ministry, then this same correlation
must also hold with respect to his second coming. For the Scripture says
in this regard that no one knows the time of this coming, not even the Son
[Matt 24:36], inasmuch as he carries forward his ministry and is bringing it
to conclusion even in the heavens, "preparing a place" [John 14:2-3] for his
disciples, "praying" [John 14:16] the Father to send the Comforter into the
world, and furthermore, according to the entire content of the Apocalypse,
determining the times and fulfillments that prepare for this second coming.
If the Father "knows" the time of the second coming, then this means that
it is accomplished according to his will, that this "knowledge" is the Father's
pre-eternal determination. In other words, we must necessarily conclude
that the Father *sends* the Son in his second coming into the world, just as he
did in his first. And just as the first sending was accomplished by the Holy
Spirit, by his activity in bringing about the incarnation, so also this second
coming is accomplished certainly not with the Son in isolation from the
Holy Trinity but rather in the Trinity's triunity, with the Father sending,
the Son being sent, and the Holy Spirit accomplishing this sending down.
Hence, there follows the dogmatic conclusion that Christ's parousia is accomplished by the Holy Spirit.

But this dogmatic truth requires further development. At the incarna-
tion, in the Son of God's descent from the heavens, this activity of the Holy
Spirit was also accompanied by the Spirit's descent from the heavens onto
the Virgin Mary: the first Pentecost. At Christ's second coming, the Holy
Spirit will not come again into the world, for he descended into it already at
Pentecost and abides in it. According to the dogmatic consciousness of the
Church (the Kontakion of the Ascension),[13] this abiding corresponds with

13. "When You had fulfilled the dispensation for our sake, / and united earth to heav-
en: / You ascended in glory, O Christ our God, / not being parted from those who love
You, / but remaining with them and crying: / 'I am with you and no one will be against

Christ's inseparability from the world in his ascension. Nonetheless, despite Christ's inseparability from the world, about which the Lord said: "Lo, I am with you always, even unto the end of the age," there will be a second coming for Christ. In a similar fashion, the Holy Spirit can play a role in Christ's second coming despite the fact that his hypostatic descent into the world already took place at Pentecost. This descent is distinct from the incarnation, and it occurs without the Holy Spirit abandoning of the depths of the Holy Trinity. Therefore, even from the heavens the Spirit participates—in accord with his hypostatic character—in the sending down of the Son from the heavens for his second coming into the world, which also occurs without the Son's abandoning the heavens. For this reason it takes place with a total fullness of activity on the part of the Holy Trinity and of each of its hypostases, each in accord with his personal quality. But that is not all. The Holy Spirit abiding in the world, precisely as the one who animates the Church as the Body of Christ, who actualizes her life in Christ, will reveal Christ to her in accord with Christ's promise: "I will not leave you orphans, I will come to you" [John 14:18]; this is precisely the promise of "another Comforter" "who will abide with you for the age" (John 14:16 and parallels). But this revelation of Christ through the Comforter necessarily extends to and includes his second coming, which the Holy Spirit prepares and summons. If in the incarnation the Holy Spirit descends from the heavens for Christ's first coming, then Christ's second coming is prepared and accomplished by the Holy Spirit already from within the world, as the Church and through the Church. This is not a one-sided act of God's omnipotence *over* the world but is instead synergistic, an act in which heaven and earth meet, the first and "second" Comforter, Christ and the Holy Spirit, to whom thus belongs a corresponding hypostatic activity at Christ's second coming, both chiliastically, over the course of the entire apocalyptically understood history of the Church, and in the eschatological event, his coming "as a thief in the night" [Rev 16:15].

This trinitarian meaning of the dogma of the parousia is disclosed only in the book of Revelation, and specifically in this multivalent and exceptionally meaningful text, "The Bride and the Lamb say: come!" The Holy Spirit who animates the Church, the Bride or the Body of Christ, summons, intercedes with groanings that cannot be uttered; and the Church, animated by the Holy Spirit, prays for this coming. The *encounter* with Christ at his second coming into the world, both the chiliastic and the eschatological, is accomplished by the Holy Spirit, in accord, of course, with the Father's

---

you!'" Translation accessed: <<https://www.oca.org/saints/troparia/2014/05/29/42-the-ascension-of-our-lord>>. —Trans.

will and the Son's corresponding desire: "even so, I come quickly." This text thus contains the dogma of the second coming of the Holy Spirit, and it is unique in this, for it concludes and seals the Word of God. "Even so, I come. *Amen*" (22:20).

And so, the book of Revelation teaches us to pray for the new coming of Christ into the world. It was this prayer that the early Church knew when she expected the "soon" coming of the Lord, in the sense of an already approaching time and not just in the sense of the present ripeness required for it, a ripeness united nevertheless with complete uncertainty concerning its date. We can say that the early Church was animated by this eschatological hope. This can be seen even in the promise of the Lord, which was, of course, understood in an eschatological sense: "truly I say to you: there are some of those standing here who will not taste death until they see the Son of Man coming in his kingdom" (Matt 16:28; Mark 9:1; Luke 9:27). Whatever the true meaning of this text, for the first generation of Christians it was understood precisely in this sense (and we hear echoes of this faith in the various letters of the apostle Paul). But as those following this first generation departed this world without the anticipation of the expected and promised parousia, the eschatological hope increasingly faded, such that later on it was completely extinguished. It is the same situation, we can say, with the entirety of historical Christianity, even in our own day. What has been retained from this eschatological state of being is only the fear of death together with the defense at the post-mortem judgment. This is how it is expressed in the prayer of the Great Litany: "For a Christian ending to our life . . . and for a good defense at the dread judgment seat of Christ, we pray." But the prayer of Revelation, "come," remains unheard to this day.

Yet it must be heard, and once heard it must become not only the object of special prayerful attention but also of a new spiritual orientation. It is nothing more and nothing less than a new (and yet at the same time primordial) feeling of life that must be reborn in Christianity, and this must manifest as a spiritual and prayerful revolution in the life of the Church—not from without, but from within. We are kept from the path to this revolution by our impotence, timidity, and stagnancy, which are mistaken as fidelity to tradition, but it is precisely this tradition that is in need of renewal. Here in a special sense we can apply this Word of God to the Church, as speaking *about* the Church: "Behold, I make all things new" [Rev 21:5]. It is not we who make it new but rather God in us, in Christ through the Holy Spirit, although this does not happen without us. But this voice once heard can no longer be forgotten, and this summons resounding in our souls must not remain unanswered. A new epoch in the life of the Church is upon us. What this means in light of the present and the future is not given to us to know. But we must learn to think and to feel eschatologically.

11

Homily on the Dormition of the Most Holy Mother of God

"In your glorious Dormition the heavens rejoice, and the angelic hosts raise their praises, and all the earth is glad."[1]

THE DORMITION OF THE Mother of God is, humanly speaking, her death, which constitutes that grievous separation of soul and body for all who die. But she did not know this grief at the hour of her death. She had beforehand already accepted, together with her Son, this grief of death by co-dying with him at the cross. This grief was exhausted and conquered by her in the light of his resurrection when she beheld the resurrected One in his glory. Thus neither did she experience grief when he left this world, ascending from earth to heaven, for she knew that this was his heavenly glorification. Before the time of her death, she fully experienced and exhausted not only earthly grief but also her own life as well. She remained on earth then not for herself but for the Church, whose bright joy and spiritual center she was. And when the hour came for her separation from the world, then was it required of her to fulfill God's universal decree: "thou art dust and to dust shalt thou return," and she gave up her spirit into her Son's bosom [Luke 23:46].[2] She

1. Sticheron for the Dormition of the Most Holy Mother of God, Tone 4.
2. Some iconic depictions of the Dormition of Mary show Jesus holding Mary's soul near his breast, as in the fourteenth-century icon of the Dormition by Theophan the Greek. —Trans.

was "translated to life, O Mother of Life,"[3] yet her dormition proved for the Spirit-Bearer to be a genuine triumph of life in the Holy Spirit. No corruption did her most pure body see, that body which bore within itself the Savior of the world. Before corruption could set in, she was raised from death by the power of Christ's resurrection and was taken up to heaven by the power of his ascension. "The angels who witnessed the dormition marveled at how the Virgin ascended from earth to heaven."[4] This is why we celebrate the dormition of the Mother of God as the *Pascha of the Mother of God*.

But is it fitting for us humans to exult in our separation from the Mother of God in her dormition? Do we celebrate when we lose in death those nearest to us, or our mother? Is it not the case rather that for us there can be *no greater grief* than this separation? And so is it not natural to imagine how much more joyful the earth and this world were when the Most Pure One lived in them? And thus would it not have been more natural for her to have remained with us on earth? But in asking such questions, we ourselves do not understand what we want and what we are requesting. The dormition of the Mother of God was an act of grace for the world, born from her love for us. In the dormition she did not desire to separate the entirety of her human nature which she gave to her divine Son. Having become the Mother of God, she remained a genuine human for whom death is the law of life, the inexorable fate of original sin. But death was conquered in her dormition, for in it she was raised by the power of the resurrection of her Son. And in her person is pre-resurrected the entire human race whom she will meet in its universal resurrection.

This resurrection became for her an ascension to the heavens in a glory both divine and "divinely fitting,"[5] and it proved as salvific for humanity as her abiding on earth was for us. Her dormition is a continuation of her work. In it and after it she abides in no less—and even with greater—closeness to humanity than when she dwelt here on earth. Now she is the Mother of all humanity, always and everywhere for the ages of ages. "In the dormition you did not abandon the world, Mother of God,"[6] the Church sings, and we must grasp this truth of revelation. The Most Pure One, abiding in heaven, "more honorable than the cherubim and more glorious beyond compare

3. Troparion for the Dormition, Tone 1. Translation accessed: << https://www.oca.org/saints/troparia/2009/08/15/102302-the-dormition-of-our-most-holy-lady-the-mother-of-god-and-ever-v>>. —Trans.

4. Zadostoinik of the Dormition, Tone 1. —Trans.

5. From the sticheron of John of Damascus, for the Great Vespers of the Feast of the Dormition. Rus. *bogolepnoj*, equivalent to Greek *theoprepes*, "worthy of God," "divinely fitting." —Trans.

6. Troparion for the Dormition of the Most Holy Mother of God, Tone 1. —Trans.

than the seraphim,"[7] is, for all that, not separated from our creaturely world. Her Son, having ascended into the transworldly heaven and sitting at the right hand of the Father, abides above the earth,[8] but the Most Holy Mother of God belongs to it, abiding at its highest limit, as the completely deified creation, "the ladder to heaven" [Gen 28:12]. She lives in the world and with the world, and for that fact she is its greatest joy. And this particular close-ness of hers is both known and felt for us first of all in prayer: she is for us "in prayers vigilant and in intercessions our immovable hope."[9] She mercifully allows us to share in her closeness to mankind through miracle-working icons and in those apparitions with which she honors mortals. Her connec-tion with the world in her dormition, that she has not abandoned the world, is a silent, mysterious, but unshakable dogma of the Church's veneration of her.

But even this is insufficient to express the complete fullness of our hope concerning her. For it is not merely that we have her palpable nearness to the world; it is also that we cannot but hope to personally encounter her in this world, which she in truth has not abandoned. When we part with a person near and dear to us, what thought more powerfully moves our heart, fills it with sweet aspiration, than the hope of meeting them again? But we, however, remain without her, since between us lies the border of death, which deters this hope. But the dormition of the Mother of God is not our separation from her in death, because in it she did not abandon the world. The Lord, leaving the world in his ascension, promised to come to it again, "in the same manner as we saw him ascending to heaven" (Acts 1:11) in his second coming in glory. And as a sort of pledge on this promise, he taught Christians to nurture in prayer their hope for this encounter. Christians are taught by the Church to summon his saving help in the Jesus Prayer,[10] to seek sacramental communion with him by communing in his body and blood. But it has been granted to us to hope for yet another encounter with him, to carry in our hearts its call, yearning, hope. We have been granted a summons that is the first and last prayer, the prayer of early Christianity and of all Christianity: "Even so, come Lord Jesus" (Rev 22:20). But we have a similar hope of an encounter with the Most Holy Mother of God, of her new coming into the world and of her return to us. And most importantly, this encounter awaits us—to the that degree we are worthy—at the hour of

7. From the Liturgy of St. John Chrysostom. —Trans.

8. See Sergius Bulgakov, *The Lamb of God*, 388–410, for more on Bulgakov's under-standing of Christ's ascension. —Trans.

9. Kontakion of the Dormition, Tone 2. —Trans.

10. A central prayer of the Eastern Christian tradition, with one of its main variants as follows: "Lord Jesus Christ, Son of God, have mercy on me, a sinner." —Trans.

death, at the border of earthly life. She has gone through the gates of death in her venerable dormition, and we believe that those ascending heavenward on this path meet her there. For this reason the dormition of the Mother of God becomes something especially intimate to us through the revelation of the death of our kin, and—we believe—in the revelation of our own death that awaits us. We also believe that the Most Holy Mother of God, who has not abandoned us in her dormition, is also near to that world beyond the grave. Together with the holy angels, with maternal love and care she guides that world and cultivates it for the coming resurrection; by her help souls grow to the measure of complete maturity, they ripen for resurrection.

But today, does our lack of faith not make it seem at times like the Mother of God has abandoned the world in these years of horrific trials, while the human race bleeds to death, brutalized by its own beastly violence? But it is precisely now that her closeness to humanity becomes more palpable, that the path for her descent to the world, for her new advent, is being prepared. It behooves us to believe and to confess that the Mother of God through her dormition is approaching her coming encounter with the world. In his second coming, the Lord enters into the world not alone but with all the angels and saints, and the Most Pure One comes at the head of this heavenly descent. The hope for this nuptial hour of the Bride and Mother of Christ is something we must carry in our hearts. And if we always pray to her: "Most Holy Mother of God, save us," then with a reverent whisper we now add this paschal prayer of her venerable dormition: "Even so, come, Most Holy Mother of God." Amen.

12

Concerning My Funeral

1 January 1941. St. Sergius, Paris[1]

I ASK THAT MY burial arrangements be *as inexpensive and simple as possible*, without any unnecessary expenses. I lack the funds, and therefore any extra expenses for my funeral would have to be taken, first of all, from my close relatives, or, more generally, from the needy to whom the money could be given as a "funeral wreath" for me, if only as a sort of recompense for my own personal callousness. I would ask that no flowers be laid [on my grave]—I do not deserve them.

"The earth is the Lord's and the fullness thereof: the world, and all they that dwell therein" [Ps 24:1]. I have no wishes concerning my place of burial, after having been exiled from my homeland where I had already chosen for myself a spot near my son's[2] grave at the Koreiz[3] cemetery. If possible, I would like to be buried in one grave alongside my wife,[4] but only if this causes no further difficulties and is generally feasible.

---

1. From 1925 until his death in 1944, Bulgakov served both as professor of dogmatic theology and dean at St. Sergious Orthodox Theological Institute. —Trans.

2. Bulgakov's third child, Ivan (Ivashechka) Sergeevich Bulgakov, died before reaching four years of age (1905–9), as a result of complications from dysentery. Bulgakov writes of his son's death in *Unfading Light*, 14–16. —Trans.

3. Koreiz is a city belonging to the municipality of Yalta in Crimea. The family of Bulgakov's wife lived in the region, and he was exiled there by the Bolsheviks from 1918–22, after which he was expelled from Russia permanently. —Trans.

4. Elena Ivanovna Bulgakova (*née* Tokmakova), 1868–1945. —Trans.

I do ask, however, that there be placed in my grave a handful of soil from my homeland, preserved in an amulet and taken from my son's grave, as well as a handful of holy soil from Gethsemane, kept in a pouch under my icons (whatever remains of this holy soil may be distributed among those who desire it).

These are all my wishes.

God's sinful priest, *Sergii.*

Bibliography

Berdyaev, Nicolas. *The Destiny of Man*. Translated by Natalie Duddington. San Rafael: Semantron, 2009.

———. *Truth and Revelation*. Translated by R. M. French. New York: Collier, 1962.

Bulgakov, Sergij. *The Tragedy of Philosophy (Philosophy and Dogma)*. Translated by Stephen Churchyard. Brooklyn, NY: Angelico, 2020.

Bulgakov, Sergius. *The Apocalypse of John: An Essay in Dogmatic Interpretation*. Edited by Barbara Hallensleben, Regula M. Zwahlen, and Dario Colombo. Translated by Mike Whitton and Michael Miller. Münster: Aschendorff Verlag, 2019.

———. *The Burning Bush*. Translated by Thomas Allan Smith. Grand Rapids: Eerdmans, 2009.

———. *The Comforter*. Translated by Boris Jakim. Grand Rapids: Eerdmans, 2004.

———. *The Eucharistic Sacrifice*. Translated by Mark Roosien. Notre Dame, IN: University of Notre Dame Press, 2021.

———. *The Friend of the Bridegroom: On the Orthodox Veneration of the Forerunner.* Translated by Boris Jakim. Grand Rapids: Eerdmans, 2003.

———. "Heroism and Asceticism: Reflections on the Religious Nature of the Russian Intelligentsia." In *Vekhi: Landmarks*, translated and edited by Marshall S. Shatz and Judith E. Zimmerman, 17–50. London: Routledge, 2017.

———. *The Holy Grail and the Eucharist (Library of Russian Philosophy)*. Translated by Boris Jakim. Hudson, NY: Lindisfarne, 1997.

———. *Jacob's Ladder*. Translated by Thomas Allan Smith. Grand Rapids: Eerdmans, 2010.

———. *The Lamb of God*. Translated by Boris Jakim. Grand Rapids: Eerdmans, 2008.

———. *Relics and Miracles: Two Theological Essays*. Translated by Boris Jakim. Grand Rapids: Eerdmans, 2011.

———. *Unfading Light: Contemplations and Speculations*. Translated by Thomas Allan Smith. Grand Rapids: Eerdmans, 2011.

McClymond, Michael J. *The Devil's Redemption: A New History and Interpretation of Christian Universalism*. Grand Rapids: Baker, 2018.

Florensky, Pavel. *The Pillar and Ground of Truth*. Translated by Boris Jakim. Princeton: Princeton University Press, 1997.

Gavrilyuk, Paul. "The Judgment of Love: The Ontological Universalism of Sergius Bulgakov (1871–1944)." In *All Shall Be Well": Explorations in Universalism and Christian Theology, from Origen to Moltmann*, edited by Gregory MacDonald, 280–304. Eugene, OR: Cascade, 2011.

Hart, David Bentley. *That All Shall Be Saved*. New Haven, CT: Yale University Press, 2019.

———. *The New Testament: A Translation*. New Haven, CT: Yale University Press, 2017.

Martin, Jennifer Newsome. *Hans Urs von Balthasar and the Critical Reception of Russian Religious Thought*. Notre Dame, IN: Notre Dame University Press, 2016.

O'Regan, Cyril. *Theology and the Spaces of Apocalyptic. Pere Marquette Theology Lecture*. Milwaukee: Marquette University Press, 2009.

Poljakova, Ekaterina. "Fyodor Dostoevsky and Friedrich Nietzsche: Power/Weakness." *International Journal of Philosophy and Theology* 78.1–2 (2017) 121–38.

Pospielovsky, Dimitry. *The Russian Church under the Soviet Regime 1917–1982*. Crestwood, NY: St. Vladimir's Seminary Press, 1984.

Rowell, Geoffrey. *Hell and the Victorians: A Study of the Nineteenth-Century Theological Controversies concerning Eternal Punishment and the Future Life*. Oxford: Clarendon, 1974.

Sandy, W., and A. C. Hedlam. *A Critical and Exegetical Commentary on the Epistle to the Romans, Volume 1, Introduction and Commentary on Romans I-VIII*. 5th ed. Edinburgh: T. & T. Clark, 1908.

Slesinski, Robert F. *The Theology of Sergius Bulgakov*. Yonkers, NY: St. Vladimir's Seminary Press, 2017.

Solovyov, Vladimir. *Lectures on Divine-Humanity*. Hudson, NY: Lindisfarne, 1995.

———. *War, Progress, and the End of History*. Hudson, NY: Lindisfarne, 1990.

Solovyev, Vladimir. *God, Man, and the Church: The Spiritual Foundations of Life*. London: James Clarke, 1974.

St. Symeon the Theologian. *On the Mystical Life. The Ethical Discourses: Volume 1. The Church and the Last Things*. Translated by Alexander Golitzin. Crestwood, NY: St. Vladimir's Seminary Press, 1995.

Tanner, Norman P. *Decrees of the Ecumenical Councils, Volume 1 (Nicaea 1–Lateran V)*. Washington, DC: Georgetown University Press, 1990.

von Goethe, Johann Wolfgang. *Goethe's Faust*. Translated by Walter Kaufman. New York: Anchor, 1990.

Williams, Rowan. *Sergii Bulgakov: Towards a Russian Political Theology*. Edinburgh: T. & T. Clark, 1999.

CPSIA information can be obtained
at www.ICGtesting.com
Printed in the USA
LVHW090753120821
694545LV00001B/1

9 781532 699658